你好，米饭，

Hello Rice, I'm Hamburger!

我是汉堡！

[美] 阿文（Kevin Smith） 著

ZHEJIANG UNIVERSITY PRESS

浙江大学出版社

阿文与好朋友在张家界比划拳脚

阿文在成都体验掏耳朵

阿文和老万，一个浙江森林的看森林人

阿文在北海市过春节

阿文爬长城，当好汉

阿文在长江三峡

前　言
Preface

　　因为小时候听说可以挖洞穿过地球，所以我开始挖洞。美国小孩儿都知道世界另一头有什么，那个"什么"就是我的目的地：中国。当时的我缺乏耐心，没继续挖。但是，我从没放弃过我的梦想。或者说，从那一天起，我就在一条想象中的龙背上坐着，直到终于到达那个遥远的地方——中国。

　　When I was young I believed people could dig straight through the Earth, so I began to dig. And every American boy and girl knew what was on the other side of the world, and that "what" was my destination: China. At the time I lacked patience, and didn't continue to dig. But I never gave up my dream. And you could say, from that day onward, I rode on the back of an imaginary dragon until I finally made my way to that faraway land—China.

在中国的第一个星期，我跟老板坐在出租车里，我看见了一头水牛在我们前面横穿过马路。

In my first week: riding in a taxi with my boss, I saw a water buffalo cross the road in front of us.

"它去哪里？"我问老板。

"Where's it going？" I asked her.

"我怎么知道，我又不是牛。"她回答。

"How would I know, I'm not a water buffalo," she answered.

很合理的答案。

What a fitting answer.

从那天起，我开始了我的冒险……

And from that day on my adventure began...

目　录
Table of Contents

成都挑战
The Chengdu Challenge 2

给面子的艺术
The Art of Giving Face 16

微笑胜于利剑
A Smile is Mightier than the Sword 24

第一天来到中国：文化冲击！
First Day in China: Culture Shock! 38

怎么跟老外聊天？
How to Talk to a "Laowai"? 60

第二个大山？并不是！
The Second Dashan? No Way! 72

顽皮，调皮，还是有道理？
Mischievous, Incorrigible or Reasonable? 84

2

对不起，中国，我没有不理你！　　　　　　　　96
Sorry, China, I Really Didn't Mean to Ignore You!

友谊：患难见真情　　　　　　　　　　　　116
Fridendship: A Friend in Need Is a Friend Indeed

化身蚊子：中国寺庙　　　　　　　　　　　130
Reincarnated Mosquito: A Chinese Temple

美貌不过是皮囊　　　　　　　　　　　　　148
Beauty Is Only Skin Deep

怎么选一个英文名？　　　　　　　　　　　156
How to Choose an English Name?

文化交流　　　　　　　　　　　　　　　　170
Cultural Exchange

三个婚礼：文化地雷　　　　　　　　　　　176
The Triple Wedding: A Cultural Landmine

怎么跟老外搞好关系？　　　　　　　　　　204
How to Develop a Relationship With a "Laowai"?

谁杀死了小孔子和小老子？——中国侦探故事　222
Who Killed Little Confucius and Little Laozi?—A Chinese Detective Story

哪里、哪里：塞了谦虚的派　　　　　　　　　234
Where? Where? A Slice of Humble Pie

一个老外的春节回忆　　　　　　　　　　248
A Foreigner's Recollection of Spring Festival

为了一份报纸，就牺牲了自己的尊严？　　　262
Sacrificing Self-respect for a Newspaper?

珠峰，谁在高原病倒了？　　　　　　　　272
Mt. Qomolangma, Who Would Succumb to Altitude Sickness?

一个老师的忏悔　　　　　　　　　　　302
A Teacher's Regret

老外在说什么？　　　　　　　　　　　312
The Foreigner Said What?

"老内"在说什么？　　　　　　　　　　322
What Did the Chinese Person Say?

神秘的现象：10 度和 20 度没有区别？　　336
A Mysterious Phenomenon: No Difference Between Ten and Twenty Degrees?

摩登的上海有条古老的龙？　　　　　　　348
An Ancient Dragon in Modern Shanghai?

4

中式专心：声音的考验　　　　　　　　　　　360
Chinese Concentration: Trial by Sound

中美的差别　　　　　　　　　　　　　　378
Differences Between China and America

Chapter 1

成都挑战

The Chengdu Challenge

成都挑战
The Chengdu Challenge

老外能吃辣椒?

Can foreigners handle chili peppers?

在中国吃饭的时候,我常常听到别人问:"他能用筷子?"当我吃任何辣的菜,比如川菜或湘菜,我就会被别人问:"外国人能吃辣啊?"我选了"能"这个字是因为问题不是会不会吃,因为所有的人都会把辣椒放在嘴里,而是外国人"能不能"承受辣椒的辣!如果我很饿,就不会再解释,我只会点点头表示:"能吃。"但是,有时我说好多国家也常吃辣:印度、韩国、墨西哥,不一而足,那里都有本地的辣椒。而且,不管在哪里,都是有的人能吃,有的人不能吃。在英文里有句话说的是:"If you can't take the heat, get out of the kitchen."意思是,如果你受不了热，那就离开厨房吧！这个俗话基本上跟承受压力有关，但是因为辣椒与热同义，我认为用在这里也是很适合的。

When eating in China, I often hear, "Can he use chopsticks?" And when I'm eating anything that contains chili peppers, for example spicy Sichuan or hot Hunan cuisine, I'm asked directly or I overhear, "Can foreigners handle chili peppers?" And I chose the word "handle" because the question isn't as much about the simple act of eating chilies, but rather, can foreigners "handle" the spice that comes with it? If I'm really hungry, and have no desire to explain, I just nod my head, "Yes." But, sometimes I bring up the fact that many countries often use peppers: India, Korea and Mexico, to name a few, each using its own local fiery peppers. And of course, no matter where you are from, some people can handle some spice, some cannot. In English we have a saying, "If you can't take the heat, get out of the kitchen." This saying is often used in situations dealing with stress and difficult situations, but as spicy peppers are synonymous with heat, I believe it works here just as well.

于是我就给自己来了一场个人挑战：任何时候去四川成都，我都想给自己一场辣的考验：一大碗水煮牛肉、一碗米饭和两瓶冰镇啤酒。

This brings me to my own personal challenge: anytime I visit Sichuan's capital, Chengdu, I give myself a trial by fire: One bowl of Sichuan's famous Poached Slice Beef Cooked in Hot Chili Oil, one bowl of rice and two cold bottles of beer.

有一次，在成都办事的时候，我从旅馆出门想寻找挑战。顺着迷宫般的小巷走着走着，我就迷路了。我发现自己在一条很普通的马路上，就是那种让人记不住的路，四周建筑都一样。路旁住着那种黑白分明的人，他们怀疑陌生人，不太喜欢改变。在那条路上我找到了我的深红色，那辣椒色的挑战。那家饭馆的装潢与外面街道的风格非常一致：装修很普通，白桌布、木椅子和不太干净的粉刷墙。我走进去的时候，正如经常发生的那样：筷子都停止了咯喇咯喇的碰撞声，嘴巴都停止了咕嘟咕嘟的吃菜声，眼睛都向我这边看了过来。

On one such occasion, when I was in Chengdu taking care of some business, I left my hostel to find my challenge. After a short time, I was lost within a labyrinth of alleys, where every street resembled the last: forgettable, functional architecture, all squares and rectangles, the kind of street where residents preferred a world that is black and white, were suspicious of strangers, and didn't welcome change. And on this unimpressionable street, where drab was the color of preference, I'd found my crimson challenge, the color of the spicy pepper. The restaurant's interior reflected the street: simple, white tablecloth, wooden chairs and whitewashed walls that weren't especially clean. And when I walked in, what was expected to happen happened: the chopsticks stopped their clicking and the mouths stopped their slurping as all eyes looked up at me.

过了一会儿，等他们对我这个陌生人的兴趣减退了以后，我点了我的挑战。那里的服务员和其他许多服务员的样子一样：年轻，有点胖，不招呼人，看得出来是真的不喜欢打工。当我一说出"一份水煮牛肉"，她没有表情地问道："是辣的。你能吃辣？"

After a short time, once the diners lost interest in this stranger who had entered their small world, I ordered my challenge. And, as soon as I said, "One order of Poached Slice Beef Cooked in Chili Oil," the waitress, young, slightly pudgy, expressionless, obviously not enjoying her work, asked flatly: "It's spicy. Can you handle spice?"

这时，饭馆的气氛又安静了下来。当其他客人都小声地说"外国人不能吃辣"的时候，我感觉我似乎站在一个很大的岩洞里，回声传到了各个角落："外国人不能吃辣。"

And just as fast, the atmosphere in the restaurant had again quieted down. And when the other customers started to whisper, "Foreigners can't handle chilies," it was as if I was standing in a big cave as their words were echoed from every corner of the room: foreigners can't handle chilies.

回声消退以后，我有点骄傲地说："没问题！"

Once the echoes dissipated, with a little too much pride I said, "No problem!"

用小拇指挖了挖耳朵，她问："微辣？"

Using her pinky to pick her ear, she asked, "Mildly spicy?"

我坚持说："不用，地道就好。"

"No, keep it authentic," I insisted.

我绝对不能把我最初的挑战改为"微辣挑战"！

I certainly couldn't change the challenge to "the mildly spicy challenge"!

她耸耸肩说："好。"

Shrugging her shoulders, she said, "Okay."

那个服务员慢慢地走向厨房说："老外点了水煮牛肉。"

The waitress walked slowly back into the kitchen saying, "The foreigner wants poached beef in chili oil."

我能听到厨子在厨房里不相信地说："老外能吃辣？"

I could hear the cook say from the kitchen with disbelief, "Foreigners can handle chilies?"

有些客人把头摇了摇。有可能他们认为我点错了，或是小看了那里的四川辣椒。一个嘴里叼着烟的秃顶胖男人坐在我前面。因为他在数着一叠发票，我估计他是老板。他透过眼镜，看了我一眼，然后按了按计算器。他模仿我的话，喃喃地说："不用，地道就好……"

Some of the customers shook their heads, perhaps believing I ordered incorrectly or that I didn't respect the Sichuan chili pepper. Sitting in front of me was a balding fat man smoking a cigarette. Because he was counting receipts, I guessed he was the boss. Through his bifocals he took a look at me, than while tapping away at his calculator, mimicking my words, he mumbled, "No, keep it authentic..."

十分钟后，服务员把一个白色大碗放在我面前。在油亮发光的川红色汤面上，刚刚被油炒过的辣椒还翻滚着，发出嘶嘶的响声。一层用辣椒、花椒和白蒜蓉做的调料浮在最上面，一点香菜漂在汤上。我很想用筷子捞几片汤面下的牛肉片。

Ten minutes later, the waitress set a giant white bowl in front of me. On the glistening surface of the Sichuan-Red broth, freshly fried dry chilies still crackled and popped with a soft pfsst pfsst hissing sound. A thin layer of Sichuan peppercorns and minced garlic covered the top. A few sprigs of cilantro floated on top. I was ready to dive in with my chopsticks and fish out one of the slices of beef that were floating just below the surface.

我夹住一片很长很厚的肉片放进嘴巴里。像在显微镜下看一只小虫子似的，我能感到饭馆的客人都在仔细地观察着我。老板轻轻敲打计算器的声音也停下来了。

I grabbed a long, thick piece and lifted it to my mouth. Like an insect below a microscope, I could feel all eyes on me as they examined my every move closely. Even the boss's soft tapping of the calculator had stopped.

我把那片肉放在我舌头上：热乎乎、鲜嫩嫩、水淋淋的肉！

I placed the piece on the top of my tongue: warm, tender and succulent!

我合拢了嘴，眼睛也跟着嘴巴闭上了，太爽了，好吃极了！

I closed my mouth, my eyes following suit, hoping to enhance the sense of taste and prolong the delicious flavor.

他们集体发出一声惊叹。

The patrons emitted a collective gasp.

我可以想象他们在想什么，他们都不相信自己看到了什么：这怎么可能？外国人刚刚在吃辣椒！如果外国人能吃辣椒，或许我们学到的一切都是假的？地球不是圆的，而是平的；扔上去的东西不一定会掉下来；南方其实是北方，北方其实是南方？外国人怎么能吃辣？？？

I could only imagine what they were thinking, unable to believe what they were witnessing: How was this possible?! Did a foreigner just eat a chili? If foreigners could handle chilies, what if everything else we've been taught was also a lie? Was the world not really round, but flat? What goes up doesn't necessarily come down? South was north and north was south? How can a foreigner eat chilies???

我嘴里几乎都是口水，猛得深吸了一口气，好像有一点儿黏在肉片上的辣椒皮被我吸进了嗓子里。当那点儿辣椒皮钻进我嗓子里，挂在我嗓子里的小东西上面（科学家称悬雍垂，像一个拳师的沙袋）。那是喉咙里最敏感的部分，当那点儿辣椒皮贴在我的小沙袋上的时候，仿佛那里正被李小龙用功夫击打一样！

My mouth nearly spilling over with saliva from savoring the initial slice for too long, I suddenly took in a deep breath. When I inhaled, what must have been a small fleck of the dried chili pepper from the top of the beef was swept into the back of my throat. Flying end over end, the small fleck of chili pepper struck the surface of that small thing that hangs in the back of our throats (scientists call it the uvula, what looks like a small punching bag). And as that area is the mouth's, possibly the body's, most sensitive spot, that miniature fleck struck the punching bag with the force of a kungfu chop delivered by Bruce Lee!

像大雾中的鸣笛一样，我的嘴巴疯狂地张开发出"吧呼"的声音。

又呼吸了好几次——"吧呼！吧呼！"我的眼球都凸出来了，恐怕快要把那些眼睛里的东西：视网膜、虹膜和晶状体都爆出来了！因为不停地咳嗽，我整个身体都抽动了。为了稳定自己，我有点重地一拳击在了桌子上。我不小心打在了筷子的一头，胖老板、厨子和其他客人，还有我，眼睁睁地看着筷子飞了出去。我的膝盖因为另一轮很严重的咳嗽撞到了桌子底部，杯子和其他的东西都咔嚓咔嚓地被撞得跳了起来。我用手捂住嘴，低沉的咳嗽声还是发了出来。我的胸部上上下下起伏着，险些喘不过气来。

Like a semi-trailer's horn bellowing it's warning through the thickness of the Chengdu fog, my mouth exploded open and out flew: "Baaah-Baaah!" And it continued, a relentless, "Baaah!" My eyeballs shot outwards, stretching that thin membrane that kept the insides: iris, pupil and yoke from exploding everywhere. Unable to stop coughing, my body twitched and danced. In an attempt to stabilize myself, I brought my fist down on the top of the table a little too hard. Accidentally striking the end of my chopstick, the other customers, the fat owner and even the chef who was peeking out from the kitchen and I watched as it shot across the room. From another round of coughing, my knee slammed hard into the bottom of the table, sending the glasses and bowls rattling loudly. Stifling the coughs with my hand, chest rising up and down, I was having a hard time catching my breath.

我的眼泪一直在流，我看到所有人的眼睛和嘴巴都惊讶地张得很大。除了我被辣得很狼狈外，周围静得连一根针掉下来的声音都能听见。

Through watering eyes, I could see that all eyes and mouths were wide open in surprise. Outside of my own personal disaster zone, you could hear a pin drop.

我的脸比四川辣椒更红，那点儿辣椒终于被一勺米饭和一杯啤酒给冲下去了。那像拖车的鸣笛声下降到了像一只感冒了的小鸭子的咳嗽声：咳！咳！

Face redder than a Sichuan pepper, the small fleck was finally washed down by a little rice and a bottle of Qingdao beer. The semi's horn was reduced to a duck with the common cold: Ack! Ack!

拿起了第二瓶啤酒，我把它靠在我额头上，满意地呻吟："啊……"

I lifted up the second bottle of cold beer and placed it against my forehead. I moaned with satisfaction, "Ahh."

其他食客的嘴巴都闭上了，又重新看着他们的对面。 我看到他们点了点头，肯定地安慰自己道：在宇宙中，一切都仍是正确的，地球还是圆的，那根掉下去的筷子怎么上去的一定还会怎么下来，南方还是南方，北方还是北方，最重要的是：外国人不能吃辣椒。

The other mouths finally shut as they went back to looking at those across from them. I watched them nodding their heads, comforting themselves that once again everything was right in the universe: the Earth was round, the fallen chopstick showing that what goes up must come down, south was south, north was north and most importantly: foreigners can't handle chilies.

"咳！咳！"

"Ack, ack!"

我真想解释一下我这剧烈的反应，那一点贴在嗓子里的小东西上面的辣椒跟能不能吃辣根本没有关系。但是，胖老板只收回了目光，摇了摇头，又低声咕哝说："不要，地道就好……"

I really wanted to explain my violent reaction, to describe the small fleck that stuck to that little thing in the back of my throat and how it had no relation to whether I could eat chilies or not. But, the boss only adjusted his bifocals and shook his head, once again muttering, "No, keep it authentic..."

"咳！"

"Ack!"

擦掉泪水以后，我继续吃饭。我的挑战才刚刚开始。

After wiping away the tears, I continued to eat. My challenge had just begun.

汤水的浓度像蜂蜜一样稠，被我用筷子夹住，一点一滴慢慢地落回碗里。肉片又粗又长，被一层很光滑的辣椒油覆盖着，下面是一些很美味、很嫩、又特别软的牛肉。我挑掉了那些四川花椒，因为不想它们把嘴唇弄麻木了，但是我非常喜欢蒜蓉的味道和口感。碰到一些看上去很辣的，我就把它放在米饭上，然后拌在一起吃。一个火红的印渍留在米饭上。

Under its spell, I watched as the broth, the consistency of warmed honey, dripped slowly from the end of a piece pinched between my chopsticks before falling back into the bowl. Each generous slice was coated in a slick layer of chili oil, which offered a flavorful introduction to the tender, extremely soft meat within. The small, round Sichuan peppercorns I left alone, not wanting my mouth to go numb under its mysterious tingly touch, but I savored the chopped garlic's flavor and texture. And if I came across a slice that looked especially spicy, I would add it to the top of the rice and eat them together, leaving a fiery red print behind on the surface of the remaining rice.

我不想骗你或者让人误会我在吹牛，实在是辣，超级辣！汗水一直从我头顶冒出来，身上汗流浃背。如果你在场的话，肯定能感觉到我的脑袋都快爆炸了！不知道我是否是一个受虐狂，但是无论多少汗水流出来，无论胃里产生多少灼热的胃酸，也不管食道已经开始被辣椒烧伤了——我发现每一片肉都比上片更好吃！我又用餐巾纸把额头的汗水擦掉，在水煮牛肉的香味中继续享受。碗里还有很多脆脆的鲜笋，但是在我看来，虽然非常有营养，但鲜笋只是一种佐料，只会让肚子感觉饱。像花椒一样，我把那些佐料剩下来了，我属虎，我需要多吃一点肉。

Now I don't want to fool you and don't think I'm bragging, because: it was spicy, really spicy! Sweat was pouring from the top of my head and under my clothes I was soaked. If you were there, you'd believe my head was about to explode from my crimson blush. I don't believe I'm a sadist, yet no matter how much sweat poured, how much bubbling and burning acid my stomach produced, and even though my throat was already scorched by the peppers, each bite was as appreciated as much as the last. I wiped my forehead yet again with a napkin as I hedonistically swam within the fragrance of the poached beef with chilies. The bowl was filled with fresh, crunchy mushroom shoots, but, in my opinion, while nourishing, the shoots were just an extra, something to fill the stomach. Like the Sichuan peppercorn, I left the filler behind as I was born in the year of the tiger and thus I needed, I craved, to eat more meat.

嘴唇烧伤了，嗓子哭了，眼睛漏水了，鼻子流涕了，头顶痒痒的，感觉肚子里有一座小火山，每分钟喷发一次——我终于把最后一点肉片吃完了。

Lips burnt, throat crying, eyes leaking, nose running, head itching, stomach feeling like a small volcano, erupting every minute, I finally finished the last strip of meat.

放下筷子，休息一会儿，我露出一个"你看吧，外国人会吃辣椒"的微笑，得意扬扬地喊道："买单。"

Letting the chopsticks rest, I released a smile that said, "look, a foreigner can eat chilies," and called out proudly, "Check, please!"

我又一次成功地完成了我的挑战！

Once again, I had successfully completed the challenge!

抬着头，我自信地走出去，骄傲地想：今晚，一个国家，啊，至少一条小马路的观念被我改变了。

Head held high, bill paid, I confidently began to leave. I thought to myself, tonight I changed a nation, well, at least a small street's perception.

门关上之前，我听到胖老板说："外国人果然不能吃辣椒。"紧接着客人都同意地回应道："嗯……没错……你说得对！"

But, before the door had closed completely, from behind I heard the boss say with conviction, "Foreigners really can't handle chilies," followed quickly by all of the customers saying in agreement, "yep", "absolutely", and "You said that right!"

站在外面，还是豪情满怀的我几乎不相信自己的耳朵！他们都是盲人吗？我刚准备转身说："我能吃辣！"但是突然，仿佛中国著名歌手宋祖英和她的辣妹子们都在我肚子里一边穿着高跟鞋，昂首挺胸，迈步前进，一边唱出那首很流行的歌曲的开头："辣妹子辣，辣妹子辣！辣妹子从小不怕辣！"我的胃里面像水泥搅拌车一样翻来翻去，有东西在胃中扭动，我一把抓住自己的后背，感觉自己得立即上厕所。

Standing outside, still puffed with pride, I almost couldn't believe my own ears! Were they blind? I turned around and headed to the door, ready to say, "But I can, and I just did!" But suddenly, as if the famous songstress Song Zuying and her army of high-heeled wearing "spicy" sisters had begun marching within my stomach, while singing the opening lyrics to the popular song: "Spicy Sisters, la, Spicy Sisters, la! Spicy sisters haven't feared spice since they were small" my insides began to churn like a cement mixer, turning end over end. As my stomach twisted into a knot, my hands grabbed my backside!

我捂着屁股快速跑回旅馆，咬着牙哭着唱："拉肚子啦！拉肚子啦！这肚子从来真怕辣！！！"

Running quickly back to my hostel, holding my behind nervously, I cried through clenched teeth, "My backside will sing! My backside will sing! This stomach has always feared the spice!" (Some things just shouldn't be translated.)

Chapter 2

给面子的艺术
The Art of Giving Face

在美国很多人知道《孙子兵法》，但是很少有人知道"给面子的艺术"。

In America many people know Sun Tzu's *The Art of War*, but few know "The Art of Giving Face".

我真的不想假装理解"面子"的文化，虽然对于这个现象的原理我懂得一点点。遗憾的是，我只知道怎么让对方丢脸，因为我有一个缺点：在我脑海里，我总把"该先思考后说话"的道理反过来执行。我常常因为自己说的话而丢脸或是让对方难堪。虽然很不好意思承认，但是我认为我只掌握怎么让人丢脸的技巧，却对给面子的技巧掌握得很少。

I really don't want to pretend to understand the culture of 'face,' but in regards to this phenomenon's principles I do understand the basics.

Regretfully, I know how to allow others to lose face, because I possess a negative trait: my mind reverses the old adage: 'Think before you speak.' And therefore often by my own words I lose face or those around me do as well. It's quite embarrassing to admit, but I believe I have mastered the art of losing face, yet know little about the art of giving face.

可是，谁能说自己从来没有让别人丢脸过？不管是不是故意的，在中国让别人丢脸简直太容易了。诸如：

But, who can say they never, no matter purposefully or not, have allowed others to lose face?

向客人、亲戚、领导之类的敬酒时把酒杯举得太高／低？

During a toast, who hasn't lifted a glass high enough or low enough to a customer, family member, leader or someone along those lines?

喝得太快／慢；吃得太少／多？

Drank too quickly or too slowly; ate too little or too much?

给不给、送不送、站不站、坐不坐？

To give or not give, send or not send, stand or don't stand, sit or don't sit?

对我来说，这实在太复杂！最初想问问别人怎么做，然后右脑问左脑，上身问下身，可想而知，接下来，连该前进一步还是后退一步都不知所措了。

In my opinion, it's simply too complicated! At first you want to ask someone else what to do, and then your right brain asks your left, your upper half asks your lower half, and as you can imagine, next thing you know you aren't even sure if you should take a step forward or backward?

可是，给面子呢？我的意思不是"给对方一根香烟就有面子"或是"敬一敬酒给对方面子"，而是真正地给面子，也许应该说，会让一个人重拾骄傲，还其以尊严。这要做到远非易事。

But, giving face? I don't mean, "giving someone a cigarette for face" or "toasting another for face" but really giving face, perhaps I should say, restoring someone's pride, returning one's self-respect. This ability is far from easy.

在中国"给面子"好像是一种艺术。所以现在我想给各位讲一个我所遇到的一位"给面子"大师的小故事 。

It seems in China, "giving face" is an art form. And, now I would like to tell you about the time I ran into a master of "giving face", his method and that day's events.

那是我第一次去那家工厂。招聘我的外贸公司跟那家工厂已经合作了六个多月，但是每次跟他们谈的时候，我都是通过我们公司的代表去翻译我所谈论的内容。我们公司的代表，是一个英国人，他的中文非常流利，那天和我一起参观那家工厂。白天大家都要工作、谈话、验货等，晚上会放松一下，有机会更了解彼此。在中国（也可以说包括美国和大多数的国家），如果想快点了解你的客户、供应商，就要加一个很简单的要素：酒！

It was my first time to visit the factory. My employer, a trading company, had been cooperating with this factory for six months. But, every time we discussed business with them, it was always done through someone who translated whatever I wanted to discuss. Our company representative, an Englishman who was fluent in Mandarin, and I visited the factory together. During the day we worked, discussed business, inspected the product, etc. In the evening we were able to relax a bit and have the opportunity to get to know one another. In China (and the United States and many other countries), if you want to get to know someone faster, like a customer or a supplier, just add one essential element: alcohol!

一天的工作完成了，我们在一张圆木桌旁坐着。我右边是英国同事，左边是工厂的总经理，在他旁边是工厂的副总，在我对面是出口公司的老板。除了我同事，他们都要热情地欢迎我。怎么欢迎呢？当然是他们敬我酒！我们喝了一、二、三、四、六、八、十杯——我都快忘记怎么数数了。我们喝的是那边的本地米酒。很快，我就喝醉了，舌头麻木了。虽然知道自己想说什么，可说出来的时候，大家都不太明白我的"醉话"！我提醒自己，不要多言，该让嘴巴做另外更重要而且非常熟悉的工作：吃东西。我们吃了扬州炒饭、狮子头、椒盐排条和几盘蔬菜。吃完后服务员送来一份西瓜。我天生就是一个健谈的人，我怎么能控制得住我的嘴呢？忍不住！但是因为已经喝了太多，脑子有点糊涂，我指着水果说：

"这是傻瓜？"

Finished with the day's work, we sat at a round, wooden table. My English coworker was to my right, the factory president to the left. Next to him was the factory vice president and across from me their export company's manager. Besides my coworker, they all wanted to enthusiastically welcome me. And how did they welcome me? Through toasting of course! We drank one, two, three, four, six, eight, ten glasses–I quickly forgot how to count — of the local rice wine. I became drunk rather quick, and my tongue went numb. I know I love talking, but when it came time for the words to come out, no one could understand my "drunken gibberish." I reminded myself, it was best to not say much, and I should give myself something more important, as well as a more familiar job: eating. We ate Yangzhou fried rice, lion's head meatballs, salt and pepper pork ribs and a few vegetables. After we finished eating, the waitress brought us a plate of watermelon slices. But, as I'm chatty by my nature, how could I control my lips? I couldn't resist! But because I drank too much, the brain was confused, and I pointed at the fruit and said, "Zhe shi shagua?" (Is this stupid ?)

我的同事、总经理、副总都疯狂地哈哈大笑起来，但没有告诉我为什么。我一说出这个词，就发现了自己的错误。我想说"西瓜"，但是因为舌头比脑子快，我不小心把西瓜的"西"说成了傻瓜的"傻"。确实很丢脸。但是我觉得没关系，因为我喝醉了，而且，普通话并不是我的母语。可是因为我常常说错话，不管是用英文还是中文，说错以后我都要找一个非常搞笑的借口，让他们知道我已经认识到自己的错误了，只是想让气氛更轻松点。所以当他们忙着笑的时候，我会努力想一想要说什么。可是当时我发现有一个人没笑，就是坐在我对面的出口公司老板。他关心地盯着我看，像是陷入了沉思。几秒过后他抬头说："其实，阿文先生说得对！在中国北方，有时候人们用'啥'（在北方表示'什么'的通俗的口语）而不是'什么'（普通话的标准用语：什么）来替代这个单词。比如'这是啥？'意思就是'这是什么？'因此，阿文没说'这是傻瓜？'他只是说，'这是什么瓜？'"

My coworker, the president and vice president were laughing madly. And no one had to tell me why: as soon as I said the word, I realized my mistake. I had meant to say "watermelon" (xi gua), but because my tongue was faster than my brain, I accidentally replaced the first character for watermelon, which is "xi" with the first word for stupid, which is "sha". Basically I pointed at the fruit and said "Is this stupid?" (zhe shi sha gua?), which was quite embarrassing. But I didn't think much of it. I was drunk. Mandarin also wasn't my native language. But because I often make mistakes when speaking, no matter if English or Chinese, I really wanted to say something funny as an excuse to let everyone know that I already knew of my own mistake, and help loosen-up the atmosphere some more. So while they were busy laughing, I was trying to think of something to say. But I had noticed one person wasn't laughing. It was the export company's manager sitting across from me. He was looking at me with concern. He looked deep in thought. After a few seconds had passed, he lifted his head and said, "Actually, Mr. Kevin said it correctly! In Northern China people sometimes use 'sha' (a colloquial term for 'what' in the north) in place of 'shen me' (the standard Mandarin term for 'what.') For example, 'This is sha?' has the same meaning as 'This is shen me?' Therefore, Kevin didn't say, 'Is this stupid?' (Zhe shi sha gua?) He only wanted to say, 'What fruit is this?' (Zhe shi shen me gua?)"

出口公司老板举杯敬酒："阿文比你们更了解北方的习惯，祝贺你，中国通。"

The export company boss raised his glass and toasted, "Kevin knows more about Northern customs than you do, congratulations, you are a Chinese master."

我们喝了一杯之后，大家都鼓掌了。

After we all drank a glass, everyone applauded.

我用手轻轻地抚摸着自己的脸：一个鼻子，两边脸颊，有点粗糙的皮肤，不长的胡子。我吃惊地说："我的亲爱的面孔，您回来了！"

I used my hand and gently patted my own face: there was a nose, two cheeks, some rough skin, some stubble. Surprised I said, "My dear face, you have returned!"

我想，我刚才碰到中国的"给面子"大师了。

I believe I had just run into a Chinese master of giving face.

谢谢您，出口公司的老板！我永远忘不了那晚的敬酒！

Thank you, export company manager! I'll never forget that evening's toast!

Chapter 3

微笑胜于利剑
A Smile is Mightier than the Sword

　　在城市中无数的小便利店里（不管是哪一家连锁店：好德、7-11、C-Store、良友、快客 或全家，它们都差不多），上方的荧光灯不停闪烁，这个故事的女英雄很骄傲地站在柜台后。她肥大的拳头支撑在很丰满的腰上，头发被煮关东做的茶叶蛋的水蒸气熏着，像烫发一样卷曲，一副眼镜架在鼻尖上，她从厚厚的眼镜片后，充满怀疑地瞄着进来的客人。她是便利店的售货员，同时又是那里的保安。全世界都用一个词语来称呼她：便利店的阿姨。

　　In one of the city's countless convenient stores (it doesn't matter the chain: All Days, 7-11, C-Store, Buddys, Kwik-Mart or Family Mart, they're all basically the same), florescent lights flickering above, the heroine of this tale stands proudly behind the counter. Meaty fists propped on ample hips, a head of hair frizzled into a permanent beneath the steam of Guan Dong steamed snacks and tea eggs, a pair of bifocals resting on the tip of her nose, she eyes the entering customer suspiciously through their thick lenses. She

IS the convenient store's salesclerk. She is its guard and protector. She is universally addressed as: the convenient store aunty.

所谓"大妈"，属于一类更大的群体，它是对说话直截了当、意志坚定不移的中年妇女的一种体面的称呼；无论是对鸡蛋打折这样的琐碎小事，还是对孩子、孙子们的交往对象合不合适，她们都充满热情；平时像有权势的女族长一样；具有热爱广场舞和爱管闲事的弱点；在小便利店里工作的阿姨在其他"大妈们"中间，几乎是无以匹敌的，她们令人畏惧和钦佩。这种阿姨以工作为傲，她的货架一直摆满，制服一尘不染；意见多，寒暄少；态度生硬，没时间胡闹。就像所有的阿姨们，她有份工作，任劳任怨。跟她们的美国同行不一样，这些便利店的阿姨们不太喜欢随便地微笑或者不期而至的闲谈。也许，这是一种文化差异的反映：中国阿姨认为跟陌生人寒暄没有必要，而只跟老客户和同事们寒暄。也有可能是由于人到中年，这些便利店的阿姨服务员，同时承担着母亲、姐妹、女儿、奶奶之类的角色，一生都在做着服务工作，内心也因此变得生硬。

Belonging to the larger class of women known as the so-called "big mamas", the respectable moniker applied to middle-aged women who've proven their ability to be outspoken and unrelenting in their opinion; equally passionate about matters as trivial as a sale on eggs to subjects as the suitability of a child or grandchild's prospective partner; often related with powerful matriarchs; with a weakness for public square dancing and busy-body like behavior; and nearly unstoppable when amongst fellow "big mamas", the professional aunty found in convenient stores across China is both admired and feared. Respect in her work, shelves fully stocked, uniform spotless and pressed; thick in attitude, light on pleasantries, gruff and little time for nonsense. Like all aunties, she has a job to do and does it without fuss or complaint. Unlike their American counterparts, these convenient store aunties aren't known for casual smiles or unexpected chitchat. Perhaps this is a reflection of a cultural difference, where a stranger does not warrant an exchange of pleasantries, which are reserved for regulars and fellow employees. Or, perhaps, as with those in middle age, acting as both convenient store aunties as well as mothers, sisters, daughters, grandmothers and the like, a life of customer service alongside domestic servitude has calloused their exteriors.

排队付钱的冷漠的客人喜欢把钱扔在柜台上，甚至都不抬头看一眼柜台后的售货员，这也可以理解，但是很遗憾，在服务员和客人中间形成了一道冷漠的冰墙。在她们的计算被质疑或者耐心受到考验或简单的问题被误解时，她们常常很快说出来，让客人感受到她们的不满。

Underappreciated, and beneath a regular stream of indifferent customers who prefer to toss their money on the counter without so much as a glance at the person behind it, it is understandable, yet unfortunate an icy wall is formed between that of customer and cashier. And at moments when her calculations are faulted or her patience tested, a question misinterpreted as a slight, she will often lash out quickly and the customer will feel her fury.

我不止一次受到过她们的训斥，忍不住想知道，孔子、孟子或者中国古代的某位哲学家不是曾经说过"刀子嘴，豆腐心"吗？在这冷漠的冰面下，不会掩盖着一些温情吗？有没有一个方法可以突破这个强硬的外表，令人感受到她珍藏的、只跟同伴和同事们分享的仁慈？您可能会问，这跟你有什么关系？有可能是因为我是一位社会科学专业的学生，而这可以作为一个关于社交的试验，而且能满足我的好奇心。或者像只想被别人接受一样简单，被阿姨们看作一个"老客人"，才有机会得到温暖的微笑。我必须试一下。

Having felt her verbal lash more than once, I could not help but wonder, didn't Confucius, Mencius or one of China's ancient philosopher's once say, "A tongue as sharp as a dagger, yet a heart as soft as tofu?" Was it not possible that there was warmth hidden beneath the icy front? Was there a way to break through the hardened exterior and feel the kindness she surely holds dear, sharing only with her fellow aunty-coworkers and regular customers? And why did I even want to try, you ask? Perhaps it is because I'm a student of social sciences and this is an experiment in social interaction, and my curiosity needed to be sated. Maybe it is as simple as wanting to be accepted, to be considered a "regular" and given a warm smile. I had to try.

我记起另外一句谚语：用蜜比用醋能捕捉到更多的苍蝇。我准备开始了。

Remembering the old saying: you can catch more flies with honey than vinegar. I was prepared to start.

便利店的门发着嘶嘶的声音滑开了，我走了进去。店里到处是各种各样的零食，背景是一堵色彩丰富的香烟拼成的墙，店员阿姨们穿着印有便利店图案的制服（按照便利店的规定，制服的颜色有浅蓝色、绿色、粉红色，等等，那位阿姨穿的是好德便利店的颜色：蓝色、白色和粉红色），正在准备迎接客人。

The door slid open with a quiet hiss and I walked in. Surrounded by a variety of snacks, a wall of cigarette boxes the backdrop, wearing the convenient stores "coat of arms", the convenient store aunty's uniform (according to the convenient store's uniform regulations: light blue, green, pink, etc. – that particularly aunty wearing the colors of All Day's: blue, white and pink), she was ready to confront her customers.

我露出了我唯一的武器———一个微笑，说："你好！"

I reveal my only weapon – a smile, and say, "Hi!"

那个服务台后的阿姨的嗓子里面像住着一只巨大的牛蛙，她吼叫出一个特别大的噪音："嗯——"

As if a massive bullfrog lived within the throat of the aunty behind the counter, she croaked out an especially noisy, "En—"

就这样，我的舌头仿佛被她那匕首一样的舌头砍下，只剩下一截苍白无力的舌尖在收银台上晃来晃去，她粗暴的回应令我哑口无言。她并不想把手伸出来接钱，我只能把十元钱放在柜台上，买了一块巧克力。

她没跟我进行眼神交流，只把找的零钱用力摔到收银台上。我把舌尖和找回的硬币从台上捡起来。第一轮，我已经输了。

And just like that, as if her dagger-like tongue had severed my own, leaving its tip rocking back on forth on the countertop, the harsh response left me speechless. Making no attempt to hold her hand out, I could only place a ten-renminbi note on the counter and buy a bar of chocolate. Without making eye contact, she slapped down my change upon the counter. I scooped up the tip of my tongue along with some change. First round and I'd lost already.

尽管那天的巧克力没有以前那么甜，但输一次也不是什么问题。长城不是在一天造成的，兵马俑也不是在一个晚上刻好的！我要坚持一下。

Even though the chocolate tasted a little less sweet that day, losing once wasn't a problem. And the Great Wall wasn't built in a day nor were the Terracotta Soldiers carved in a single night! I had to persist.

第二天我跟她打招呼说："你好！"

The second day I greeted her with, "Hello!"

她用漠然的眼睛看了下我，回答："哪里好？"

Disinterested eyes said, 'What's good about it?'

第二轮我又输了。我静静地吃我的巧克力。

I lost on the second day as well. I ate my chocolate bar in silence.

第三、第四、第五、第六、第七轮，我都输了。有时候她甚至不愿用令人不快的"嗯"跟我打招呼。我的信心受到了打击，不像以前那么乐观了。我低估了她的决心。我买的巧克力只是一个安慰奖,糖也不甜了。

The third, four, fifth, sixth and seventh time were also losses. Sometimes, she wouldn't even greet me with her unpleasant bellow "en." My confidence had taken a hit, and I wasn't as optimistic as before. I had underestimated her determination. The chocolate had become nothing but a consolation prize, sugar without the sweet.

但是,我承诺过不会放弃!阿姨肯定没有那么冷漠,除了会发出那个"嗯",她肯定会说话。我没见过她跟同事开玩笑?没听过她骂客户?柜台前后的距离没那么远,对吗?我的坚持,并且穿过横亘在我们之间的冷漠的峡谷。

But, I promised myself that I wouldn't give up! The aunty certainly couldn't be that cold and of course could utter more than that single sound "en." Haven't I seen her joking with her coworkers? And, haven't I heard her curse out customers? The distance between the front and the back of the counter wasn't that far, was it? I had to persist and cross the chilly chasm between us.

在第八次战斗中,当我又一次说"谢谢你!"时,她用一句含糊的"欢迎下次光临",代替了之前的牛蛙式吼叫。

During the eighth battle, when I once again said, "Thank you!" in place of the bullfrog's bellow I heard her say vaguely say, "Welcome back again."

真不可思议!如果没有搞错,我刚刚听到了一个破裂的声音!冰层里出现了一条裂缝?那天,我的巧克力里有点甜味了。

Unbelievable! If I wasn't mistaken, I'd just heard a crack! Had a fissure in the ice appeared? That day a little sweetness returned to my chocolate bar.

几个星期过去了。有时候我又被她打败。但另一些时候我改变了战术，局势就推进了。一次我以为自己差点就要穿透那层冰了：阿姨向我微笑了！但是，我很快就意识到是自己错了，她只是想用舌头把一块卡在牙缝间的菠菜挑出来罢了，并不是冲我微笑。

A few weeks had passed. Sometimes I'd lose the battle. But other times I'd alter my tactics and advance. One time I thought I had almost broken through the ice: the aunty smiled to me! But, I quickly realized that I was mistaken and she had only wanted to use her tongue to pick out a piece of spinach stuck between her teeth. She hadn't smiled at me.

每次对视，我总是礼貌地说"你好""多少钱？"或"谢谢"等。给她钱时，不管是纸币或硬币，我都把钱放到她手里，而不是扔在柜台上。而她找钱时，即使我伸出了手，她也经常无视，直接把钱放在柜台上。可有时候，不知道是否是故意的，她也会把钱放到我伸出的手里。即使是这最微小的胜利，也是值得的。

Making eye contact every time, I'd always politely say, "Hello!" or "How much?" "Thank you," and so on. When handing her the money, no matter if coins or paper, I'd place the change in her hand, not throwing it onto the counter. And even though I'd extend my hand, she'd often ignore me and put the change directly on the counter. But sometimes, unsure whether or not it was on purpose, she'd put the change directly into my extended hand. Even the smallest victory is worthwhile.

几个月过去了，我几乎要放弃了。事实上，我也意识到，在大城市里住的时间越长就越冷漠，我最近也开始对陌生人吼叫"嗯"。笑容也比以前少了。很可能这是每一个在农村里长大的男孩儿在搬到大城市后，必须经过的自然演变。也许纽约、巴黎、上海都一样，大城市的人没有时间来感受小城镇人的迷人风情，每一张他们看过的脸，无非就是一张有着两个眼睛和一些洞洞的纸。可是，春天来了，冬天的寒冷也消失了。在小鸟的唱歌下，风中弥漫着清新的花的香味，我心里想，不，不是想，是需要，需要再舞动一下。

A few months had passed and I had nearly given up. Actually, I realized that the longer I lived in the big city, the more indifferent I became, and I had recently begun croaking the same, "En." Producing smiles was also no longer as easy as previously. Perhaps this is the natural evolution every small town boy must make when adjusting to life in a big city. New York, Paris, Shanghai, perhaps one in the same, big cities with little time for small town charm, where passing faces are nothing more than blank sheets of skin with two eyes and a couple of holes. But spring had come and winter's cold touch had vanished. Beneath a little bird's song, the smell of fresh flowers blowing in the wind, my heart wanted to, no, it didn't want to, it needed to, my heart NEEDED to dance once more.

激情再次被点燃，我猛地把门打开——其实商店的门都是自动打开的——喊："大城市，你不能打败我！"

Passion reignited, I threw open the doors – well, actually they just automatically opened – and shouted, "Big city, you won't beat me!"

我的力量完全恢复了，我又站在柜台前。阿姨站在柜台后，面无笑容，只盯着我看。我信心满满地说："你好，阿姨，今天的天气真漂亮！"

My energy completely restored, I once again stood before the counter. The aunty was standing behind the counter, not smiling, just staring at me. I confidently said, "Hello aunty, the weather really is nice today!"

便利店阿姨的脑袋突然摇了起来，似乎她想咳嗽，拍了拍胸口。接着，她就咳了：像一个蝴蝶快要破茧而出，她的脸上绽放出美好！她露出了一个迷人的微笑，说："是啊，真漂亮！"她的眼睛立刻变得比太阳更加光亮！她的头发也变得更有光泽，皮肤也更加迷人。

The convenient store aunty's head suddenly shook, and she patted her chest as if she were about to cough. And then, she did: like a butterfly emerging from its cocoon, her face exploded with beauty! She revealed an attractive smile and said, "Yep, it really is beautiful!" And immediately her eyes grew brighter than the sun! Her hair grew more lustrous and her skin more glamorous.

瞬间，那道冰墙融化成了地板上的水坑。

In a flash, the icy wall had become nothing but a puddle.

她变成了以前的那个小姑娘，笑着撒娇说："帅哥，巧克力呢？"

Turning into the young gal she once was, she said coquettishly, "Hey handsome, where's my chocolate?"

她重生了！！微笑确实胜于利剑！！

She was reborn!! The smile truly is mightier than the sword!!

我在尽享荣光的时候，想象着在她年轻时，多少男人为之倾倒。这时，另外一位客人快步走过来厉声叫道："中南海香烟，一包。"

Relishing in the glory, imaging that she must have been quite the catch in her youth, another customer quickly walked up and snapped, "A pack of Zhong Nan Hai cigarettes."

她的笑容消失了，眼睛、头发、皮肤的颜色褪去了。液体又变成了固体，那层冰恢复了，阿姨用低哑的声音说："嗯。"

Her smile vanished, the color of her eyes, hair and skin faded. Liquid returning to solid, the icy front restored, she croaked, "En."

我摇了摇头，仿佛我知道了那个顾客所不知道的事，对自己笑了，我享受着这种感觉：我终于成了一个老顾客，正在跟便利店的阿姨共享一条亲密纽带。

Shaking my head, and as if I knew something that he didn't, I smiled to myself, relishing in the fact that I had finally become a "regular" and now shared an intimate bond with the convenient store aunty.

我记不得那天的巧克力是什么味道，可能是因为没有任何东西会比那天体验过的更甜蜜：我赢得了她的尊敬，为了表示感谢，她回报给我她的魅力，和一颗用豆腐做的心。

Can't say I recall how the chocolate tasted that day, but perhaps that was because nothing could have been sweeter than what I'd experienced: I had earned her respect and she thanked me with her guarded, yet willing to share charm, and exposed a heart made of tofu.

Chapter 4

第一天来到中国：文化冲击！
First Day in China: Culture Shock!

　　红灯亮了，车辆却仍然穿行着。首次尝试过马路，我紧张地往前走着每一步，差点被一辆绿色桑塔纳出租车撞到，于是我赶紧退了一步，可是那辆车的司机还按了喇叭。我不懂为什么他要按喇叭，交通灯不是红色的吗？退回到路旁，我看别的行人都在勇敢地过马路。行人灯闪着令人愉悦的绿色，但好像不只是行人想接受那闪光的小绿人的欢迎，还有这里的车子！每一次看到行人们几乎快要被小汽车、公共汽车、摩托车等撞到的时候，我就退缩了。但是，除了他们的衣服被灰尘弄脏了以外，没人受伤，大家都成功地过了马路。我又开始过马路。走了几步后，一辆慢吞吞的、土气的拖拉机颠簸着开过来。为了躲过又黑又浓的尾气，我跳回到一辆绿色人力三轮车的夹缝中间。司机生气地按响了喇叭，强壮的腿用力踩在刹车上，那辆三轮车踉踉跄跄地骑了过去。我又回到路边，看到行人灯变成了红色。但是有几个行人，我不知道他们是因为看不见还是非常勇敢，不理信号灯坚持过马路。有些车减速了，有些车不减速；有些行人停下了，有些不停。在大太阳下，温度简直超过 40 度，但是我身上似乎已经干了，没有汗水流出来。我向前走一步，又退一步，又走，又退……我只能跳起这种难看的二步舞！

The traffic light was red, however cars continued to go through. On the first attempt to cross the road, nervously stepping forward, I was nearly struck by a green Santana taxi, and quickly took a step back. The driver hit his horn. I couldn't understand why he hit his horn. Wasn't the traffic light red? Back on the curb, I watched other pedestrians bravely walk across the road. The pedestrian light flashed a welcoming green. But it seemed it wasn't just the pedestrians who accepted the little flashing green man's offer, but the cars as well! Every time I saw a pedestrian nearly clipped by a car, public bus, motorbike, etc., I'd flinch. But, outside of clothes dirtied by dust, no one was hurt and all successfully crossed the road. I began to cross the road again. After a few steps, a very slow, very rustic tractor chugged by. In order to escape its thick black exhaust, I jumped backwards directly into the path of a green three-wheeled pedicab. The driver angrily ringing his bell, strong legs pedaling hard, the pedicab swung madly around me. Once again I'd jumped back. Standing back on the curb again, I saw the pedestrian light change to red. But a few pedestrians, unsure whether they were blind or really brave, continued to cross against the light. Some cars slowed. Others didn't. Some pedestrians stopped walking, while some didn't. The temperature easily surpassed forty degrees, but with my body seemingly dried out, there was no sweat to be seen. I took a step forward, followed by a step back, another forward, and another back. I could do nothing but dance an ugly two-step.

在一个离我家乡几千公里的十字路口，我低垂着头。好遗憾，自己连如何过马路也不懂。

At an intersection thousands of kilometers from my hometown, my head hung low. How pathetic, I didn't even know how to cross a road.

由于无法过马路，我走到附近一个像飞机场一样宽、楼顶是弓形的建筑里。可那儿没有飞机，都是蔬菜。在菜市场的铁皮屋顶底下，熏肉、扔掉的烟头和霉烂的味道都窜进我鼻子里。在很多被人乱扔掉的红色塑料袋上，黑虫子飞来飞去。不知道是因为温度高还是里面的空气难闻，我呼吸困难，嗓子非常干燥。我想了想，可还是记不得自己上一次喝东西是什么时候了。我的嘴唇都皲裂了。一个卖西瓜的中年胖女人盯着我看。我对她微笑，她也微笑回应了。在她旁边，一个卖黄瓜和白菜的男人指着我，嘴里喊一些我听不懂的话。卖西瓜的又向卖黄瓜和白菜的喊了一声。接着，他们开始大声嚷嚷，其他卖菜的人也参加了进来。突然大家都大喊大叫起来，而我什么都听不懂。我头很痛，而且很渴。

Unable to cross the road, I walked over to a nearby structure that was as wide as an airplane hanger with the same arched roof. Instead of an airplane it was full of vegetables. Under the vegetable market's tin roof, the smell of warm raw meat, discarded cigarette butts and mildew hung before my nose.

Black flies hovered above the discarded red plastic bags. Not sure if it was from the temperature or the air inside, but it was hard to swallow. My throat was really parched. I thought for a moment, but I couldn't remember the last time I had something to drink. My lips were chapped. A fat middle-aged woman selling watermelons was staring at me. I smiled at her. She smiled back. Next to her a man selling cucumbers and cabbage pointed at me and began to shout things I couldn't understand. The watermelon seller began to shout towards the man selling cucumbers and cabbage. In turn, he began to shout at her. Other vegetable sellers joined in. Suddenly everyone began to shout and yell. I couldn't understand anything. My head was throbbing and I was dying of thirst.

靠在菜市场的墙边上是一个卖香烟和日用品的小摊子。摊子的后墙上挂着几个斜着的货架。货架上有可口可乐、橙汁之类的饮料。我又渴得咽了咽口水。

Against the vegetable market's wall was a small stall selling cigarettes and daily necessities. Hanging on the stall's back wall were a couple of sloping shelves. On the shelves were Coca-Cola, orange juice and other similar drinks. I swallowed dryly.

我说："你好。"

I said, "Ni hao."

他发出了一个声音。有可能是对我的回答，但是也许他只想把嗓子清一下。

He let out a sound. Perhaps it was an answer, but he also might have just been clearing his throat.

我开口准备继续用中文说话，但是除了英文单词，没有一句中文说得出来。我对这并不感到意外，那时候，我只认识一个汉语短语：你好。由于嗓子越咽越酸痛，我指着一瓶沾满灰尘、像是橙汁的饮料，伸出食指和中指说明自己要两瓶。他朝我喊了一些话。我摸了摸额头，根本不懂为什么今天大家都要大声说话。我不知道该做什么，就伸出两根手指，向那瓶饮料指了一下，又说："你好。"他一边挑着饮料一边又喊了些什么。终于他挑对了那瓶饮料并把它递给我，同时又说了些什么。我没法说中文，只好用英文说："我不懂。"他喊得更大声了。根据语气，我觉得他不高兴了。我把一些皱巴巴的人民币从我的口袋里拿了出来，向他伸出手，耸了一下肩。他拿走几张纸币。我不知道那是多少钱，因为我对人民币还不熟悉，但是希望他对我能像陌生人对一只三条腿的小狗那样，仁慈一点。说实话，那时候我渴死了，更重要的是这两天——48 小时，我的睡眠却没超过两个小时，我真的不在乎他拿走多少钱。我用英文说了谢谢，他喊叫着回应了。站在他小摊子的太阳伞下，我打开盖子，一口气就把里面温热的液体喝光了。

I opened my mouth, ready to continue using Chinese, but other than English words, no Chinese came out. This wasn't too surprising, as at the time, I only knew how to say "ni hao" in Chinese. Increasingly sore with each swallow, I stuck out my index and middle finger to show that I wanted two, pointing at a bottle completely covered in dust which looked to be orange juice. He shouted something. Rubbing my forehead, I really couldn't figure out why everyone was speaking so loud today. No idea what to do, sticking out two fingers, I pointed at the bottle and again said, "Ni hao." He'd choose one, while at the same time shouting something. Eventually he chose the right one and handed me the bottle. He spat out some words. I couldn't do anything but say in English, "I don't understand." He shouted louder. From his tone, I guess he really wasn't happy. I pulled a few wrinkled renminbi from my pocket. Stretching my hand out towards him, I shrugged my shoulders. He took a few bills. I didn't know how much, I still wasn't used to Chinese currency, but as a stranger would treat a small dog with only three legs, I was hoping he'd show a little mercy. Actually, at that time, dying of thirst, and more importantly not having slept more than two hours in the past forty eight hours, I really could not care less how much he took. Using English I thanked him. He shouted back. Standing below his stall's umbrella, I immediately opened the bottle and drank every drop of the warm liquid.

在被困在这条马路过不去之前，我已经经过了四十多个小时的旅程：克利夫兰到芝加哥，芝加哥到洛杉矶，洛杉矶到香港，再坐巴士到深圳，又上飞机飞到广西北海，最后在一个新房子里过了一个不眠之夜。我跟行尸走肉一样，筋疲力尽、跌跌撞撞地回到了我的新家。

Prior to being trapped by an impassable road, over a period of forty hours of travel: Cleveland to Chicago, Chicago to Los Angeles, Los Angeles to Hong Kong, a bus to Shenzhen, once again back on board a plane for Beihai, Guangxi, followed by a sleepless night in a new home, I already had become a walking zombie. Nearly fainting from exhaustion, I staggered back to my new home.

大约十几分钟后，也有可能更久——已经记不清楚，我走到家门前。在走进新房子的一楼的时候，那气味让我回忆起了外面那个菜市场：霉烂味很重，这有可能跟亚热带气候有关，但至少没人大声嚷嚷。在一个角落里，我看到一个老奶奶坐在一把看起来很不舒服的木头椅子上。我看上去像是这里的入侵者。我露出紧张的微笑，就好像自己在图书馆里那样，低声地说："你好。"她看着我，点了点她那个不但小，而且皱纹比干掉的苹果更多的脑袋。我想，有可能我进错地方了，这不是我的新房子？

About ten minutes later—it could have been longer, nothing was very clear—I reached my door. And as soon as I entered my new home via the first floor, the atmosphere reminded me of the market outside: the smell of thick mildew. Perhaps it had something to do with the subtropical location. At least no one was shouting. In one corner I saw an old grandmother sitting in what looked to be a very uncomfortable wooden chair. Feeling as though I was an intruder, smiling nervously, as if I was in a library, I whispered, "Ni hao." She looked at me, and nodded a head smaller and with more wrinkles than a dried apple. I thought to myself, perhaps I made a mistake and this wasn't my new home?

不知道该说什么，或该做什么，我只想去我的房间。我蹑手蹑脚地上三楼去了。听说在这栋房子里有些人住在二楼，其他住在四楼。我住的是三楼。我几乎走不动了，全身不舒服，筋疲力尽，我真不想遇到别人，只想到一个没有人大声嚷嚷的房间里去。

Not sure what to say or what to do I thought I should go to my room. I was told some people lived on the second floor and others on the fourth of this house. Mine was the third floor. With my legs almost unable to continue and my entire body sore, mentally drained, I really didn't want to run into anyone. I only wanted to enter a room where no one was shouting.

进入房间，把门锁上以后，我往床上一倒，像一块又重又平的石头轰然倒在地上一样，我的屁股砰的一声落下。我又尝试着在新床垫上放松了一下。

After entering my room and locking the door, I fell back towards my bed, and like a heavy, flat rock smacking against the ground, my backside landed with a thud. I attempted to get comfortable on my new mattress again.

那块床垫，还被塑料膜包着。没有柔软的棉布，也没有枕头，我的脸直接贴在塑料上；没有床单，我全身贴在塑料包装膜上。过了一会儿，我又努力调整姿势，看到前面有一个布满灰尘的、被太阳晒褪色的小红灯。它就挂在电视机的边上。我无法入睡，于是拿出还在袋子里的遥控器打开了电视。电视上出现了一个很漂亮、头发造型完美的女歌手。她唱歌的背景中士兵一边行进、一边向不停被挥舞着的很大的中国国旗敬礼。因为她穿着军装，我估计她在大声唱着一首爱国的歌曲。*我从来没看过这种音乐频道，但我知道一件事情：中美的音乐频道完全不一样！

The mattress was still wrapped in plastic. With no soft cotton and no pillow, my face stuck to the plastic surface. With no sheets, my entire body stuck to the plastic film. After a while, shifting my body yet again, I looked over at a small, dusty Chinese lantern that had faded in the sun. It hung from the side of a TV. Unable to sleep, I used a remote control that was still in its bag to turn it on. On the screen appeared a beautiful woman with perfectly sculpted hair, not a hair out of place. In the background soldiers marched as they saluted a giant waving Chinese flag. Because she was dressed in a military uniform, I figured she must be singing a patriotic song. While I've never seen a music television station like this, I can certainly say: Chinese and American MTV were completely different!

我往右边滚。我的皮肤从黏着的塑料包装膜上慢慢地剥离下来，呲呲的响着。我从卫生间的门里看进去，那个我非常熟悉的马桶和很舒服的坐便器都不在，只有一个瓷洞对着我。昨晚新老板说过，在我住的地方有一个西式马桶，但是那扇门被锁起来了。新老板说因为那家房东对她说等我搬出去以后他们要用，所以不想被别人弄脏了。

---

*后来我才发现电视上穿着军装的歌手是宋祖英，她唱的歌曲叫《爱我中华》。
Later I discovered that the singer on the TV dressed in a military uniform was Song Zuying, and the song she sang was "Love My China".

I rolled to my right. My skin slowly peeled away from the plastic cover making an awful sound. I found myself looking into the bathroom. The toilet I was very familiar with and its comfortable seat weren't there. A ceramic hole stared at me. Last night my new boss had told me that there was a western-style toilet here, but that door was locked. My new boss said that the home's landlord told her that after I moved out they would like to use it, so they don't want others to dirty it up.

眼皮很重，头更痛了，我捏了捏鼻梁。我开始后悔我的决定：来到中国。

Eyelids heavy, a migraine growing, I pinched the bridge of my nose and rubbed. I began to regret my decision: the decision to come to China.

我闭上眼睛，开始回忆，才明白我本来对中国的期望跟现实完全不一样。天真的是，我愚蠢地把中国想象成电影里的世界，特别是一个被美国好莱坞创造的中国化世界：想象过我将住在一条很窄的小巷里，路面是鹅卵石做的，两侧是连成排的房子，房子的上面有很复杂的图案，都是上个朝代的艺术家用刀雕刻而成的。我错误地以为每一个石板做的倾斜的屋顶上都会挂着红灯笼。下午，天气不冷不热，我站在竹子阳台上，穿着一套后面绣着一只彩色老虎的丝袍，喝着一杯绿茶，我愉悦地欣赏小巷里非常有趣的舞龙舞狮活动、武术动作、北京杂技。接着是很多美女，她们头发乌黑发亮，穿着合身的旗袍。最后到处都会有鞭炮和烟花放起火！好像这不是现代的中国，至少不是北海市。好莱坞还没来到北海。

Closing my eyes, I had a chance to recollect, and I understood too late that my original expectations of China and reality were completely different. Naively, I foolishly imagined an overly "Chinese-like" China that was more fit for a world found in a movie, in particular a Hollywood produced movie: I imagined I would live in a narrow lane, the road's surface cobblestone, both sides lined with connected houses. The outsides of the homes would be covered in intricate designs carved by the blades of a former dynasty's craftsman. I wrongly believed that there would be red Chinese lanterns hanging from the edges of sloping slate roofs. On afternoons which were neither cold nor hot, I'd stand on a bamboo balcony. Dressed in a silk robe with a colorful tiger embroidered on the back, drinking a cup of green tea, I would happily watch a vibrant parade as it took place in the alley below: dragon and lion dances, martial arts, Beijing acrobats, followed by beautiful women, jet black, shining hair, adorned in form-fitting qipaos. At the end, firecrackers and fireworks would explode everywhere. It seemed this wasn't modern day China or at least not in Beihai, Guangxi. Hollywood had yet to have arrived in Beihai.

我看着行李，感觉很失望。

Feeling quite disappointed, I looked at my luggage.

我精神疲惫地走到窗户边。从栅栏的窗户看向对面：除了一个房子贴了粉红色的瓷砖以外，外面没有其他好看的。

My spirit depleted, I shuffled over to the window. I looked through the window's bars: other than a building's pink tiles, there was nothing.

一只苍蝇飞下来，在栅栏上落下。一双复眼盯着我。

A fly flew down and landed on one of the bars. A pair of compound eyes stared at me.

我又转头看了看我的包。

I turned back and looked at my bags again.

仿佛不喜欢这里的环境，苍蝇飞出去了。我想像它那样，想成为它的搭档，陪着它飞出去。外语培训学校原来说我可以住在一套公寓房里，现在却把我安排在一个我显然不喜欢住的房子里，在一座好像大家都在生气、只会大喊大叫的城市，更别提还有一条无法通过的马路！是，我做了一个新的决定：跟随着那只苍蝇，我也要飞回家。

As if it didn't like its surroundings, the fly flew off. And just like that, I wanted to become its companion, to join it and fly away. The English training school had originally said I could live in an apartment, but instead I was placed in a home that obviously wasn't welcoming, in a city where apparently everyone was angry, a city that only wanted to shout and scream, not to mention a street that couldn't be crossed! Yep, my decision was made: following the fly's lead, I would also fly home.

我拿着两个大包。电视上的美女已经唱完了。

I picked up the two bags. The beautiful woman on the TV had stopped singing.

站在门旁，我听见门后传来几个低沉的声音，其中一个明显是女性的响亮的声音。一定是之前被美女唱歌的声音遮盖了，以至于我没早点听见。他们至少是两个人，一个男的和一个女的。他们在一起低声地说话。不用猜都知道他们正在讨论什么："他在干什么？要偷走什么？估计想用我们的干净马桶！"

Standing next to the door I could hear hushed voices, one of which was clearly a woman's, coming from behind the door. They must have been hidden by the woman's singing and that's why I hadn't heard them earlier. There were at least two, a man's and a woman's. They were whispering to one another. No need to senselessly guess what they were discussing: "What's he doing? What's he want to steal? Bet he's planning on using our clean toilet!"

我又向窗户外看了一眼。不行，窗户有栅栏，我可不是那只小苍蝇，不能从窗户逃跑。我沮丧地想着，那些栅栏是防止人从外面进入的，但是似乎这房间像监狱一样，也防止人出去。但是，就算自己能从窗户爬下去，然后呢？连这里的马路我都不知道如何过去，又怎么敢指望自己能找到一辆出租车带我去飞机场？更重要的是，如果最后我能找到的话，怎么说清楚让司机带我去机场？用双手展开模仿飞机飞起来，在原地打转，嘴里发出引擎的声音希望他能明白我的意思？

I glanced back at the window. Nope, the window had bars, and I wasn't that little fly. I couldn't escape through the window. Sadly I thought, those bars were for keeping people from entering, but as if this room was a prison cell, they also kept people from leaving. But, even if I could climb down from the window, what would I do after? I couldn't even cross a road here, so how could I dare think I could find a taxi who would be willing to take me to the airport? More importantly, if I found one, how could I explain that I wanted him to take me to the airport: spread my hands and imitate an airplane taking off, spinning in circles, my mouth making engine noises hoping he'd understand my meaning?

这根本不是我第一次出国，我不是什么都不了解的无知国外旅客！这也不是第一次失去自己的方向，可是为什么我不禁啜泣？

This certainly wasn't my first time abroad, and this visitor wasn't so ignorant that he was totally clueless! And this wasn't the first time I'd lost my way, so why was I whining?

我站着没动，肩膀耷拉着，包在地板上放着，不知道该做什么，我的视线又回到电视上。电视上正在播出一则推销中国的广告。虽然我完全听不懂，但是我越看越感兴趣：有着异域风情的景点和名胜，令人难忘的长城，无数的兵马俑永远警觉地伫立着，翠绿色梯田里的水稻在阳光下闪闪发亮，旅客们在广阔的沙漠上骑着骆驼……一切都像我的梦想中的那么有魅力。

Standing, but not moving, shoulders sagging, the bags back on the floor, not knowing what to do, my eyes went back to the television. What appeared to be a commercial advertising China came on. I couldn't understand a thing, but the more I watched, the more captivated I became: exotic locales and the country's famous spots; the unforgettable Great Wall of China, the countless Terracotta soldiers forever standing vigilant, vibrant green rice terraces and their rice paddies shining in the sunlight, tourists riding camels through a vast desert, they were all as enchanting as the places in my dreams.

最终，门后的说话声停止了。我把耳朵贴在门板上，能听见他们的脚步声越来越轻了。他们走下楼去，然后楼下的大门砰地被关上了！我赶紧向房间的窗户跑去。我在窗帘的后面躲起来，隐藏起自己，偷偷看了看那两个刚刚在我的门后小声嘀咕的主人。他们是一个年纪大点的男人和一个好像是他的老婆的女人，样子都长得差不多：矮个子，身材比较结实，面带愁容，正站在楼下抬着头仔细观察我的窗户。我的新房东彼此喊了一些话以后，就向拐角处走去，消失了。

Finally the voices behind the door had stopped talking. Ear pressed against the door, I could hear their footsteps getting quieter as they went downstairs. After reaching the ground floor the front door slammed shut with a bang! I quickly ran over the to the room's window. Hoping to conceal myself, I hid behind the window curtain and spied on the owners of the whispering voices who had recently been behind my door. A middle—aged man and what looked to be his wife—both similar in appearance: short, blocky figures, faces scowling—stood below and looked up as they scrutinized my window. After shouting something at one another, my new hosts walked around a corner and disappeared.

我又看起了电视：漂在一条小河上的一只木船上的旅客正兴奋地欣赏着一个古老的水乡。河边，很多穿着长裙的美女在相互泼水，山上的寺庙一半被云海笼罩着，充满神秘色彩……类似的迷人场景连续播出来。尽管这两天我的想象力好像因为失眠和时差退化了，但是现在我能重新感觉到想象力，我的激情渐渐又开始复苏。我又回顾了一下来中国之前的想法：也许某一天有机会在著名的少林寺练习功夫；有机会跟中国人享受丰盛的宴会，能尝试各种各样的正宗中国菜肴——在冬天吃北京烤鸭，夏天吃广东点心。就这样，我来到我梦想中的地方！电视上播放的那些冒险将会接踵而来！反正，北海不是一个海边城市：在大太阳和蓝蓝的天空下有没有海滩的烧烤晚会和小小比基尼女郎跳来跳去呢？因为只看过这个城市的很小一部分，甚至都不能算一个街区，我有什么权利判断整个城市，甚至整个国家呢？

I looked back at the television: floating on a small river in a wooden boat a group of excited tourists enjoyed an ancient river town, along riverbanks wearing long dresses beautiful girls splashed each other with water, mysterious mountain temples half-hidden in a sea of clouds, and other similarly enchanting places continued to be shown. Even though these two days may have cast my imagination aside through insomnia and jet lag, I could feel my imagination, my passion slowly return to life. Once again I began to think about how I felt before I had arrived in China: hadn't I thought that perhaps someday I'd have a chance to study Kungfu at the famous Shao Lin Temple? I'd have the chance to enjoy colorful banquets with Chinese people, tasting any and all authentic Chinese cuisine, from Peking duck in the winter to Cantonese dim sum in the summer? And just like that, I had arrived in the place I had wanted to arrive in! The potential adventures shown on the television were endless! Anyways, wasn't Beihai a beach city: under the hot sun and blue skies on the beaches wouldn't there be barbeque parties and small bikinis jumping around? Having only seen a small part of a city, which didn't even quantify as a city block, what right did I have to judge an entire city, let alone an entire country?

我感到极度的振奋，我小心地站在厕所里，怕自己不小心踩到马桶里。我用冷水洗了澡，身心像一个花蕾在春天里轮回了。虽然卫生间没有肥皂，但是从克利夫兰市起飞，到大约四十多小时之后的现在，我终于又感到身体干净了。旅行的污垢和今早的怀疑被水冲走了。

My spirit feeling extremely lifted, standing carefully over the toilet fearful I might accidentally step in, I took a cold shower, and like a flower in the spring, my mind and body were reborn! And while there was no soap in the bathroom, for the first time since a departure that began in Cleveland, approximately forty hours earlier, I finally felt completely clean again. Alongside the grime from traveling my earlier doubts were washed away by the water.

我想，这个决定是不是我自己的选择？学生、新老板和她的培训学校是不是希望我来？难道我没有责任心？昨晚我认识了新老板，她一句难听的话也没对我说。确实，我住在一个好像不欢迎我的房子里。难道我一个大男人躲在门后、窗帘后不羞耻吗？

I thought, wasn't this decision my own own? And, aren't many students, a new boss and her training school expecting my arrival? Didn't I have a sense of responsibility? And, when I met my new boss the previous evening, she hadn't shouted a thing, not even once. And, sure, I was living in a home that didn't seem welcoming. But, was I without shame, a grown man who hid behind doors and curtains?

因为没有毛巾，我用早上穿破的衬衫把身体擦干，精力充沛地打开行李包的拉链，拿出我最喜欢的衬衫和一条新内裤。包一下子开了，我的新生活随之迸发开来！我把棒球帽戴上，满血复活地出门了！

Without a towel, using the shirt I'd worn that morning to dry myself off, with fresh vigor, I opened the zipper on my bag and pulled out my favorite shirt and a clean pair of underwear. My bag having burst open, I was ready to allow life to follow suit! Pulling on my baseball hat, totally energized, I was off!

在外面，我用帽子挡住大太阳，不一会儿就又走到今天早上挑战的地方：那个无法通过的十字路口。快到的时候，我听到右边有像一个又大又丰满的虫子打在车窗上的啪嗒声。我转向那个声音的方向，只见一只巨大的黑水牛拉着木板车慢步过来。坐在车上的是一个拿着小鞭子的农民：一顶宽边草帽遮住了他的大半张脸，他皮肤黝黑，像老皮革一样粗。他疑惑地盯着我看，然后吐出很大一口痰。潮湿的痰撞在路面上发出啪嗒一声！太了不起了！我碰到一个真真正正的农民，一个非常地道的农民！也许是因为一种冒险家的快感，或者内心的浪漫主义，或者自己由于缺乏睡眠而迷糊了，但是我相信，在那一刻，不管"发现"什么事情，都令我印象深刻！想象着他脑子里会有多少有趣的故事，我想试试模仿一下他的动作，也吐一口痰。可是我嘴巴太干了，只能吐出一点点口水，在我的下巴上可耻地挂着。我很高兴地对他打招呼："你好！"他没有回答，只点了点头。那很完美！那黑水牛不理我，继续散步过去了。

Outside, my hat blocking out the strong sun, in no time I was again walking towards this morning's challenge: that impossible to cross intersection. Nearly there, to my right I heard what sounded like a big, plump bug smacking against a car's windshield with a splat. I turned in the direction of where the splat struck the road. And what did I see but a huge black water buffalo pulling a wooden cart strolling forward. Sitting on the cart was a farmer and his little whip. A wide brimmed conical straw hat concealed half of his sun-tanned face, the skin rough as old leather. He eyed me suspiciously, then spat out a big slimy wad of spit. It smacked wetly on the pavement–splat. Outstanding! I'd just run into an authentic, salt of the earth Chinese farmer! Perhaps it was due to an adventurer's high, the romanticist within or I was just delirious from a lack of sleep, but I believe, at that moment, no matter what I would have "discovered", it would have left a deep impression! Imagining the many interesting stories he must carry in his mind, wanting to try and imitate his attitude—rough, yet totally free of societal manner—I spat myself. But, my mouth was too dry, and I could only spit out a little, and it hung shamefully from my chin. Nonplussed, I happily greeted him with a, "Ni hao!" Besides a slight nod of his head, he didn't respond. It was perfect! The black water buffalo ignored me and continued to saunter by.

红灯的时候,不出所料,车子都随便开过去了。谁在乎? 我自言自语。在越南的胡志明市市中心,混乱比规律更正常,我也照样开摩托车; 在菲律宾,八个随身带刀的流氓围着我,威胁我让我滚开; 在自己生活的阿拉斯加后院差点被公驼鹿踩死……我还怕什么! 在我旁边等着六七个准备过马路的人。我躲在这个小队伍里面: 人多势众。好像想保护我一下,他们离我更近了。灯绿了,我们开始慢慢过马路。没人喊叫,车子在行人的前面和后面开过去了,我们终于穿过了那条路! 我想大家都应该互相祝贺,但是一过马路,其他六个行人就向他们自己的目的地走了。

The streetlight was red, but as expected, cars continued to pass through as they liked. Who cares, I said to myself! In the center of Vietnam's Ho Chi Minh City, a place where chaos was more common than order, hadn't I ridden a motorbike with confidence? In a rough part of the Philippines hadn't eight thugs who more than likely were armed with knives surrounded me as they threatened me to get lost? Had I not nearly been trampled to death by a bull moose in my Alaskan backyard? What was I afraid of! To my side was a group of six to seven people waiting to cross the road. I secretly moved in between the group: safety in numbers. As if they wanted to protect me, they moved in closer. The light was green, and becoming one, we started to slowly cross the road. No one shouted. With cars passing in front and from behind our group, we eventually crossed the road! I thought we should congratulate one another, but after crossing the road, the six people went their separate ways.

站在那条路的另一边，欣赏着路边漂亮的南方棕榈树，我才意识到天气不是那么热，这里正是非常舒服美好的夏日。我深吸一口气，露出一个很开心的微笑。那微笑代表心满意足，是意识到自己真的做出了正确的决定的那种满足。我往前一步，开始一辈子难忘的冒险之旅！

Standing on the other side of the road, admiring the attractive southern palm trees that lined the streets, realizing that it wasn't as much hot, as just what it should be on a summer's day, I took a deep breath, and revealed a happy smile. The smile represented total satisfaction, the kind of satisfaction you find once realizing that you truly had made the correct decision. I took a step forward and began a once in a lifetime adventure!

Chapter 5

怎么跟老外聊天?
How to Talk to a "Laowai"?

广州火车站，两个姑娘的对话——

Guangzhou Train Station, two young ladies' dialogue:

姑娘甲："老外。"

Young lady 1: "Laowai."

姑娘乙："哪里？"

Young lady 2: "Where?"

姑娘甲："后面。"

Young lady 1: "Behind you."

姑娘乙："我应该说点啥？"

Young lady 2: "What should I say?"

姑娘甲："我不知道。"

Young lady 1: "I don't know."

我笑着在她们的背后说："我也不知道。"

From behind them I said with a smile, "I also don't know."

她们都呵呵地笑着说"Sorry"，就跑开了。

Giggling they said, "Sorry," and ran away.

很多好奇的学生认真地问："老师，怎么跟外国朋友说话？如何跟外国同事交流？" 对我来说，这个问题是有点奇怪——虽然您读下去就会更明白我的想法——可我还是需要回答一下这个问题。

Many curious students ask in earnest, "Teacher, how can I speak with foreign friends? How can we communicate with foreign coworkers?" To me, this question is a little strange—continue reading and you will better understand my feelings—but I still should respond to this innocent question.

在下面我写了一些 Do's & Don'ts：有些很搞笑，有些你可以试试，有些最好避开。

Down below I wrote some "Do's and Don'ts": some are hilarious, some you can try and some are best to avoid.

第一，语言和文化有差异，可没有物种差异。

Number One: Language and culture have differences, but there's no difference in species.

不要忘记，我们的最大区别是我们的语言。可是如果你会说英文，即使只会讲一点，这个问题就大大地减少了。嗯，是的，我们还在文化上有一些差异，可是，美国和英国、南非和印度呢？英文都是我们的母语，只是文化都不一样罢了。所以别怕，只要开口，大多数的外国人都不是坏人。如果你说错，不要担心，他们不会咬你。

Don't forget, our biggest difference is language. But if you can speak English, even if only just a little, then this problem is greatly reduced. And, yes, there is still the difference in culture. But, what about the United States and England, South Africa and India? For all of us, English is our native tongue, but our cultures are different. So don't be afraid, just open your mouth. Most foreigners aren't bad people. If you say something wrong, don't worry, they won't bite.

第二，"May I be your friend?" 如果在中文里听起来比较奇怪，也许在英文里也是奇怪的。

Number Two: "May I be your friend?" If in Chinese this sounds a little strange, perhaps in English it sounds strange as well.

说实话，这句话不仅很诚恳，而且是很友好的。不幸的是，诚恳和友好看上去容易有奇怪的感觉。可是，在我的"中国生活"中，偶尔有几个陌生人一走到我面前就说这句话。假如你不觉得很奇怪，我问你，要是在中国，你走到一个你不认识的人的前面说"咱们交个朋友？"的话，对方会想什么？会觉得你很奇怪。如果你是女的，他会想你是……

这么说或许不太好，但估计你能猜到他会怎么想。但在聚会、网上聊天时可以用，对方会乐意接受你友好的邀请，至少在大多数时候会。可是，要是在路上直接说呢？请先考虑一下怎么开始对话。

Frankly speaking, not only is this sentence sincere, but it's also friendly. Unfortunately, sincere and friendly can just as easily come across as strange. During my "China Life", I've had strangers walk up to me and ask this question. And if you don't think this is strange, well, let me ask you, if in China you walked up to another Chinese person you don't know and asked, "Want to be my friend?" what would they think? Maybe they'd think you were crazy. If you were a female, he may think you are…sorry, I think you can guess what he'd think, etc. But at a party, on the internet, etc., it's okay to use, and the person you are speaking to will happily accept your offer of friendship. Well, most of the time at least. But, on the street, direct to a stranger? Please consider for a moment how to begin talking with them.

第三，"今天天气很好。"
Number Three: "Beautiful day, isn't it？"

不错，这是闲聊，可是还要看环境／情况。如果是在路边等巴士的情况下，可以这样说。在晚会时你可以这样开始对话："嘿，你怎么认识某某人？"或者用我们都非常熟悉的这个基本介绍："您好，我叫阿文。"（当然不要用我的名字。）等火车的时候："现在是几点钟？"看见别人独自吃饭，可以说："想跟我们一起吃吗？"（最好是先看清楚情况再讲。）给你说几个尽量要避免的例子：在上海外滩骑车等红灯时一个小伙子对我说："小菜一碟。"我看了一眼他的手里是否拿着一块蛋糕，但并没有。好像他想使用一句美国的俗语"小菜一碟（It's a piece of cake.）"（那句话的意思是"很容易做"。）跟一个外国人交流，可是他的话绝对没有上下文。再举一个例子。有一次坐在饭店的时候，一个老人用英文问我："美国人？"我回答："是。"他用中文再问我："旧金山有很多同性恋？" 根本没有上下文。我最后举的例子是："阿文，在你业余时间你喜欢修理屋顶和修理篱笆吗？"什么？就算你的英文课本里有些很古老的或者根本没人使用的短语，你也不必真的使用它们。反正，许多英文课本比奶奶的裤袜更古老。

Not bad, this is small talk. But you still need to look at the environment/situation. If you are standing by the side of the road waiting for the bus, you can say something like this. At a party you could start a dialogue with, "Hey, so, how do you know so and so?" And we are all familiar with this basic introduction, "Hi, my name is Kevin." But, don't use my name of course. How about waiting for a train, "Do you have the time?" If watching someone eating alone, you can say, "Would you like to join us?" It's best to first look at the situation, then speak. Let me give you some examples that you should do your best to avoid: biking on Shanghai's Bund I stopped for a red light and a young man said to me, "It's a piece of cake." I glanced at his hand to see if he was holding a piece of cake. There wasn't any. It seemed he wanted to communicate with a foreigner using the common American saying "It's a piece of cake," (which means something was easy to do) but what he said had absolutely no context. Another example: once while sitting outside of a restaurant, an old man asked in English, "American?" I answered, "Yes." Then in Chinese he asked me, "Does San Francisco have many gay people?" Zero context. And for my last example, "Do you enjoy fixing rooftops and mending fences in your free time?" What did she just ask me? Just because some old fashion or awkward sentences may be found in your English textbooks, that doesn't mean you must use them. Anyways, most English textbooks are more out of date than your grandmother's pantyhose.

第四，"我可以帮你什么忙吗？"
Number Four: "May I help you?"

我估计你们多少都碰到过迷路的外国人：张着嘴巴，拿着一张倒置的地图走来走去，搔搔头——都是国际通用表情："帮我！我迷路了！"要是你问那个迷路的外国人是否需要帮忙，他们肯定会感谢你的关心。然后你就可以用英文给他们指路。

I estimate that you have all run into this kind of foreigner at least two or three times: mouth hanging open, holding a map and walking back and forth as he scratches his head—which are all the international signs for: "Help! I'm lost!" If you want to ask if they are lost and whether they need your help, certainly they will appreciate your concern. After that you can use English and show them the way.

第五，"对不起！"
Number Five: "Excuse me！"

要是你看到外国人掉了东西，在他后面可以喊："对不起！"但是，请你不要说："您好！"如果只说"您好！"他有可能会不理你，因为他不知道为什么他看不到的人会突然喊："您好！"

If you see a foreigner drop something, from behind them you can call out, "Excuse me!" But please don't just shout 'Hello!' If you only say, "Hello!" maybe they will ignore you because they don't know why someone they cannot see suddenly shouts, "Hello!"

第六，"那件毛衣很漂亮。"
Number Six："That's a beautiful sweater."

谁不喜欢恭维？这样开始交流简直是太容易了。因为大家都知道女孩子最好的朋友就是恭维，所以可以说"我真喜欢你的发型"或"请问，你的鞋子是在哪里买的？"恭维也受男孩子的欢迎，比如"你很帅"（女孩子对男孩子说）或"手表很好，有故事？"（男孩子对男孩子）当然还有最经常听到的："你的中文非常好。"（不分性别）无论是一种夸张的恭维或者是想给对方面子，一句表扬总是会让气氛轻松一点或者能打破沉默。

Who doesn't like a compliment? To begin talking this way is really easy. And because everyone knows a compliment is a girl's best friend, you could say, "I really love your hairstyle " or "Excuse me, where did you buy those shoes?" (said to a girl) Compliments are also popular with men: "You are very handsome." (girl to boy) "Nice watch. Does it have a story? " (man to man.) And of course there is the most commonly heard, "Your Chinese is very good." (either sex) Whether it is exaggerated flattery or a face-giving measure, a compliment always lightens the mood and breaks the ice.

第七， "可以跟你练习我的英文吗？"
Number Seven: "May I practice my English with you ？ "

当然问话的人没有觉得不好意思，只是想练习他的英文。可是很多人都很忙，可能会误会你的意思，也许会以为你是要求他们教你英文，让人感觉这是一种工作。更好的方法是问他："你好吗？ "对，非常简单。"新来到这个城市？让我做第一个欢迎你的人……"欢迎他来到你的城市，这样不也能练习你的英文吗？还不会令人感觉到是一种工作！

Of course the one you are talking to won't think this is bad and only believes you want to practice your English. But everyone is busy, and they might misunderstand, perhaps believing that you are requesting that they teach you English. It will make the person feel it's like a job. A better way to ask is, "How are you?" Yes, very simple. "New to the city? Let me be the first to welcome you to...." like welcoming them to your city. In this way aren't you practicing your English? And it doesn't leave the other person thinking it's a job!

第八，你好与你好啊

Number Eight: Hello and Halloo

和外国人／老外打招呼的时候，请你用眼神跟他们交流，然后向他们微笑地说出"Hello"。

When greeting a foreigner/laowai, please make eye contact, then smile in their direction and say, "Hello!"

请不要在他背后喊："Hello！"

Please don't: Shout from behind, "Hello！"

也不要不停地说："Hello，Hello，Hello。"

Without stopping say, "Hello, Hello, Hello."

不要大声地喊叫："Halloo!"

Loudly shout: "Halloo!"

也请不要向老外吹口哨或拍手。我们不是小狗。

Also please don't: Whistle or clap your hands towards a laowai. We aren't little puppies.

也不要用"嘿"或"哦"，或者另外一些比较奇怪的，或是陌生的发音。

As well as: "Hey" or "Oh" or other relatively strange and unusual sounds.

第九，"我很好，你呢？"
Number Nine: "I'm fine, thank you. And you?"

如果你不巧地说出这最简单、最自动的答案，先打自己一耳光。把这部分内容再读一遍。假如对方已经用过这两个句子，然后你还是不经意地说出："我很好。你呢？"你应该立刻找到最近的窗户跳出去。

If you accidentally speak out this simplest, most automatic response, first slap yourself. Then please read again, 'How to talk to a laowai.' If the person you are speaking to already used these two basic sentences and you followed by accidentally saying, "I'm fine, thank you. And you?", then you should immediately seek out the closest window and jump.

当然我是开玩笑的。不要跳窗。跪下去，向你曾经的英文课本叩头一千次。

Of course I'm only joking. You don't need to jump out the window. Please kneel down and kowtow towards your previous English textbook one thousand times.

最后，我想说，我意识到大多数的中国人对外国人都是礼貌的。除了"第八"的 halloo 以外，他们大多数时候是真心想交朋友，练习自己的英文等，万一冒犯了对方，很可能也不是故意的。

Finally, I'd like to say, I realize that most Chinese are very polite to foreigners. Besides Number Seven's "Halloo", they are all more than likely earnest attempts at a friendship, wanting to practice one's English, etc. and if they have offended someone, it was more than likely not their intention.

好的，我说完了！现在我必须马上出门把屋顶和篱笆修理一下！

Okay, that's enough! Now I need to get outside ASAP to fix rooftops and mend fences!

Chapter 6

第二个大山？并不是！
The Second Dashan? No Way!

看电影的时候，谁没幻想过成为一名演员？摇身一变你就能成为任何"人物"：英雄、国王、军人，甚至是外星人！简单来说，不管想成为什么人物，在电影世界中，根本没有限制！

When watching a movie, who hasn't fantasized about becoming a movie star? You could transform into anything: a hero, an emperor, a soldier, even an alien! To put it simply, no matter what role you'd like to act out, in the world of movies, there are no limits!

不幸的是，不是每个人都能当演员，社会还需要理发师、办公室员工、医生，等等。

Unfortunately, not all of us can become actors. Society still requires hairdressers, office workers, doctors, etc.

可是，非常意外的，有一天，在中国的好莱坞，这个难得的机会终于来敲我的门了。

But quite unexpectedly, one day, in China's Hollywood, this hard to come by opportunity finally came knocking at my door.

可是，难道他们用我是因为我有白皮肤，因为我是外国人，仅此而已？不是因为我演技好？好吧，该让你，我的读者来判断那是因为我的肤色还是我天生就是演员。

But, did they use me because I had a white face, because I was foreigner and nothing more? And not because I had any actual acting talent? Okay, I should allow you, the reader to decide if it was because of my white face or my natural ability to act.

先来介绍一下我的表演经历。

First, I will introduce my acting resume:

1. 2003 年，云南省昆明市郊外，一处秘密的场所
1. 2003, Yunnan Province, Kunming suburbs, a secret location

电影片名：我忘了。不，电影不是叫《我忘了》，我只是记不住叫什么。很明显，那不是部大片。

Movie Title: I forgot. And, no, the name of the movie wasn't *I Forgot.* I just can't remember its name. Apparently that movie wasn't a blockbuster.

情节：法国人在云南造铁路，欺负本地人。

Plot: France building a railroad in Yunnan, harassing the locals.

主角：曹操（美国演员）

Leading Role: Cao Cao (American actor)

我的角色：法国军人，土地测量员。你可以想象一根瘦瘦的胡萝卜穿着很破旧的军装。真难看，可那就是我的样子。

My Role: French soldier, land surveyor. Imagine a skinny carrot dressed in an old, ragged soldier uniform. It was really unattractive, but that's what I looked like.

历史简介：20 世纪初，法国人在云南造铁路时，因为要利用当地农民的土地，把他们的房子拆掉造铁路，结果与当地农民发生冲突。

Time Period: At the beginning of the twentieth century, when the French were building a railroad, to utilize the local farmer's lands, they knocked down their property to build the railway. As expected, they clashed with the local farmers.

我的小镜头：我测量那里的土地时，农民对我和我的中国保镖进行阻挠。事情演变为暴力场面，农民用农具攻击我和我的保镖。导演命令我喊："我是法国人，别打我！"我的保镖也喊："我是中国人，别打我！"可是我太紧张，无论用中文说或英文说，仿佛嘴里塞满三明治，怎么都说不清楚！真丢人！导演烦躁地对翻译说："告诉他，不要紧张，不管他说什么，我们都要把他的台词配音一下。"

My small scene: As I was surveying the land, the farmers confronted my

Chinese bodyguards and I and began to obstruct us. Things would turn violent and the farmers would attack my guards and I with farm tools. The director told me to say, "I'm French, don't hit me!" And my guards would also shout out: "I'm Chinese, don't hit me!" But, I was too nervous, and no matter in English or Chinese, as if my mouth was stuffed full of sandwiches, nothing I said came out clearly. It was really embarrassing. Irritated, the director told his interpreter, "Tell him, don't be nervous, no matter what he says, we will still dub over his words."

2. "云南欢迎你" 广告
2. "Welcome Yunnan!" commercial

不值得一提（我的镜头只有 0.5 秒钟长）。

Not worth mentioning (my part was 0.5 seconds long).

3. 香港电视剧
3. Hong Kong Television Drama

不值得一提（因为不能控制脸上的动作或者由于我红彤彤的脸色，我被导演剪掉了）。

Not worth mentioning. (Because I couldn't control my facial movements or the color of my glowing red face and I was removed by the director.)

看起来我不是第二个大山。

It would seem I wasn't the second Da Shan.

那时，我敢打赌我连演一块石头也不行，我的信心十分低迷！

At that time, my confidence was so low that I'd have bet I couldn't even have played the role of a rock!

但是，几年后，突然一个难得的机会又来敲我的门了。

But, a few years later, suddenly that once in a lifetime opportunity once again came knocking at my door.

在一个新的导演——王力宏的导演下，我又当了一次演员！

Under the direction of a new director, Leehom Wang, I once again was an actor!

故事是这样的：在一个卡拉 OK 酒吧唱歌时，我的英国朋友碰到几位演艺圈人士，有演员、制片人和导演。其中一位对他说："我们需要两个老外当演员，你能帮助我们吗？"

The story went like this: while singing at a Karaoke bar, my English friend bumped into some people involved in show businesses, actors, producers and directors. And one of them said to him, "We need two foreigners to act, can you help us out?"

他当然说："肯定的，没问题！"

Of course he said, "Sure, no problem!"

4. 2009 年，上海，璞丽酒店

4. 2009, Shanghai, Puli Hotel and Spa

电影片名：《恋爱通告》

Movie Title: *Love in Disguise*

情节：爱情故事，一位有名的演员扮演学生追求学院院长的女儿。

Plot: Love story, a famous actor plays a student who is pursuing the dean's daughter.

主角：王力宏、陈冲

Leading Roles: Leehom Wang, Joan Chen

我的角色：扮演一个西方投资人，陈冲的朋友。穿上正装，化装、造型后他们说我可以了。看了镜子，我想，我头发本来就有发型，可是化完装以后就像一个小孩子刚被妈妈用口水把他的头发拨平似的，一点也不好看。

My Role: playing the role of a western investor, and Joan Chen's friend. I was dressed in formal attire. After make-up and hair styling, they said I was ready. Looking in the mirror I thought, my original hairstyle had personality, but now I looked like a little boy who'd just had his hair slicked down flat by his mother's spit. I looked awful.

我的小镜头：我们四个外国人，其中包括一位美国男生（我的英国朋友没时间）和两位扮演我们的老婆的女演员（她们两个是俄罗斯的高中学生，好尴尬）在那所五星酒店参加一个 VIP 晚会，等着祝贺陈冲和王力宏扮演的角色。我的"老婆"高个子，皮肤白白的，化着浓妆。除了她带过来的朋友以外，她对我们都非常冷漠。在英文里我们叫这种女生：冰雪公主。

My small scene: Four foreigners, including another American male (my English friend couldn't make it) and two female actresses who were playing the roles of our wives (they were both Russian high school students—talk about awkward) were attending a VIP party at the five star hotel. Everyone was waiting to play out their roles and congratulate Joan Chen and Leehom Wang. My "wife" was tall, had very white skin and way too much make-up. Other than the friend she'd brought along, she was extremely cold to us. In English we call this kind of female an ice princess.

灯光、摄影机、开拍!

Lights, camera, action!

王力宏穿着一套白色服装，他的表演一结束，就和一位台湾演员跟着陈冲（上海的一位上了点年纪的，但非常引人注目的女演员），走到我们的前面来了。我拥抱着陈冲用英文说："真棒，Joan！"吻了一下她的脸颊。

After Leehom Wang's performance ended, wearing a white suit, he, a Taiwanese actor and Joan Chen (Shanghainese actress, middle-aged, but a striking lady) walked up to us. I hugged Joan Chen and said in English, "Joan, that was great!" and kissed her once on the cheek.

"咔，再来第二次！"助理导演喊道。

"Cut, take two!" the assistant director shouted.

王导演对我们四个说："伙计们，你们的激情在哪里？给我们点激情，没错！"

Director Wang said to us, "Guys, where's your passion? Give me some passion, alright!"

在我旁边，是我的"老婆"。

Next to me, my 'wife' growled.

然后，陈冲笑着鼓励我们说："让我们来点乐趣，叭——叭——叭——哺！"

After that, Joan Chen encouraged us, laughing, "Everyone, let's have some fun, va-va-va-voom!"

我"老婆"露出一个冷冰冰的、不自然的微笑。

Next to me the ice cracked, allowing my "wife" to reveal a small, chilling tight smile.

"开拍！"

"Action!"

"真棒，Joan！"我又吻了一次她的脸颊。

"Joan, that was great!" I kissed her cheek again.

"咔，再来第三次！"导演喊道。

"Cut, take three!" the director shouted.

"真棒，Joan！"我又吻了一次她的脸颊。

"Joan, that was great!" I kisser her cheek again.

"演完了！"导演喊。

"That's a wrap!" The director shouted.

亲完后我对自己发誓，我永远不会洗这双嘴唇！

After kissing her I promised myself, I'd never wash my lips again!

几个月过后，这部电影上映了。

A few months later, the movie came out.

我们公司的老板请我和我的同事们去电影院看我的"首次登台"！

Our company's boss treated my coworkers and I to the cinema to see my "debut"!

我们都坐在同一排的座位上等待我的镜头出现。发现我的镜头快要出现时我兴奋地对大家说："小声一点好吧，这是我的镜头！"

We were all sitting in the same row waiting for my scene to appear. Noticing my "chance" was about to begin I excitedly told everyone: "Quiet down, this is my scene!"

几秒钟过去了，然后一分钟、几分钟也过去了。

First a few seconds passed, and than a minute, followed by a few more.

右边的同事转头向我问道："阿文？"

The coworker to my left turned to me and asked, "Kevin?"

左边的同事转头问我："你在哪儿啊？"

The coworker to my right turned to me and asked, "Where are you?"

我只能试图把脸放在爆米花的盒子里掩藏一下。我的镜头被剪掉了。

I could only attempt to hide my face inside the popcorn box. My scene had been cut.

第二个大山？我望尘莫及啊！

The second Da Sha? Not even close!

我又失败了。

Once again I failed.

但是，不是每一天都有机会亲吻电影明星！非常感谢您，陈冲女士。

But, it isn't everyday that you get to kiss a movie star! Thank you very much, Ms. Joan Chen.

Chapter 7

顽皮，调皮，还是有道理？
Mischievous, Incorrigible or Reasonable?

　　读大学时西班牙语老师给我打分的时候这样对我说："对于西班牙语，即使你不会说、不会听、不会读、不会写，也不要担心，就好像我不会弹钢琴的女儿一样。" 她是什么意思呢？我估计她想说学语言不是我的优势，不过没关系，因为人无完人。但是她为什么说这个来鼓励我，我不知道。

　　While studying Spanish in college, my professor handed me my exam score and told me this："In regards to the Spanish language, even if you can't speak it, understand it, read it and or write it, don't worry, you are just like my daughter, only she's no good at playing the piano." What did she mean? I believe she wanted to say that studying languages wasn't one of my talents, but that it was okay because nobody is perfect. How exactly was that encouraging, I really don't know.

好几年后我希望证明她是错的！我刚来到中国的时候很想学习汉语，可是当时除了两个最简单的短语"你好"和"谢谢"外，我什么都不会说，听、读和写也不会。对，虽然这种学语言的感觉与从前相似，不过我认为，汉语比西班牙语难学三倍！教过我的老师肯定会说这个挑战是一项不可能完成的任务。

Many years later I hoped to prove her wrong! Just after arriving in China I wanted to study Chinese. At that time, excluding two simple phrases, "ni hao" and "xie xie," I couldn't say, understand, read or write anything. Yep, it was like *déjàvu*! Only that I thought studying Chinese was three times more difficult than Spanish! The teacher who had taught me in the past would certainly say this challenge was: Mission Impossible.

我教英语的外语培训学校提供了免费的中文课。可是，我承认，我从来没当过好学生，我的学习经历乏善可陈，记忆力和注意力跟跳蚤一样短。可我很想参加，因为想早一点跟本地人讲话。我必须抓住这个机会！

The foreign language-training center where I was teaching English provided free Chinese classes. But, I should admit, I've never been a good student, my academic history was fairly poor and my memory and attention span were shorter then a gnat's. But I really wanted to attend, as I wanted to be able to communicate with the locals as soon as I could.

为了尊重老师，好好改过自新，我准备好了我的学习用品：一支新钢笔、一本小笔记本和一个完全"开放"的脑子。 走进教室里，我安静地坐在我的椅子上，我的背挺得很直。我很愿意听老师的话，会尽最大努力去学习中文。 除了我，还有两位加拿大的学生。她们是三个星期之前来到中国的。我们都是这里的英文老师。

Wanting to show respect to the teacher, and really wanting to turn over a new leaf, I prepared my study materials: a new pen, a small notebook and a very open mind. Entering the classroom, I quietly sat down in my chair, my back straight. I was really willing to listen to the teacher and to try my hardest to learn Chinese. In addition to myself, there were two Canadian students. They arrived in China three weeks earlier. We were all English teachers.

老师开始讲了。可我应该先给你们介绍一下我老师的样子和她的性格。她是学校的英文助教。她个子一点也不高：她的身高只到我的手肘，而且非常瘦。因为她说话的声音是那么小，我几乎听不见。我第一天来学校的时候，她还没有足够的信心跟我交流，她很害羞。可是我没想到她还有恐怖的另一面。在教室里，她会拿出她的秘密武器：她的铁腕！

The teacher began. But first, I should introduce my teacher and her personality. She was the school's assistant teacher. She wasn't tall in the slightest: the top of her head was equal to the height of my elbow, and she was really thin. Because she was so soft spoken, I usually couldn't hear her. From the first day that I arrived at the school up until now, she still hadn't enough confidence to communicate with me, she was that shy. I never would have thought she had a frightening other side. In the classroom she was about to pull out her secret weapon, her iron fist!

她上课的时候会认真地用中文说："学生们好。"

Once class began, she said seriously in Chinese, "Hello students."

我不明白，只能耸耸肩，给她一个很诚实的微笑。

I didn't understand and could only shrug, giving her a very sincere smile.

她看了我一眼，也看了其他同学一眼，很冷漠地跟大家打招呼，一点笑容也没有。

She looked at me, then looked at the other students. It was a very cold greeting, without so much as a smile.

她花了几分钟哇啦哇啦哇啦哇啦说话。谁知道她在说什么？

She spent a few minutes babbling away. Who knew what she said?

哇啦哇啦说完后，她转身开始在黑板上写东西。她写下了几行字。因为都是汉字，还不如看一碗面条翻倒在桌子上，至少还能看明白。可汉字呢？它们简直太复杂。我的眼球还没开始转动，就已经累了。黑板上的东西我一点也看不懂。

After she finished babbling, she turned around and began to write on the blackboard. She wrote down a few lines. Being that they were all Chinese characters, seeing a bowl of overturned noodles on a table would have been easier to understand as at least I would know what I was looking at. But Chinese characters? They were simply too complicated. My eyes hadn't even started moving and they were already exhausted. I couldn't understand anything on the blackboard.

我举手用英文说："对不起，老师，我看不懂。"

I raised my hand and said in English, "Sorry, teacher, I don't understand."

她一边不停地写着什么，一边用英文认真地回答："你有两个同学。"

Without stopping whatever she was writing, she responded sternly in English, "You have two classmates."

我想，我的两个同学在中国只待了三个星期，已经能看得懂了？她们都是天才吗？！可是，我没那么老实，我往她们那边挪了一下并小声地问："你们看得懂？"

I thought, my classmates have only been in China for three weeks and they could already understand? It would seem they were both geniuses! But, I wasn't that naïve and turning to where they sat I asked quietly, "Can you understand?"

她们两个同时说："我们看不懂。"

They said together, "We can't understand."

她们都比我年轻，大约 25 岁左右。她们明显很不耐烦，其中一个继续说："每一节课都这样。老师用我们看不懂的汉字写一些句子。这就是她的教学方法。"

They were both younger, around twenty-five years old. Clearly frustrated, one continued to say, "Every class is like this. The teacher writes down sentences using Chinese characters we don't understand. This is her teaching method."

我不敢批评老师。为了不忘记，我提醒自己：我已经改过自新了，不想再做不听从老师建议的学生了。可是，我忍不住想：好奇怪的教学方法。如果一点也看不懂，我们怎么能学会呢？我们总要从基础汉语，中文里的"ABC"开始学习吧。

I didn't dare criticize my teacher. And in case I forgot, I reminded myself, I had turned over a new leaf, and didn't want to once again become the student of my youth who paid no attention to teachers' suggestions. But, I couldn't help but think, this was a really strange method. If we couldn't understand a thing, how could we study? We should begin with the fundamentals, the Chinese "ABC's".

不自觉地，我又举手问："老师，她们也看不懂。"

Unconsciously, I raised my hand again and asked, "Teacher, they also don't understand."

她立刻转身气愤地盯了我一眼，不耐烦地说："我还没写完。"

She immediately turned around and glared at me, saying impatiently, "I haven't finished writing."

我无法控制快到嘴边的话，说道："可是，老师，我们都看不懂。你可以用拼音吗？"

Unable to control the words that were coming out of my mouth, I said, "But, teacher, none of us can understand. Can you use pinyin?"

"拼音你看得懂？"

"You can understand pinyin?"

"看不懂。可是我会读。"

"I can't understand. But I can read it."

"可以，但没用。"她继续写着。

"Okay, but it is of no use." She continued to write.

我想，这是什么理由？

I thought what kind of reasoning was this?

"好的，我们开始吧。"

"Okay, let's begin."

开始什么？怎么开始？我们一点也不懂黑板上写的东西。

Begin what? How could we begin? We couldn't understand a thing written on the blackboard.

我是真的想尊敬老师的，可我好像有调皮的天性。

I wanted to respect the teacher, but it seemed my natural instinct was to be troublesome.

"老师，可以把那些句子翻译成英文，然后写在它们的下面吗？"

"Teacher, could you translate those sentences into English, and then write the sentences below?"

那时候，大家都看出那老师有点不高兴了。

At that moment, everybody could see the teacher really wasn't happy.

老师开始用英文翻译那些句子的意思。她气呼呼地写，用掉了三支粉笔，粉笔头都狂怒地打在黑板上，才写下来。她快要发火了！

The teacher began to translate the sentences. She wrote with indignation, using up three pieces of chalk, their tips banging against the blackboard furiously, before she was finished. She was about to explode.

写完后，我真的不能相信自己的眼睛了。

After she finished writing, I couldn't believe my own eyes.

黑板上写的句子是：我想买一份法国报纸给我老公看。（是用英文写的）

Written on the blackboard was the sentence: I want to buy a French newspaper for my husband.

这个中文句子的难度太高了，更不用说它是一个很奇怪的句子。

The level was too advanced, not to mention it was quite a strange sentence.

我无法保持沉默，就又举手问："老师，不好意思，可是我只会说'你好'和'谢谢'。教我们那么复杂的句子有什么用？你没教我们怎么说'多少钱？''厕所在哪里？'这些都比黑板上的句子更有用。"

Unable to remain silent, I raised my hand again and asked, "Teacher, excuse me, but I can only say, 'ni hao' and 'xie xie'. What's the point of teaching us such a complicated sentence? You haven't taught us how to say 'how much?' 'Where's the bathroom?' both of which are much more useful than the sentence on the blackboard."

"它们都有用。 也许不是今天，但是某一天会用到。"

"They are all useful. Perhaps not today, but someday they will be."

她的回答有些道理，可是不是学走路之前都要先学会爬吗？

There was some reason to her response, but don't you need to learn to crawl before you can walk?

"老师，不好意思，可是对我来说，一点用也没有。我在中国，为什么要买法国报纸？而且，我是男生，我为什么有老公？"

"Teacher, excuse me, but in regards to me, it's not useful in the slightest. I'm in China, why would I want to buy a French newspaper? Furthermore, I'm a man, why do I have a husband?"

老师发火了，对我说： "好了，如果你不喜欢，你可以出去。"

The teacher lost her patience and said to me, "Okay, if you don't like it, you can leave."

我没想到看起来那么甜美的姑娘会用如此强硬的铁腕控制她的教室。

I never would have thought that such a sweet young girl could use such an unrelenting iron fist to control her classroom.

"好的，我出去。"

"Okay, I want to go."

"好的，你出去吧！"

"Okay, get out!"

"我出去了！"

"I'm leaving!"

我对同学说："对不起。"然后我走出了教室。

To my classmates, I said, "Sorry." After that I left the classroom.

真不幸，我的老习惯似乎又回来了，我还是小时候那个顽皮的男孩子。

Unfortunately, it seemed my old habit had returned, I was still that troublesome boy from my childhood.

几年后我成了那个老师结婚时的伴郎。老师，如果您有读这本书，您愿意原谅您这个有点讨厌的学生吗？

A few years later I was the best man at that teacher's wedding. And, teacher, if you are reading this book, are you willing to forgive a slightly obnoxious student?

虽然我还是没买法国报纸……或者找一个老公，可是现在我会用中文来说了！

94

I still haven't bought a French newspaper…or found a husband, though I can now say both in Chinese!

Chapter 8

对不起，中国，我没有不理你!

Sorry, China, I Really Didn't Mean to Ignore You!

在 2010 年世博会期间，我从上海坐长途巴士到浙江省慈溪市出差，偶然间生了中国的气。

During the World Expo held in 2010, I took a long distance bus from Shanghai to Cixi in Zhejiang Province for business, and accidentally angered China.

那天下午慈溪的事情办完后，临上车回上海时我跟着其他乘客们在排队，感觉越来越担心。我看着一个收票的服务员，她像在军事训练的女中士一样，表情比牛头犬更烦燥，声音像机器人的声音一样冷漠，不带感情。她重复着发出一个很机械的声音："身份证。"怎么回事，已经被售票的问过了，可现在检票还要问？她的认真态度，让我们觉得这不是简单地快要上车回上海了，而是在办理入境和海关检查，进入其他国家。

That afternoon after finishing things in Cixi, before boarding the bus back to Shanghai, standing in line with the other passengers I became more and more concerned. And what was the reason for my growing concern: I watched a ticket collector, one that resembled an army drill sergeant, face grumpier than a bulldog's, with a voice that sounded more robot than human, cold, emotionless. She repeatedly emitted an automatic response, "Identification." I couldn't help but wonder what was going on as I had already been asked by the ticket seller, and now the ticket collector was asking as well? From her serious demeanor you'd think we were about to pass through immigration and customs to enter another country, not simply to board a bus returning to Shanghai.

轮到我时，她站得很直，显得威武又雄壮。她机械地重复道："身份证？"

When it was my turn, standing straight, body thick and sturdy, all shoulders and chest, she emitted her automatic response, "Identification?"

我回答："没有。我是外国人。"

I answered, "I don't have one. I'm a foreigner."

她又用牛头犬似的烦燥面孔盯着我，用那个机械的嗓音重复道："护照？"

The bulldog's grouchy face glared at me, but she continued to use the same automated voice, "Passport?"

没小法，我又说："没有。" 我把笔记本电脑拿出来说："但是笔记本里有我护照的扫描复印件。"

No choice, I again answered, "I don't have it." I pulled my laptop out and said, "But I have a scanned copy on my laptop."

似乎被冒犯了，她机械般的声音被破坏了，变得生动了一点。她竟然有点生气地说："那不行！"

As if offended, her automated script broke apart, and becoming a little animated, she unexpectedly said angrily, "Unacceptable!"

我被她的语气惊呆了，话暂时卡在嘴里，我说："可是，我每一次都使用笔记本里的扫描复印件。在售票台也用过。"

Surprised by her tone, my words temporarily caught in my mouth, I said, "But I use the scanned copy in my laptop every time."

她讽刺地回道："每一次都是世博会？"

She responded sarcastically, "Is it the World Expo every time?"

我说："啊，不是？"

Me, "Ah, no?"

像母亲看着想顶嘴的孩子，她以责备的目光看着我。显然那是一个反问句。

Like a mother watching a child who was thinking of talking back, she gave me a reproachful look. Apparently it was a rhetorical question.

恢复平静后她说："先生，如果没带护照，就不能进入上海。您别无选择。必须马上去公安局。"

After regaining her composure, she said, "Sir, if you didn't bring your passport, you cannot enter Shanghai. You have no other choice. You must go to the public security bureau at once."

一听到最后面的三个字,我的胃都开始抽筋了。她刚才说公安局?要去公安局?不管在什么国家,谁喜欢去一个让你自己和警察待在一起的地方?对我过于夸张的想象力来说,公安局只有两样东西:警察的怀疑和冷漠的牢房!我忍不住开始担心起来:我还需要工作,今晚必须跟客户联系,明天有几个会议要参加,我不能坐牢!

After hearing those last three words, my stomach immediately did a back flip. Did she just say the public security bureau? I had to go the public security bureau? No matter the country, who likes to go somewhere that involves you and the police? To my overactive imagination, the public security bureau was two things: suspicious police and cold prison cells! I couldn't help but begin to worry: I still had work to do, I had to contact customers that evening and there were meetings I must attend tomorrow. There was no way I could stay in jail!

然后那个发号施令的检票女中士指了指汽车站的门口方向。我只听清零星的几个词:"去外面,左拐,对面。"走到门口时,我听到她在背后喊:"嘿!"转过身我看到她手指向一个服务窗口,厉声说:"那边!"

Then the bossy ticket collecting drill sergeant pointed in the direction of the bus station's entrance. I only heard a small part: "go outside, turn left, across the way." Walking over to the entrance, from behind I heard her shout, "Hey!" I turned around and saw her hand pointing towards a customer service counter. She snapped, "There!"

　　我想说："你刚才不是让我去外面？"但我无法说出，因为她立刻又扬着马戏团里驯兽师拿着的鞭子一般的胳膊。我这头狮子胆敢吼叫就要被打哑了！她不耐烦地指向那边。那边？我不懂那边有什么，但是最好不要问为什么，她一定会再训我一顿。

I wanted to say, "Didn't you just say I should go outside?" But I didn't have a chance to respond as she immediately snapped her arm like the fierce whip of a circus lion tamer. The lion was silenced before it dared to roar, let alone whimper. She pointed impatiently in that direction. There? I didn't know what "there" had, but I figured I'd better not ask why, because I'd certainly get another earful.

　　那个服务窗口是巨大的。但只有一个很低、很小的窗口让乘客们跟坐在窗后的工作人员交流。我笨拙地弯下腰，脸一半压住窗户，嘴冲着小窗口里，不懂该说什么，就说："你好，她说——"

The customer service window was massive. But there was only a single very low, extremely small hole in the window that a customer could use to speak with the customer service girl sitting behind the counter. Awkwardly bent over, half my face pressed against the outside of the window, sticking my mouth through the small hole, not knowing what to say, I said, "Hello, she said—"

窗后一个年轻可爱的姑娘笑着说："票。"

From behind the window, the young, cute girl said with a smile, "Ticket."

我给了。

I gave it to her.

"退票？"

"Ticket refund?"

"什么？"

"What?"

"退票？"

"Ticket refund?"

"可以退票？"

"Can I refund my ticket?"

"可以退票。"

"Yes you can refund your ticket."

扣了几块钱，她就给我退了票。

Minus a few yuan, she refunded my ticket.

突然，仿佛她就站在我的耳朵里，女中士的声音传过来："好的！跟着我！"不知道什么时候，她已经来到我身旁。窗后坐的女孩咯咯地笑起来，对我说："再见。"我们离开窗口前，女中士朝窗后的女孩望了一眼，说："小心点！"

Suddenly, as if she was standing within my ear, the female drill sergeant hollered, "Alright! Follow me!" Not sure when, but she was already by my side. The girl behind the window giggled and said to me, "Bye bye." Before leaving the front of the window, the female drill sergeant flashed an eye at the girl and said, "Watch it!"

我像一个被老师提着耳朵的顽皮小学生，公安局成了校长办公室，检票员成了老师，好尴尬。指导我走出汽车站后，检票员说："你看看，那边是公安局。"顺着她的强壮的手臂所指的方向，我看了看。但是，没看到她在指什么。

Like a naughty student, ear pinched between the teacher's fingers, a public security bureau replacing a principal's office, the ticket collector led the way. It was pretty embarrassing. After leading me outside the bus station, she said, "Look, there's the public security bureau." I looked in the direction her sturdy arm pointed towards. But, I couldn't see what she was pointing at.

不知道该怎么称呼她，我说："阿姨，我看不到……"

Not sure how to address her, I said, "Aunty, I can't see…"

她自言自语地低声说："老外。"就拉着我的手臂，我们两个穿过了马路。

She mumbled quietly, "Foreigners," and then pulling my arm, the two of us crossed the street.

说实话，我有一点儿被她粗鲁的动作感动了，尽管我惹了一堆麻烦，她还想帮助我。不知道这是否是她的工作职责，我估计不是，但是非常感谢她陪我去。

Actually, I was slightly moved by her fierce actions. Even though I was a lot of trouble, she still wanted to help me. Not sure whether or not it was one of her job responsibilities, I'm guessing it was not, but I really did appreciate her accompanying me.

到了公安局门口，她带我去一个小服务亭，给一些坐在里面的警察解释为什么带我来。她和里面的警察都向我摇了摇头。一个问："带护照了吗？"女中士替我回道："没有！"

Reaching the public security bureau's entrance, she took me to a small service kiosk and began to tell the police officer sitting inside why she brought me here. She and the police officer both looked towards me and shook their heads. One asked, "Brought his passport?" The female drill sergeant responded for me, "No, he didn't!"

那个问问题的警察出来了，说要我跟着他进公安局。我想先对女中士说声感谢，可当我转向她时，我发现她已经走开了。好像她连一分钟时间也不肯浪费，必须回汽车站保持警惕。

The police officer who asked the question came out and said I should follow him into the public security bureau. I wanted to first express my gratitude to the female drill sergeant, but when I turned towards her, I discovered she had already left. It seemed she didn't have a minute to waste and had to return to the bus station and remain vigilant.

在里面，不知道那是登记台、处理部还是其他小部门，但五个警察坐在一张长桌子后看着我。

Inside, not sure if it was the registration counter, administration or another department, but five police officers were sitting behind a long desk looking at me.

其中一位年纪稍大一些的警察，估计是他们的主管，名牌上写着李什么什么的，对我说："护照没带？"

One of the police officers, a little older than the rest, more than likely their supervisor, the name tag showing Chen something-something, said to me, "You didn't bring your passport?"

我："没带。"

Me, "I didn't bring it."

他："为什么没带？"

Him, "Why didn't you bring it?"

我："我认为扫描的复印件就够了。"

Me, "I thought a scanned copy was enough."

他："你叫什么？"

Him, "What is your name?"

我："凯文。"

Me, "Kevin."

他："什么？"

Him, "What?"

我："凯文。凯旋的凯，文化的文。"

Me, "Kevin. Kai as in the kai in kaixuan, wen as in the wen in wenhua."

他："什么？你会写你的名字？"

Him, "What? Can you write your name?"

我："会。"说实话，除了我的名字以外，我基本不会写汉字。

Me, "I can." Actually, besides my name, I pretty much can't write Chinese.

当我开始写名字时，那四个还坐着的都站起来，几个在外面的警察也走进来，都围绕着主管。一写完，大家都一起朗读：凯文。

Starting to write my name, the four still sitting stood up and a few from outside walked in and they all crowded around their superior. As soon as I finished writing, everyone read it out loud together, Kevin.

他："贵姓？"

Him, "Family name?"

我："史密斯。"

Me, "Shi mi si (Smith)."

他："什么意思？"

Him, "What's the meaning?"

我："不，不是什么意思，是史密斯。"

Me, "No, not 'shen me yi si,' it's shi mi si."

他："我说了。"

Him, "I said that."

我有点糊涂地问："说了什么？"

A little confused I asked, "You said what?"

像耐心用完了，他眯着眼，说："会写吗？"

As if his patience was used up, he narrowed his eyes and said, "Can you write it?"

我："啊，我忘记怎么写。"

Me, "Ah, I forgot how to write it."

似乎不太相信，他打量着我的脸等了几秒钟。我不知道该怎么回答。

Looking like he didn't really believe me, he looked my face up and down and waited a few minutes. I didn't know how to respond.

"反正，我的护照上没有中文姓名，只有英文的。"

"Anyways, my passport doesn't have a Chinese family name, only an English one."

他有点恼火，说道："唉，"接着说，"那怎么拼写？"

Somewhat vexed, he said, "Oh boy," and continued, "Here we go again. How do you spell it?"

我："KEVIN。K—E—V—I—N。"

Me, "KEVIN. K-E-V-I-N."

他："K—B？"

Him, "K—B?"

我："E。"

Me, "E."

他："V？"

Him, "V?"

他后面一个年轻的，也许是新手的警察喊出："B—BOY！B—BOY！"

From behind a younger police officer, perhaps a new recruit shouted, "B-BOY! B-BOY!"

年轻的那个被其他同事嘲笑了。主管翻了个白眼。新手低下头又用英文说："Sorry。"

The young man was heckled by his coworkers. The superior rolled his eyes. The new recruit lowered his head and said again in English, "Sorry."

我继续："E。"

I continued, "E."

他放下了笔，说："太烦了。"

Putting down the pen, he said, "Too much trouble."

他站起来，从桌子后走过来，说："好的，过来吧。"我跟着他去了别的房间。

He stood up and came out from behind the counter and said, "Okay, let's go." I followed him to another room.

里面有几台电脑和两个中年人。主管用本地话跟一个只有几根毛盖在头顶上的警察说了一些我听不懂的话。年纪大的警察命令我坐下。

Inside were a few computers and two middle-aged men. The superior spoke to one of the officers who had nothing but a few hairs combed over his bald head in the local language which I didn't understand. The older police officer ordered me to sit down.

今天的老对话又出来了——他："没带？"我："没。"他："为什么？"我："我以为……"反应都一样：另外一双眼睛又怀疑地盯着我。

Today's familiar dialogue came up again: him, "You didn't bring it?" Me, "No." Him, "Why not?" Me, "I thought…" The reaction was the same: another pair of eyes stared at me suspiciously.

递给我一支钢笔，他说："写下你的英文姓名吧。"

Handing me a fountain pen, he said, "Write down your English name, family and given."

没写完第一个字母"K"，那张纸就被笔划破了。

Before I finished writing the first letter，"K", the paper was torn by the fountain pen.

他看了我一眼，我不好意思地说："不好意思，这张纸太破……"他眼睛睁大了，表示我不要看不起他的用品。还好，我接下来说的是："我的意思是，我不知道怎么用钢笔。"

Glancing at me, I apologetically said, "Sorry, the paper's too poor--." His eyes grew big, implying that I shouldn't look down upon on any of his stuff. Fortunately, I continued by saying, "What I meant is, I don't know how to use a fountain pen."

他不停地摇了摇头："什么？不知道怎么用？"他摇头说，"轻一点，好吗？"

Him, "What? You don't know how to use it?" Shaking his head back and forth, he said, "Gentler, okay？"

即使纸太薄了，质量太差了，我也不该提出。反正，我是真不知道怎么用钢笔，在美国年轻人不学这个。我缓慢而仔细地写了下去。

Even if the paper was too thin, the quality too poor, I didn't need to mention it. Anyways, I really didn't know how to use a fountain pen. In

America young people never learn how. I wrote slowly and cautiously.

然后他把纸举起来，贴近了看。他把眼镜调整一下，在电脑里输入我的资料。仿佛眼镜没用，他还是离电脑屏幕很近，坐在他旁边，我又开始想象中国的监狱生活：饭是什么味道？床硬不硬？最恐怖的可能是像好莱坞电影里一样，牢房狱友要我当他的——"老婆"？！

He lifted up the paper and held it close to his eyes. Adjusting his glasses, he entered my information into the computer. As if the glasses were useless, he got very close to the computer screen and began to search. Sitting next to him, I once again began to think about what life would be like inside a Chinese prison: what would the food taste like? Would the beds be hard? And the most frightening possibility, was it like the Hollywood movies, where my cellmate would want me to become his—wife?!

查到了我的资料，他转向我，装出一本正经的口气开始询问："想不理我们的规定？想不理中国的法律？"

After looking up my information, he turned towards me, and assuming a humorless manner, he began the interrogation, "Do you want to ignore our regulations? Do you want to ignore Chinese law?"

我还在想象着一个很恐怖的监狱爱情故事，我结结巴巴地说："不——不是，我认为……以为……啊，上次……啊……下次……"

Still imagining a horrific prison love story, I stuttered out, "N…no, I thought…thought…uh, last time…uh…next time…"

他严厉地继续问："在美国，你也不管那边的规定？"

He continued to ask sternly, "If in America, would you ignore the regulations?"

我："什么规定？"

Me, "What regulations?"

他："这些有关身份证、护照的规定。"

Him, "These regulations, the ones related to identification, passports."

我："哦。我不知道。"

Me, "Oh. I don't know."

他有点生气了，吃惊地问："不知道？！这是什么意思？"

Slightly losing his temper, he asked in surprise, "You don't know?! What does that mean?"

我天真地回答："不清楚我们有什么规定。"

Too naive, I answered, "I don't know our regulations clearly."

他："不可能！"

Him, "Impossible!"

虽然我不想顶嘴，但禁不住想诚实回答，我说："有可能。"

Not wanting to talk back, but unable to resist responding innocently, I said, "It's possible."

突然在我肩膀上，我母亲的形象出现了。她坐在我肩上，生气地对我说："儿子，至少这一次给我闭嘴！"

Suddenly an image of my mother appeared on my shoulder. Sitting on my shoulder, she told me angrily, "Son, at least this once, would you please shut up!"

似乎不敢相信他的耳朵，老警察对我再三低声地说："有可能？"

As if he couldn't believe his ears, the old police officer quietly said again and again, "It's possible?"

在老妈的影响下，我最终说："是，不好意思，是我的错。对不起中国。"

Under my mother's influence, I finally said, "Yes, sorry, that was my mistake. Sorry China."

他疑心地看了我一会儿，在一张纸上写了几个我看不懂的句子。有可能是说："这老外太笨。依我看来，除了能把他自己炸飞了，他没聪明到把别的东西引爆。他不危险。让他回上海去。"

Eyeing me suspiciously for a brief moment, on a piece of paper he wrote down a few sentences I couldn't read. Perhaps the sentences said, "This foreigner is really stupid. In my opinion, besides blowing himself up, he wasn't clever enough to blow anything else up. He's not dangerous. Allow him to return to Shanghai."

他把纸递给我，说："好了，你能回上海。给检票员看。下一次记得带护照。" 然后他就挥了挥手赶我走。

Holding the piece of paper he gave me, he finally said, "Okay, you can return to Shanghai. Let the ticket collector see this. Next time bring your passport." And then he waved me away.

我向汽车站走去，走过公安局小服务亭的时候，里面的警察把头伸出亭窗外说："请下次再来！"

When I walked by the small service kiosk on my way back to the bus station, the police officer inside stuck his head out the kiosk's window and said, "Please come back again!"

真奇怪！

Talk about strange!

我最后想说，这真是我的错。对不起中国，我不会再不理你们的规定！

Finally I want to say, this really was my mistake. Sorry China, I will not ignore your regulations again!

一个月以后，我又坐着长途巴士去慈溪出差，想确认一下自己带好了护照，我拍了拍口袋。突然意识到：早上因为时间很急，我喝牛奶喝得太快，不小心把牛奶都溅到衣服上，所以那件衬衫被我换了。好可惜，我的护照还在那件衬衫的口袋里留着。

One month later, sitting on the long distance bus once again returning to Cixi for business, wanting to double check that I had brought my passport, I patted my pocket. Suddenly I realized, because time was really tight that morning I had drunk some milk too quickly and carelessly spilled it on my shirt. So I had changed the shirt. Which was a real shame because my passport was still in the pocket of that shirt.

请下次再来……

Please come back again...

Chapter 9

友谊：患难见真情

Fridendship: A Friend in Need Is a Friend Indeed

在远离岸边的礁石上，两个老朋友正坐着钓鱼。

On a boulder far from the shore, two old friends sat fishing.

左边是西方，右边是东方；一双蓝眼睛，一双棕眼睛；一头又乱又卷的金发，一头又直又整洁的黑发；一个高个子，一个矮个子；一个身材有点瘦，一个身材有点胖。相反，但互补。他们都穿着纽扣解开的夏威夷衬衫和沙滩短裤，脚上的拖鞋在爬礁石时，都弄丢了。

On the left was the west. On the right was the east. One pair of blue eyes. One pair of brown eyes. One had messy, curly, blond hair. The other had straight, neat, black hair. One was tall. The other was short. One was a little thin. The other a little fat. They were opposites, yet complimentary. They both wore Hawaiian shirts, the buttons opened, and a pair of beach shorts. The flip-flops they had been wearing were lost when they had climbed onto the boulder.

在我们头上，闪电划过天空，天黑了下来，接着传来很可怕的雷声。

Over our heads, the lightning flashed against the sky as the day began to darken, followed by a frightening thunderclap.

透过超大的 20 世纪 90 年代样式的眼镜片，我的朋友看着我着急地说："这里不安全！快要下雨了！"

Through a pair of over-sized, Nineties-style glasses, my friend looked at me and said anxiously, "It's not safe here! It's going to rain!"

我轻松地回答："没事，雨就是水。"

I responded casually, "It's nothing, rain is just water."

"雷电呢？"他问。

"And what about lightning?" he asked.

"没事，但……"

"It's nothing, but…"

他说得有道理。

He had a point.

如果我当初已学会一句中国的古话：患难见真情，我肯定会说出来，因为那非常适合当时的情景。可那时我还不太会说中文。

If I had early on mastered this ancient Chinese saying, "A friend in need is a friend indeed." I would certainly have said it out loud, because it definitely fit that situation. But at that time I couldn't really speak Chinese.

我们两个铁哥们坐在一个又硬又粗，而且有点高——五米左右高度的大礁石上。石头上面被锋利的、破损的贝壳覆盖。我们爬上去的时候正值退潮。可是现在不是。我们离海岸大约有一两百米左右。是的，我不反对他的观点，当然快要下雷雨了。但是，我们在海产市场买的虾饵已经挂在钩子上，两根鱼竿在我们的膝盖上休息，鱼线放在海里，一大瓶红星二锅头已打开了。现在怎么能放弃？ 我们才刚刚开始！

The two of us, solid buds, sat on the hard, rough and fairly high boulder which was approximately five meters in height. The rock's surface was covered in a layer of sharp, broken shells. When we had climbed up it was low tide. But it wasn't now. We were about two hundred meters from the coast. Yep, I didn't disagree with his opinion: it definitely was about to thunderstorm. But, the shrimp bait we had bought at the wet market already hung from our hooks, our rods were resting on our knees, the fishing lines were cast into the sea and a large bottle of Red Star Erguotou had already been cracked open. How could we quit now? We'd only just begun!

"兄弟，别担心。我比你高。所以，如果这里有雷击，肯定只能打到我。"

"Brother, don't worry. I'm taller than you. Therefore, if lightning strikes here, of course it will only strike me."

我喝了一口白酒，擦了擦嘴后，递给他。

I drank a mouthful of the white spirit, and after wiping my mouth, I handed it to him.

他喝了一口后，道："哈，对啊！"

After he drank a mouthful he said, "Ha, that's right!"

烈酒留在我们的喉咙里，我们一起皱了一下眉头，骄傲地说："男子汉！"

The strong spirit hitting our throats, both wrinkling our brows, we proudly proclaimed, "Manly men!"

轰！突然，我们的周围电光闪闪，雷声隆隆。我全身的汗毛竖了起来，脸色苍白。

Boom! Suddenly all around us lightning flashed and thunder rumbled. All the hairs on my body jumped up. My face paled.

"哇，那么近！你怕吗？"他大声喊道。

"Whoa, that was close! Are you scared?" he shouted.

"怕？怕是什么意思，我都不知道！"我撒谎。幸运的是天色近黄昏，几乎黑了，他看不到我的汗毛竖着或者我的脸色发白。

"Scared? I don't even know the meaning of scared!" I lied. Luckily it was near dusk, the day nearly dark, so he couldn't see my hairs standing up or the color of my face.

我看着大海，海的颜色变暗了，波浪不大。在海平线上我看不到任何捕鱿鱼的船或者挂在甲板上吸引猎物的又亮又圆的灯泡。他们肯定比我们聪明，已经回到安全的码头了，准备在船舱里修补渔网，等待风暴过去。

I looked at the sea. Its color was darkening. The waves weren't overly big. I couldn't see any squid boats or the many bright, round lights that hung from their decks to lure their prey, on the horizon. Certainly they were wiser than we were and had already headed home to safe ports, and prepared to wait out the storms inside their crafts mending fishing nets.

他用食指把眼镜推上鼻子，用手肘轻推我说："别想太多，好吧。"

Using his index finger to push his glasses up, nudging me with his elbow, he said, "Don't think too much, alright."

我真佩服这位亲爱的朋友。我不需要说任何话，可是他都知道。

I really admired this dear friend. I didn't have to say anything, but he knew.

他把那瓶二锅头高举起来说："为渔民干杯！"

He raised the bottle and said, "A drink for the fisherman!"

我真尊敬坐在我旁边的人。他的故事在中国的一些地方司空见惯，但是在我的国家却不多见。他小时候很贫穷，他不得不蹲在农村的路边卖水果。而当其他孩子骑自行车时，他骑的是水牛。但是，归功于他父母的努力工作、吃了很多苦，他从小努力学习，终于走出了那个小镇。

I really did respect the man sitting next to me. And while his story may be common in some parts of China, it is not common where I come from. When he was young he was quite impoverished, and he had no choice but to squat by the side of a country road selling fruits. And while other children rode bicycles, he rode a water buffalo. But, due to his parents' hard work, enduring many hardships, and focusing heavily on his studies from a young age, he eventually was able to leave his small town.

除了我们的个人背景以外，有人说我们两个一模一样：都喜欢泡妞（虽然都不成功），都喜欢喝酒、讲故事，都尊敬家庭，爱吃川菜，喜欢打羽毛球，在工作上我们总是喋喋不休，而且相信必须努力工作。我们都是单身，都没有孩子，家人都不在我们所住的城市。当年我们都被女孩子伤害了，尝过失恋的味道。虽然我们建立友谊的时间不是很长——一年半左右，但我们同甘共苦，除了男女之情，可以说我们分享过大多数的感情。他是我的好朋友，同时也是我的好榜样。

Outside of our individual backgrounds, some said we were one in the same: we both loved chasing girls, though neither was successful, we both loved a drink, telling stories, respected our families, liked Sichuan cuisine, played badminton, were both garrulous and in regards to work, we believed that you must work hard. We were both single, neither had any children and our families did not live in the city we lived in. That year we were both hurt by girls and had tasted rejection. And even though the length of our friendship wasn't overly long, about a year and half, from happiness to shared pain, excluding the romantic, you could say our friendship had shared most every emotion. He wasn't just my good friend, but also my role model.

回到我们目前的情况：天完全黑了，下着大雨。半瓶酒被喝光了，可我们还是没钓上一条鱼。也许是因为我们的鱼饵都滚下海里去找不到了，反正，我们的鱼线都勾住了，鱼竿没用。似乎我们还有另一个相似之处：我们都不太会钓鱼！

Getting back to our current situation: the day had turned to night. It was raining heavily. Half the bottle had been finished. We hadn't caught a single fish. Perhaps it was because we couldn't find our bait, possibly having rolled into the sea. Anyways, our lines were tangled and our rods useless. Seems we had something else in common: neither of us could fish!

事实上，去海、河、湖边钓鱼的活动只是一种借口。百万年来，从史前人到现代人，男人利用过这个借口逃避社会责任：家务活、唠叨的老婆/女朋友、抱怨着的孩子、工作，等等。不管在哪方面有压力，男人有时候真的需要，也应该逃离到另外的地方去休息。很多男人选择钓鱼：因为孩子不太喜欢，他们感觉钓鱼很无聊，所以那里很安静；女人不太喜欢，她们也觉得很无聊，而且很脏，所以那里更安静。没有老板，没有工作，没有交通堵塞，只有友谊、一瓶红星二锅头和大自然。完完全全的幸福。

In all honesty, a trip to the sea, river or lake's edge to fish is just a kind of excuse. Millions of years ago, man used this excuse to escape society's responsibilities, household chores, nagging wives and/or girlfriends, complaining children, work, etc. No matter which aspect, if it involved pressure, sometimes man really needed, and deserved to escape it all if for only a brief moment to rest elsewhere. Children didn't like it because they felt fishing was too boring, so it was quiet. Females didn't like it because they also felt it was too boring and a dirty activity, so it was even quieter. And in that regards, who could nag him? No bosses, no assignments, no traffic, only friendship, a bottle of Red Star Erguotou and Mother Nature. Total bliss.

"你吃吧。"朋友递给我一包花生米说。从他和另外的中国朋友那里我学会了，不管是什么东西，都该提议先给对方。

"Have some," my friend said handing me a bag of peanuts. From him and other Chinese friends, I learned, no matter what it is, you should first offer it to the one next to you.

我们时而交谈，时而各自沉思。

Sometimes we spoke. Sometimes we kept to our own thoughts.

我的朋友把手搭在我的肩膀上笑着说："阿文，听我说，除了屁股底下锋利的贝壳和这狂风暴雨以外，这样享受生活，我们一点也没有压力！"

My friend put his arm around my shoulder, smiled and said, "Kevin, listen to me, besides the sharp shells under my butt and this crazy thunderstorm, when enjoying life like this, there isn't even an ounce of pressure!"

我们为这句话举杯。

We celebrated what he said with another swig.

我们唱了歌，说着互相的过去、现在和未来。

We sang, and talked about the past, present and future.

雨下得越来越大了，我们都湿透了。可是这里的夏天闷热，所以一点也不冷。

The rain was heavier and heavier. We were both soaked. But the summers here were really muggy, so we weren't cold in the slightest.

雨终于停了，暴风雨过去了。尽管所有的衣服都湿透了，我们俩都活着。

The rain eventually did stop. The thunderstorm passed. Besides our clothes being completely drenched, we were alive.

我们都抬起头来看了看那晚的星星，它们一颗接着一颗地从云层后出现了。

We looked up at the evening stars, as they popped out from behind the clouds one by one.

"最后一口你喝吧！"他把酒瓶递给我。

"Finish the last swallow!" my friend said, handing me the bottle.

"好的！"我喊道，喝光了酒，我还打了一个嗝出来。

"Okay!" I shouted, finishing the bottle and releasing a belch.

"我们的酒没了，花生米吃光了。我们应该离开这里。可是，你看看，现在已经涨潮了。你准备游回到海岸？"

"Our drink is gone and the peanuts have been eaten. We should leave this spot. But, look, it's already hightide. Do you plan to swim back?"

我笑着回答："当然！"

I laughed and answered, "Of course!"

实际上，因为水面不高，水深及腰部，所以我们能慢慢涉水走回去。但是海底表面不是沙滩，而是石头，而在石头表面上覆盖着像那刚离开的高处一样的锋利而破损的贝壳。我摸了摸自己的臀部，酸痛的屁股提醒着我它们是如何锋利。拖鞋早就被海水冲走了，我们只能一边喊出"嘿""啊""哎哟"和一些我不敢分享的脏话，一边很痛苦地往回走。我们终于回到沙滩上，脚上被锋利的贝壳割伤了很多处，流了很多血。因为已经有点晚了，在一个刚下了暴雨的远方海滩，我们正为怎么回到城里去而犯愁。

Actually, because the water level wasn't really that high, the depth only up to our waists, we were able to slowly wade back. But the seabed wasn't sand but rocks, and the rock surface was covered in more of the same sharp, broken shells that had covered the perch we had just left. Rubbing my backside, my sore rear reminded me how sharp they were. Flip flops long lost to the sea, we could only shout out "Oh!" "Ouch!" "Oh my!" and a few words I don't dare to share as we made our way painfully back. Eventually back on the beach, we saw that our bare feet had been cut to shreds by the sharp shells and a lot of blood poured out. As it was a little late, the beach was remote and a thunderstorm had just passed, we were unsure how to get back into town.

悲叹完了以后，伤口像是被沙子堵住了，血止住了。在这样的形势下，我们看到一个很不得其所的东西。有可能是由于出血过多，脑子糊涂了，我们居然发现一辆粉红色的凯迪拉克敞篷车停在那里的停车场。我们向那辆车一瘸一拐地走过去。一个小伙子坐在保险杠上吸烟。他说他是那辆车的司机，而那是一辆婚车，用于送新人去景点拍照。司机同意送我们回去。我朋友问："你们的客人呢？"司机回答："就是你们两个！"我们看了一眼对方，一齐说："老婆，你先上！"

After we finished moaning, the wounds seemingly clotted with sand, the blood having stopped flowing, we saw something quite out of place considering the situation. Perhaps it was due to a loss of blood and my mind playing tricks on me, but we noticed a pink convertible Cadillac sitting in the parking lot. We hobbled over to the car. A young man was sitting on the bumper smoking a cigarette. He said he was the driver of the car and it was a wedding car, which took lovers to scenic spots for photos. The driver agreed to take us back. My friend asked, "And where are your clients?" The driver responded with, "they are you two!" Not wanting to look a gift horse in the mouth, we looked at one another and said simultaneously, "Wife, after you!"

在那辆车上，我的好伙伴睡着了，我也昏昏欲睡。我答应自己，我将永远记得那个晚上。

In the car, my good buddy sleeping, feeling drowsy, I promised myself that I would never forget that evening.

非常感谢你，我亲爱的朋友，你提醒了我友谊的真正含义。

Thank you very much, my dear friend, you reminded me what the meaning of friendship really was.

Chapter 10

化身蚊子：中国寺庙
Reincarnated Mosquito: A Chinese Temple

我盘腿坐在一把矮凳子上。因为凳子在不断地晃动，我害怕会倒下来撞到这家寺庙中众多的镀金菩萨，我努力寻找我可以依靠的"物"。又差点往后倒下去，我想，该死，我需要的"物"到底在哪儿？

I sat cross-legged on a low stool. With the stool constantly rocking back and forth, fearful I would tip over, crashing into the temple's many gold-plated Buddha, I struggled to find my object. Nearly falling backwards again, I thought, dammit, where is my object?

在浙江省临安市附近的一座寺庙里，一位澳大利亚和尚轻松地说："集中精力在你想要的'物'上，直到它围绕着你。"

In a temple near Lin'an in Zhejiang Province, an Australian monk, said relaxingly, "Concentrate one's energy on your object until it surrounds you completely."

在我左边的一位泰国男孩，20岁的年轻弟子，一直含含糊糊说些我听不清楚的祈祷词。为了使自己注意力集中，我偷偷祈祷他小声一点，因为在他的喋喋不休下，我找不到我的"物"。我的鼻子好痒，我的背也很酸痛。

To my left a young man from Thailand, a twenty-year old apprentice, continuously mumbled prayers that I could not comprehend. In order to focus my attention, I secretly prayed that he would pray a little quieter, as I couldn't find my object under his jabbering. My nose itched horribly. My back ached.

突然，我耳边居然有一个声音在温柔地呢喃："在顺境中修行，永远不能成佛。"我虽然看不见，但是能想象我耳旁一位小菩萨坐在一片荷叶上漂着的形象。

Suddenly, in my ear I unexpectedly heard a voice whisper gently, "Practicing religion in favorable conditions, one will never become Buddhist." I couldn't see it, but I could imagine the image of a small Bodhisattva floating on a lotus leaf outside of my ear.

在令人窒息的炎热下，我的脑子已经被烧坏了。我不理那个我凭空想象出来的声音，而是在努力思考我依靠的"物"到底是什么：我的"物"是地板？是另外一个修行者？我闭上眼睛，潜入我的脑海里努力思索，是上面的木梁？是它们上面挂着的长长的彩色旗帜？我用手指摸了摸眼睛，压住眼皮，一道闪过的红光终于让我想起了我的"物"！

My brain already fried beneath the stifling heat, I ignored the voice I had conjured up and focused on what my object was: was it the floor? Another disciple? Closing my eyes, I looked inwards and thought hard, the wooden beams overhead? The long, extraordinarily rich and colorful banners that hung from them? Rubbing my eyes with my fingers, pressing my eyelids, a flash of red light allowed me to finally find my object!

早先，在寺庙的酷热条件下，我感觉时间过得很慢，师傅要我们寻找一个"物"，然后在那个"物"上集中精神一会儿。我按字面意思去找了一个，伸展了一下僵硬的脖子，在大厅的另外一面，我找到了我的"物"：一张挂在墙上的古老卷轴上的红印章。如果他指的是找一个灵性的或感性的"物"，那么，我已经失败了。

Early on, beneath the temple's sweltering conditions, feeling that my life had already run out as time slowed to a crawl, the master requested us to seek out an object and then to concentrate on that object. I literally sought an object. Once again stretching a tightening neck, on the other side of the main hall I found my object: a red stamp on the surface of an ancient scroll hanging from the wall. If his point was to find a spiritual or emotional object, then I had already failed.

师傅问道："它带着什么气味？"

The master asked, "What scent did it possess?"

印章在玻璃片下，闻不到，但是我能想象到那种布满灰尘的、淡淡的霉菌味。

The stamp was beneath glass, and couldn't be smelled, but I imagined it was covered in dust and smelled a little moldy.

我突然想打喷嚏。但我怕会干扰别人的注意力，所以忍住了。

Suddenly I had the urge to sneeze. But I resisted, fearful of breaking others concentration.

我禁不住想象其他人选了什么。

I couldn't help but imagine what the others had chosen.

一去想其他 13 个坐在师傅周边的人选了什么"物"，我就失去自己的"物"了。我继续思考：其他人选了什么样的"物"？他们在把注意力集中于自己的"物"时是否都能找到自己内心的宁静？会像我一样难找吗？

As soon as I started to think about what objects the thirteen others sitting around the master had chosen, I had lost my own. Having lost it, I continued to wonder: what kind of object did everyone choose? While focusing on their objects, are they able to find their inner peace? Are they having a hard time finding it like me?

一滴汗水沿着我的脊柱流了下来。

A bead of sweat ran down my spine.

我左眼张开一点，偷偷看看其他人。13 个人都有不同的沉思状态。一位四川女孩，头发几乎和尼姑的一样短，她露出的微笑比弥勒佛的还安详，容光焕发。如果她突然长了一千只手，我就会相信她是观音转世！在我对面的一个荷兰男人好像已经陷入了深度冥想。我觉得他随时都可以轻轻浮起。一位金发的美国加州姑娘，眼睛睁着，往前看着，可似乎已经上升到了另外一个境界，我看不见她在看什么。在我左边那位泰国小伙子，背特别直，仍然喃喃自语着。好像就连那位刚从纽约市飞过来的中年犹太女人也能在热浪下冥想，哪怕在脸上化着浓浓的妆，脖子、手腕、手指上都戴着很俗气的珠宝的情况下，她的专注力还是比我的厉害！

I opened my left eye and spied on the others. The thirteen were in different states of meditation. A girl from Sichuan, her hair nearly as short as a female monk's, wearing a smile more serene than that of the happy Buddha, was practically radiating with spiritual essence. If her body suddenly sprouted one thousand arms I would have believed that she was the reincarnate of Guan-yin, the Bodhisattva of Compassion! Across from me a Dutchman had already sunk into a profound state of meditation, and I believed that at any moment he would begin to levitate lightly. A blond girl from California, eyes open, staring ahead, seemed to have already transcended to another plane and I was unable to see what she could. To my left, the young Thai, back perfectly straight, continued to mumble. It would seem even the middle-aged Jewish woman who flew over from New York City could meditate in this blistering heat. And even though her face was covered in makeup, or that her neck, wrists and fingers were covered in gaudy jewelry, her concentration skills were better than mine!

我的胃痉挛了。我很担心自己快要放出一个响屁。

My stomach was cramping up. I was worried I was about to release a loud fart.

师傅问道："你们感受到了吗？"

The master asked, "Can you feel it?"

我全身感到黏黏的。

My entire body felt sticky.

开始寻找我们的"物"之前，寺庙大师傅，一个看上去很仁慈的老人，给我们送来了非常可口的西瓜。他想让我们在这炎热的天气里休息一下。说来奇怪，虽然所有的人都设法不把一滴西瓜汁洒落在寺庙的地上，但我周围还是都被西瓜汁弄湿了。等我把那片西瓜吃光时，我的手、腿和脚上都满是果汁。15分钟之后，那些果汁变得黏黏的，迷人的甜蜜味道覆盖在我的皮肤上。

Before we were asked to seek our objects, the temple's head master, a benevolent-looking old man, had brought in watermelon slices for everyone. They were a refreshing break from the heat. Strangely enough, even though no one had managed to spill a drop of watermelon juice on the temple floor, the area around me was soaked in watermelon juice. By the time I had finished eating the piece, my arms, legs and feet were completely covered in juice. Fifteen minutes later, the juice had become a sticky film, with a particularly attractive sweet aroma that covered my skin.

说曹操，曹操就到！

And speaking of the devil!

我耳朵里传来一只蚊子的嗡嗡声。接着它在我的脚趾上落下。仿佛我的腿变成了飞机场的停机坪，紧接着，第二、三、四、五只蚊子也降落了下来。

A mosquito buzzed in my ear. Then it landed on my toe. And as if my leg had become an airport's landing strip, immediately following the first, a second, third, fourth and fifth also made their descents.

我再一次丧失了专注力，这次是因为被蚊子咬了，我咕哝道："该死！"

Concentration lost once again, this time due to mosquitos, I murmured, "Dammit!"

又有十只蚊子加入了在我腿上的野餐，似乎我的血就是它们的主菜！很快我腿上露出的部分都布满了蚊子。我正举起手准备攻击，却被那个在我耳朵旁的热爱和平的小菩萨的说法稳住了："救人一命，胜造七级浮屠。"可是，我现在还是人类，不是那么纯洁：在心里的黑暗角落，我一边骂了它们的祖先，一边把它们都打死了！遗憾的是，心里所发生的事跟现实中一点关系也没有。我的身体变成了活着的血库。

Another ten mosquitos joined the picnic on my leg, my blood seemingly the main course! My exposed legs were quickly covered in mosquitos. Raising my hand ready to strike, the words of the small peace-loving

Bodhisattva filled my ear steadying my hand, "Saving a life is better than building a seven-story pagoda." But, I was currently still human, not so pure and honest: and in my dark recesses of my mind I cursed their ancestors, as I swatted them to death! Regrettably, what happened within my mind had absolutely nothing to do with reality and was of zero use. My body had become a living blood bank.

不知道是否由于我终于找到了自己的"物"，或蚊子都吃饱了，或者冥想时间到了，我精神集中了一会儿，最后，仁慈的师傅说："好了，活动结束了。"

Not sure if it was due to the fact that I had eventually found my object, finally able to concentrate briefly, or the mosquitos had eaten their fill or the time for meditating had concluded, but a merciful master said at last, "Okay, the activity has finished."

我虽然没有找到灵感，却也没做杀生者。

I hadn't reached enlightenment, however I also hadn't become a murderer.

但是，那晚真正的考验还在后面。而我还有机会将手上沾满血腥。

But, I had yet to have faced the night's real test. And there was still a chance I would bloody these hands.

由于在寺庙生活，和尚都不允许喝酒、看电视、打牌或出门泡妞，而且更重要的是，每天早上必须起得特别早进行祈祷，晚上八九点钟大家就都睡觉了。因此，我们也入乡随俗。因为一楼的房间都住满了，我在二楼跟一位加拿大朋友共住一间房。除了我们两个和另外两个女人以外，所有的人都在一楼住。楼上的温度简直比楼下热了 10 度，直逼 40 多度。我们没有空调，但至少每一个房间有一个大电风扇。我上了厕所，刷了牙，回到房间发现我们连大电风扇也没有。我的室友说它被泰国的小弟子拿走了，说是拿给那位来自纽约市的中年犹太女人。我们给她取了个外号叫"大城纽约"，因为她坚持住单人房间，不跟陌生人共住。不幸的是，电风扇不够，而泰国弟子认为我们两个是绅士，所以需要把我们的电风扇给她。我们两位绅士真想把那位泰国小弟子从二楼的阳台上扔下去。小菩萨回到我的耳旁轻轻地说："静下心来冥想……"小菩萨没机会说完，被我挥手拂去了。阿弥陀佛。

Due to the fact that life in a monastery for a monk doesn't allow for drinking, watching TV, playing cards or heading out to chase women, and more importantly, every morning they must start praying quite early, they go to bed at eight o'clock. Therefore, when in Rome, do as the Romans. Because the first floor's rooms were full, I shared a room on the second floor with a Canadian friend. Other than two women and the two of us, everyone was staying on the first floor. The temperature upstairs was practically ten degrees warmer—pushing it to over 40 degrees. We didn't have air conditioning, but at least each room had a large electric fan. I went to the bathroom, and brushed my teeth. When I returned to our room, I discovered that we didn't even have an electric fan. My roommate said that the fan had been taken away by the Thai disciple. He said he was giving it to the middle-aged Jewish woman from New York City, who we had nicknamed: Big City New York, because she insisted on having a private room and wouldn't share a room with a stranger. And unfortunately, as the electric fans were not enough, and because the Thai disciple believed us to be gentleman, he needed for us to give ours to her. The two gentlemen really wanted to throw the Thai disciple from the second floor balcony. The small Bodhisattva returned to my ear and said gently, "To indulge in fantasy, one…" But she didn't have the chance to finish as I shooed her away. Amitabha. (May the lord Buddha preserve us.)

临睡前，我下楼去对我女朋友和她的澳大利亚室友说晚安。她们两个说："我感觉有点凉，你呢？我们先把电风扇关一下，看一看是否需要，好吗？"我惊讶地想，感觉有点凉？先关一下？你们不知道楼上的温度大约是40度？你们不知道楼上多闷热，甚至连灰尘也不敢飞动？在心里，我也把"大城纽约"从阳台上扔了出去。小菩萨像一只小蚊子一样唠叨说："根本不必回头去看咒骂你的人是谁。如果有一条疯狗咬你一口，难道你也要趴下去反咬他一口吗？"我想，能不能从什么神圣的阳台上把她和漂着的小荷花扔出去？阿弥陀佛。

Prior to going to bed, I went downstairs, wanting to say goodnight to my girlfriend and her Australian roommate, I overheard the two of them saying, "I feel a little cool, what about you? Let's turn the fan off for now and see if we need it, okay?" Shocked, I thought, you feel a little cool? Turn off the fan for now? Don't you know that the temperature upstairs was around forty degrees? Did you know it was so humid upstairs that even the dust wouldn't dare to float about? Mentally, I also threw Big City New York off the balcony. The little Bodhisattva became as annoying as a mosquito and said, "Don't look back to see who has cursed you. If you have been bitten by a dog, do you plan on getting down on the ground and biting the dog in return?" I wondered, from what heavenly balcony I could throw her and her small floating lotus? Amitabha.

我们俩都脱去内裤，各自躺在床上，慢慢地陷入自己产生的汗水坑中。过了一段时间，在房间的黑暗中，我室友站起来把房间的小窗户打开了。我立刻被一件蚊子做的被子盖上了。我用脏话喊叫："你％￥＃＠干什么？"小菩萨又回来了，低声说："没有缺憾的世界，也就没有圆满。"我根本不理会她，挥了挥手把她吓走了，再祈祷说：阿弥陀佛。

Both stripped to our underwear, the two of us lied on our respective beds, slowly sinking into our own puddles of sweat. After a short time, in the room's darkness, my roommate stood up and opened a small window in the room. I was instantly covered in a blanket of mosquitos. I cursed him shouting, "You %$#@, what are you doing?" Returning, the little Bodhisattva whispered, "In a world without fault, there is no satisfaction." Completely unable to comprehend her, I waved my hand wanting to scare her away and prayed again: Amitabha.

室友说自己热死了，而且没有蚊子打扰他。他把窗户关上了。估计是希望我能快睡觉，然后再开窗。他给了我他带来的安定药片。可是那种药片不是天然的，佛教里不准用。我又被蚊子咬伤了。小菩萨的声音像被蚊子咬住的伤口一样，那么刺耳，那么恼人，一直缠着我的耳朵：

"每一种创伤，都是一种成熟。"我抱怨地反对："成熟似乎是一种被过于推崇的品德！"我吃了两片。阿弥陀佛。

My roommate said he was roasting and that no mosquitos were biting him. He closed the window. Guessing he wanted me to fall asleep quickly so he could then open the window again, he gave me some Valium that he had brought. But, because that kind of medicine wasn't naturally made, Buddhism forbid it. I was bitten again by mosquitos. As if as irritating and irksome as the mosquito bite, constantly lingering around my ear, the small voice said, "Every kind of wound is a kind of maturity." Complaining, I objected, "It would seem maturity is an overrated virtue!" I swallowed the two pills. Amitabha.

我的室友和我花了两个小时谈论了很多话题：是否相信因果报应和轮回，怎么把"大城纽约"从小窗户扔出去，是否能扔得卜，等等。我终于睡着了。12点，我被蚊子咬醒，意识到我全身又被那件蚊子做的被子盖上了。半醒半睡间，仿佛还在噩梦中，我的手在一位少林寺的武术大师的控制下，拳头像雨点般打在自己身上，击打一只又一只的蚊子。结果很显然：一百多只蚊子惨遭屠杀！小菩萨果然很失望地说："好好地管教你自己，不要管别人。"我试图打击她，讽刺地嘟囔道："你呢？没有别人要管？"阿弥陀佛。

My roommate and I spent the next two hours discussing many topics: whether or not we believed in karma, reincarnation, how to throw

Big City New York out the small window, whether or not she would fit, etc. I eventually fell asleep. At twelve I was woken by mosquito bites. I quickly realized that my entire body was once again covered in a blanket of mosquitos. Half awake, half asleep, seemingly still within a nightmare, my hand under the control of a Shaolin Temple martial arts master, my fists rained down upon my body, crushing the mosquitos one after another. And the results were clear: I had brutally massacred over one hundred mosquitos! Understandably very disappointed, the little Bodhisattva said, "Teach yourself well; do not try to teach others." Attempting to strike her, I sarcastically muttered, "And you? Don't you have someone else to teach?" Amitabha.

血洗之后，我往左边看了一眼：我室友又站在开着的窗户前面。他说："不好意思，我热死了。没发现蚊子飞进来。"我们两个公然地诅咒"大城纽约"，接着一齐再三说出："阿弥陀佛。"

After the massacre, I glanced to my left: my roommate was again standing in front of the open window. He said, "Sorry, I was roasting. I hadn't noticed that mosquitos had flown in." The two of us openly cursed Big City New York, then we repeated in unison, "Amitabha."

我又睡着了。两点钟又被咬醒了。蚊子做的被子又回来了。想彻底消灭蚊子，我再度化身少林寺的武术大师，剁碎了所有敢飞进我们房间的蚊子！想着这一定是人间地狱，我不断地说道："阿弥陀佛。"小菩萨好像知道不宜向我说话。室友又站在开着的窗前说他热死了，而且没有蚊子咬过他。我骂了他，他把窗户关上了。我们都心不在焉地说："阿弥陀佛。"

I fell asleep again. At two o'clock I was once again awoken by mosquito bites. The mosquito blanket had returned. Wanting to annihilate the world's mosquitos, once again transforming into a Shaolin Temple martial art master, I chopped to bits any mosquito that dared to fly into our room! Thinking this must be hell on earth, I said continuously, "Amitabha." It seemed the little Bodhisattva knew it was inadvisable to speak to me. My roommate was again standing in front of the open window saying he was roasting, and that no mosquitos has bitten him. I cursed him. He closed the window. Absent-mindedly, we both said, "Amitabha."

我又睡着了。

I fell back asleep.

三点半我被清晨祷告的撞钟声惊醒了。我的室友站在开着的窗户前面。显然，我的血已经被吸光了，或者所有的蚊子都被我杀掉了，因为这次我没有被蚊子做的被子盖着。我问室友他睡觉了没有，他给了一个我不宜透露的回答。仿佛他也有自己的小菩萨，他忏悔地说："阿弥陀佛。"

At three thirty, I was awoken by the sound of the gong announcing morning prayer. My roommate was standing in front of the open window. Apparently, my blood had been sucked dry or I had murdered every last mosquito, because this time I wasn't covered in a blanket of mosquitos. I asked my roommate how he slept. He used some language to respond that I don't dare print. It would seem he also had his own little Bodhisattva, as he repented, "Amitabha."

坐在床的一边，我挠了挠全身，一个又一个地把蚊子压碎的小尸体拂去，我只能想，和尚生活不太适合我。

Sitting on the side of the bed, scratching my entire body, wiping off the crushed little bodies of the mosquitos one by one, I could only think, the life of a monk didn't really suit me.

小菩萨飞在我耳朵旁，听上去她要训斥我说："盲人摸象。" 小声音一说完，像那些折磨我的蚊子一样，她就被我不耐烦的手压扁了。耐心没了，我说："你的意思是这样摸吗？"

Flying beside my ear, sounding like she wanted to reprimand me, the little Bodhisattva said, "Like a blind person touching an elephant." As soon as the little voice finished, it was squashed flat much like the mosquitos that had tortured me by an impatient hand. Patience depleted, I said, "Did you mean touched like that?"

看着那一朵朵"小荷花"飘飘落下，我知道有一点可以肯定的是：我的业力要完蛋了。

Watching the small lotus float downwards, I knew one thing for certain: my karma was finished.

按照善有善报、恶有恶报的因果，我下一辈子很可能是：第一天我将化身为蚊子，第二天被一个大傻瓜打死了！

In accordance with "good is rewarded, evil is punished", I could more or less predict my next life: on the first day I will be reincarnated as a mosquito, and on the second, I will be flattened by an idiot.

请原谅我，菩萨，我没准备好大彻大悟。

Please forgive me, Buddha, I am not ready for enlightenment.

阿弥陀佛。

Amitabha.

Chapter 11

美貌不过是皮囊
Beauty Is Only Skin Deep

在广西北海住的那些年里，我经常跟几个本地朋友在夜市的路边一边吃烧烤一边喝啤酒。和往常一样，当我们坐在那里时，有一位很瘦的12岁的小女孩走过来想卖鲜花给我们。可是，我们都是男的，谁会想买一朵玫瑰送给同性？白天我有时候在路上会看到她的父母——她的脸非常像她父亲，像两个勺子：圆圆的、光滑的、扁扁的——在路上来回地骑三轮车收废旧物品。很明显她的家庭生活艰难，他们需要女儿做童工。我们有时会买一罐雪碧或可乐给她喝，让她坐下休息一段时间。坐在我们旁边，她的小腿挂在椅子下来回摇摆，眨巴着一双很大的眼睛好奇地看我们四个用英文交流。她开心地喝可乐时会变成一个无忧无虑的小孩，暂时忘记她需要卖花吗？我真的不知道，希望如此。过了一年后她换了工作，开始弹吉他和唱歌给客人听。她简直是不会唱，真难听。可是我们四个怎能拒绝她？给她几块钱，她就露出了纯洁的笑容，唱一首歌。

During my years in Guangxi, Beihai, some local friends and I would often sit by the roadside at our regular night market eating barbecue and drinking beer. And as usual, a thin twelve-year old girl would walk by trying to sell us roses. But, as we were all men, who wanted to buy a flower for the other? During the day I would sometimes see her father—her face an exact copy of her father's, like twin spoons: round, smooth and flat—on the road carting recyclables back and forth. It was quite easy to see their family's economic situation. We all knew their life was hard, and that they needed their daughter to work. Sometimes we'd gladly buy her a Sprite or Coca-Cola and let her sit for a bit to rest. Sitting next to us, her short legs swinging below the chair, a pair of big, blinking eyes curiously would watched the four of us as we used English to communicate. Did she happily drink the cola and for a short period forget that she should be selling flowers and could be a regular carefree child? I really don't know, but I hoped so. After a year she had changed jobs and began playing the guitar and singing songs to customers. She really couldn't sing though and sounded awful. But how could the four of us refuse her? For a few yuan she'd flash her innocent smile and sing out a song.

第二年冬天圣诞节前夕，在一家小饭馆，我跟一个美女第一次约会。我们对话还算好，没什么特别，就是两个人感觉有点别扭，因为不知道说什么。过了一会儿，在窗外，我看到那位小女孩。她的小吉他挂在肩膀上，一些乐谱卷在她的小手里。她微笑着向我们挥挥手。我招手让她进来。她高兴地说："叔叔，你好！"然后她向我的约会对象也看了一眼。我问她："想听什么歌？"她转身，对我认真地说："你不明白，你不认识她。她想骗你。"因为想让小女孩也听明白她刚才在说什么，她用中文又说："她想骗你。"

During the winter of my second year, Christmas was fast approaching. In a small restaurant, I was on a first date with an attractive girl. Our conversation was okay, nothing special, as we were two people who felt slightly uncomfortable because we didn't know what to talk about. After a while, I saw the little girl outside the window. Her small guitar was hanging from her shoulder, some sheet music rolled up in her hand. She waved towards us smiling. I waved her inside. She said happily, "Hi uncle!" Then she glanced at my date. I asked my date, "What do you want to hear?" My date turned towards me and said seriously, "You don't understand, you don't know her. She wants to trick you." Because she wanted the little girl to understand what she just said, she said it again in Chinese, "She wants to trick you."

她说完这话后，那位小女孩的微笑就像一根被风吹过的蜡烛一样，立刻熄灭了。从她的大眼睛里能看出来她想跑出去，可是小身体冻住了，仿佛她忘记了怎么跑。即使已经尝过了艰苦的味道，但在我看来，这个小女孩仍保有善良和纯洁。我的约会对象呢？在我眼里，她的美貌变得丑陋，而且她心里黑暗的一面也呈现出来。我的内心呢？颜色变成冒烟的鲜红色了。为什么呢？因为我气得热血沸腾！当时，我的血和内心都起火了！

After she said those words, like blowing out a candle, the little girl's smile was extinguished. In her eyes you could see she wanted to run away, but her little body was frozen and it was as if she had forgotten how to run. Even though she'd already tasted the bitterness of life, in my opinion, the little girl symbolized kind-heartedness and innocence. And my date? In my eyes, her beauty had suddenly turned ugly and the color of her heart had become apparent: black. And my own heart? The color turned a bright, smoking red. Why? My blood was boiling! And, at that time, my blood, including my heart, burned with anger.

如果我约会对象的样子和语气是想表示别的意思，比如，她只想保护我，可能我会接受她最初的反应。也许她觉得我过分信任一个对她来说的陌生人。而且，我知道中国有很多骗子，可悲的是，有时候他们只是小孩子。如果真是这样，我可以介绍她们两个认识，解释这个误会。但是，她就是瞧不起那个小女孩，从她的语气里真的能听出她的漠视。很明显小女孩无法选择她自己的生活，为了帮助家庭，她只是唱着歌，弹着她的小吉他，哪里是骗子？什么样的人会那么快就看不起另外一个人，特别是一个挺可怜的小孩子？

If my date's facial expression and tone of voice expressed, for example, that she only wanted to protect me, maybe I could have accepted her initial reaction. Perhaps she considered me too trusting of what she considered to be a stranger. And I know that there are a lot of scam artists in China and sadly, sometimes they are even children. And, if that truly was the case, then I could have introduced the two of them and explained the misunderstanding.

But, she was looking at the little girl with disdain. And from the tone in her voice you really could hear total disregard. It was very obvious that the little girl hadn't chosen this life and was only trying to help her family by playing a few songs and strumming her little guitar. What kind of person could look down on another that quickly, especially a poor child?

我的脸像蒸汽机吹响的喇叭一样，我发火了！我对约会对象生气地说："我不明白？我不认识她？骗我？我大概一年前就认识她了！跟你呢？才两天多！如果你问我，我会说她真棒！你怎么能伤害那么小的女孩？而且，如果你让我选谁离开，我选你！"

My face was like a steam engine blowing its horn, and I exploded! To my date I said angrily, "I don't understand? I don't know her? Trick me? I met her over one year ago. And you? Only two days ago! If you ask me, she's great! How could you hurt such a small girl? Furthermore, if you would like me to choose who leaves, I'll choose you!"

从我的语气和表达，那位小女孩明白了我的意思。

From my tone and expressions, the little girl understood my meaning.

她的笑容慢慢回来了。我向她点了点头，鼓励她弹吉他。然后，她控制住情绪并开始唱歌。一开始，她显得有些紧张，可是后来越唱越大声！尽管她的歌唱得不好听，但她的声音还是让我冷静多了。

Her smile slowly returned. I nodded in her direction, encouraging her to play. Then, restraining her feelings, she began to sing. At first, she sang nervously, but gradually she sang louder and louder! And even though she sang terribly, her voice calmed me down.

我的约会对象呢?

And my date?

可以想象到，晚上剩下来的时间真的很不舒服。如果约会对象一直用一双"要杀死你"的眼睛瞪着你，你吃饭能吃得开心吗?

As you can imagine, the rest of the night was quite uncomfortable. If your date stared at you with daggers for eyes, could you have enjoyed your meal?

是的，也许自己该花几分钟给她解释一下我跟那位小女孩认识的过程和她的背景之类的，可是谁想对牛弹琴?

Yes, perhaps I should have spent some time explaining how I met the little girl, her background, etc., but who would cast pearls before swine?

没有第二次约会了。

There was no second date.

Chapter 12

怎么选一个英文名？

How to Choose an English Name?

　　名字不仅是一个人的名号，还能让对方知道你的国籍，也能反映你的性格和文化背景。通常我们的本名，是上代人传下来的，被认为很吉祥，有那个时代的特征，或者只因好听。除了本名，有时候亲友也会给你起绰号。而且不要忘了，有时候为了表达个性和创意我们也会给自己取名字。无论是本名、绰号或是一个自取的名字，从根本上看，我们的名字实际上是一种个人标签，在任何社会场合让大家都知道怎么称呼你。我认为名字是非常实用的。举个例子，在对话中，如果你对朋友提起另外一个不在场的人说："嘿，我昨晚碰到那个个子高、汗毛多的人。"朋友未必能猜出他是谁。但如果你点出名字："嘿，我昨晚碰到阿文。"那你朋友立刻就明白了。另外，住在一个强调集体主义的国家里，父母常用老二、老三、老四叫孩子；在餐厅和公司里，你的名字被替换成了一个号码，比如67号，很自然会让人家认为自己只是一个号码。这样，我就能理解为什么选英文名能给人家一个新的感觉，特别是当你自己挑选的时候。当学习新的语言的时候，也能让你感到距离那个语音更近（比如学西班牙语期间我挑选了Julie，我最喜欢的棒球运动员的西班牙名）。但最终，无论出于什么原因：创新精神也好，让客户、不认识的或者刚交的新朋友更容易记住你是谁也好，想更容易融入社会也好，取名时请考虑如下条件。

A name isn't just a person's title, it can allow others a little insight into your nationality. It can also reflect your character, culture and background as well. In general, given names are passed down by the generation before you, they are thought to be auspicious, a reflection of that time period or simply just because they sound nice. In addition to given names, sometimes family and friends will also give you a nickname. And let's not forget, sometimes when wanting to express your creativity or individuality, you will choose your own name. No matter if a given name, nickname or one that is self-given, fundamentally, our names are effectively a kind of individual label, which allows people to know how to address you no matter the social setting. I believe names are very practical. Let me give you an example: during a coversation, if you bring up someone who isn't on the scene, and there's no name to use, "Hey, yesterday I ran into that tall guy with all the hair," you can't be certain if your friend will be able to guess who it is. Using a real name, "Hey, yesterday I ran into Kevin," will allow the friend to know right away. Furthermore, living in a country that stresses collectivism, where the parents will often use Number Two, Three, Four to call their children, or in the restaurant and offices where your name is replaced with a number like 67, it is only natural that some people may feel as though they are nothing but a number. Therefore, I can really understand why choosing an English name can give a person a new feeling, especially from one you chose yourself. When studying a new language, it can also allow you to feel closer to that language (for example when I was studying Spanish I chose Julio, the Spanish name of my favorite baseball player). But, finally, no matter stemming from which reason: an innovative spirit, to better help customers, people you don't know or to new friends you just met to better remember who you are or simply wanting to more readily blend into a particular society, please consider the following conditions:

看文化的差异：
Look at cultural differences:

有一次，一个供应商的女销售代表打电话给我说："你好，我是Naughty！"

我立即忍不住想象出一个从头到脚穿着紧身性感黑皮衣的女销售，手里拿着一条长鞭，诱人地小声说："过来吧，小男孩，你今天太调皮，要打你屁屁！"

你想问为什么会那样想？我特别色吗？绝对不是，至少我不会是最色的。可在西方，对于孩子，Naughty 只是顽皮、调皮；而对于女人，意思就没那么单纯了。因此，不要给自己取这种名字。

One time, a new supplier's sales representative gave me a phone call and said, "Hello, I am Naughty!"

I couldn't help but immediately imagine a sales girl dressed head to toe in tight, sexy black leather, a long whip in one hand, seductively whispering, "Come here, little boy, you've been very bad, and I need to spank you!"

Why would I think like this, you ask? Do I have a dirty mind? Absolutely not, at least no more than the next man. But in the west, in regards to a child, NAUGHTY just means mischievous or obstinate, but in regards to a woman, the meaning is not that simple. Therefore, you really don't want to give yourself this name.

看年龄多大：

Look at the age:

"你好，我是 Princess（公主）、Monkey King（孙悟空）、Batman（蝙蝠侠）、Barack Obama（巴拉克·奥巴马）！"

在小学里，选这些名字都挺可爱，但是到高中、大学、毕业后找工作的时候，你肯定不会想要在打电话的时候对潜在的客户或新老板说："您好，我是 Superman（超人），您有什么要求？"

不要误解我，我很喜欢 Superman。小时候他是我的英雄。但是，如果你没穿着蓝紧身衣、红内裤，并且没打算救我的命的话，我并不想跟超人合作。飞走吧，超人！

"Hello, I am Princess, Monkey King, Batman, Barrack Obama!"

In elementary school, everyone chooses really cute names, but when you get to high school, college and finding a job after graduation, you certainly don't want to answer the phone call of a potential client or a new boss and say, "Hello, I'm Superman, what can I do for you?"

Don't get me wrong, I love Superman. When I was young he was my hero. But, if you aren't wearing a tight blue body suit, red underwear and don't plan on saving my life, I really don't want to work with Superman. Hit the road, Superman!

看语音：
Look at the language:

女孩子："嗨，我是 Yuki！"

我："嗨，Yuki，这算什么名字？"

女孩子："英语啊。"

我："不是日语吗？"

女孩子："是啊，但这是我英文名。Y-U-K-I，你看，都是英文字母。"

我："哦，好的。但不要说这是你的英文名，应该说这是你的名字或日本名。"

别忘记，很多语言都用"英文字母"（叫罗马／拉丁字母），比如法语、德语等。名字里有"英文字母"并不一定是英文名。

Girl, "Hi, I'm Yuki!"

Me, "Hi, Yuki, what kind of name is this?"

Girl, "It's English."

Me, "It's not Japanese?"

Girl, "Yep, but it's my English name. Y-U-K-I, see, they are all English letters."

Me, "Oh, okay. But don't say this is your English name, just say this is your name or your Japanese name."

Don't forget, many languages use "English letters" (called Roman or Latin characters): Russian, French, German, etc. A name isn't an English name just because it has "English letters".

看英文单词的本来意思:

Look at the original meaning of the English word:

她："你好，我是 Tomorrow（明天）！"

我有点好笑地回答："很高兴认识你，明天，我是今天，这是我的朋友昨天，后天还没来。"

这太混乱了。

对方被你的名字弄糊涂了，因为这本来是一个很普通的，天天用的单词，不是名字，所以你就不要用了。

Her, "Hello, I am Tomorrow!"

Smiling, I answer, "Very nice to meet you, Tomorrow, I am Today and this is my friend, Yesterday! The Day After Tomorrow hasn't arrived yet."

It's just too confusing that way.

If the person you are talking to is confused by your name, because originally it is a normal, everyday word, not a person's name, you really shouldn't use it.

看背景:

Look at the background:

他: "你好, 我是 Jefferson Thomas Smith!"

我: "你好, 你不是中国人?"

他: "什么意思?"

想把名字变成英文是因为新名字很时尚或让客户更方便地称呼你, 但是改变姓呢? 那不行。第一, 应该保留自己的背景, 给祖先点面子; 第二, 如果不是演员, 就不要随便改变姓, 不要戴起 "面具" 隐藏真实 的你! 我知道, 我的姓名 (Kevin Smith) 太普通了, 很多人, 从潜在 的客户到潜在的供应商都有一半不相信我的姓名是真的。

Him, "Hello, I am Jefferson Thomas Smith!"

Me, "Hello, aren't you Chinese?"

Him, "What does that mean?"

Wanting to change your name to an English one to try a new name as its currently quite fashionable or to make it more convenient for a client when

addressing you is fine, but changing your family name? That's not right.
First, you should retain your background, your ancestor's pride; second, if
you aren't an actor, it's really not that easy to change your family name, and
you don't want to wear a "mask" and hide who you really are! And I should
know as my given and family names are really too common and many
people, from potential customers to potential suppliers half disbelieve my
names are real.

你的姓消失了？
Your family name has vanished?

我看他邮件签名和名片上的英文名是 Bob，没有姓。

于是我给他公司打电话问："你好，Bob 在吗？"

秘书／Bob 的同事："谁？他贵姓？"

我："我只知道他是 Bob。"

秘书／Bob 的同事："谁啊？中文名是什么？"

我："我只知道他是 Bob。"

这让我怀疑自己打错了。

如果对方看不懂中文或者你原来只提供了你的英文名，交流就会出
现困难。如果你是 Lady Gaga 或 Madonna，一个名就好，但是估计你
不是，我没听说过叫"Bob"的名人。

Looking at his e-mail signature, and the English name on his business card, I see: Bob. There's no family name.

Giving his company a phone call I ask, "Hello, is Bob there?"

Secretary/Bob's coworker asks, "Who? What's his family name?"

Me, "I only know that he is Bob."

Secretary/Bob's coworker says, "Who? What's the Chinese name?"

Me, "I only know that he is Bob."

I suspect that I dialed the wrong number.

If your recipient can't read Chinese or you only listed your given name, a communication problem will come about. If you are Lady Gaga or Madonna, a given name is enough, but I figure you are not, as I haven't heard of a famous person named, "Bob".

看性别：

Look at the sex:

一个声音又粗又低沉，特别男性化的人，却说："我叫 Mary。"

我："Merry Christmas 的 Merry？ M-E-R-R-Y？"

他："不，是 Mary，M-A-R-Y。"

我不好意思地问："你知道这是女性的名字吗？"

觉得有点丢脸，他不高兴地回答："我知道。"

现今，我们的性别不像以前那么黑白分明，但是至少查一下你的英文名是否符合你的性别。

A very manly voice, deep and loud said, "I'm Mary."

Me, "Merry of Merry Christmas? M-E-R-R-Y?"

Him, "No, it's Mary, M-A-R-Y."

I responded hesitantly, "Do you know this is a female's name?"

A little embarrassed, he said unhappily, "I know."

Nowadays, gender differences aren't as black and white as before, but we should at least choose an English name that matches our sex.

看道理:

Look at reason:

他: "你好，我是 XYZCBA。"

我: "你叫什么？"

他: "XYZCBA。你念不出来吗？"

我: "我没听说过。"

他: "可这是英文，自创的！"

我: "哦，好的，我的中文名是⊠！"

他: "这不是中文啦！"

我: "可这就是中文，自己创造的！"

他: "哦，明白了。" 他不好意思地回答。

我鼓励你自己创造，可是，你的创造总该符合点逻辑吧。

Him, "Hello, I am YXZCBA."

Me, "What is your name?"

Him, "XYZCBA. You can't say it?"

Me, "I haven't heard it before."

Him, "But this is English, I created it myself!"

Me, "Oh, okay, my Chinese name is: ☒ !"

Him, "That's not Chinese!"

Me, "But this is Chinese, I created it myself!"

Him, "Oh, I understand," he responded embarrassingly.

I encourage you to exercise your creativity, but add some reason to the creative process.

现在，我再说一次，请你不要误解我的意思，我并不想扼杀你的创造力！比如，我的国家美国是世界上最巨大的熔炉之一：南美、欧洲、非洲、亚洲等地的人都移民到美国，渐渐混在一起。然后他们的名字都可以算是美国名，但带有本国特色或者文化根源。所以在美国，即使他/她是美国人，他/她仍然能用也能说自己的名字是中文名、法国名、韩国名，等等，因为要保留个人的背景、个人的认同感之类的，这是他们的权利。这些名字有些没有改变，而其他的自然而然地在新的文化环境下改变了，或者混在一起了，还有一些被蚕食了。因此美国老师第一天来点名的时候十分困难，会面对很多很复杂的发音，要猜猜如何才能说得对：Xue（中国人）、Schwarzenegger（德国人）、Kuczynski（波兰人）、Nikolaevna（俄罗斯人）、Enwelumokwu（尼日利亚人）、Ng（越南人）、Cheyenne（美国印第安人），等等。所以点到我的姓名时，实际上老师也不出意料地松了一口气，觉得最简单，非常无聊地说："Kevin

Smith." 我只能给出一个无趣的答案: "在。" 我真嫉妒那些听起来很有趣的姓名。好吧，至少我的中间名很有特色。

At this point I'd like to say once again, please don't misunderstand me, as I really don't want to stifle your creativity! For example, take a look at my country, the United States, which is one of the world's largest melting pots: names from South America, Europe, Africa and Asia have all immigrated to the USA and gradually blended together. Afterwards they can all be considered American names with original characteristics and/or cultural roots. So in the USA, even though he/she is American, they can still use and say their name is their Chinese, French or Korean name, because it is their right and prerogative to want to maintain their individual background, personal identity and what not. Some names don't change, others naturally change or mix beneath the new cultural surroundings while others are totally consumed. American names become very difficult to spell and say as they become more creative. Therefore, the first day of roll call for American teachers is really difficult, and they have to face many complex, hard to pronounce names which they must guess how to say correctly: Xue (Chinese), Schwarzenegger (German), Kuczynski (Polish), Nikolaevna (Russian), Enwelumokwu (Kenyan), Ng (Vietnamese), Cheyenne (American Indian), to name a few. So when my name is called, it is no surprise that the teacher breathes a sigh of relief as she says the simple, quite boring name, "Kevin Smith." I can only give the anti-climatic response, "Here." I really envy those with colorful names. Well, at least my middle name is unique.

另外，还有一件事，如果你不想选其他国家或者语言的名字，也是非常正常的。很有可能第一、第二、第三次，你需要付出一些耐心帮助对方明白怎么发音，向其介绍名字有什么历史。或者在你的名片上或邮件的联系方式中，在你姓名后的括号里写下你的英文（或者你所住国家，如意大利、西班牙、日本的语言）名字。

In addition, there is one more thing, if you don't want to choose another country or language's name it is completely normal. It's very possible that for the first, second or third time, you will have to patiently help others to understand how to pronounce your name and give them an introduction to the name's history. Or on your business card or within your email contact information, after your name, in parenthesis you can write your English (or depending on the country you are living in, an Italian, Spanish, Japanese, etc.) name.

这是我个人的意见，如果你坚持选 Mr. Smileyface 008，你就选吧。规则就是让人来打破的！

This is just an individual opinion and if you insist on choosing Mr. Smileyface008, then go ahead and choose it. Rules are meant to be broken!

Chapter 13

文化交流
Cultural Exchange

　　一个周六的早上六点钟，我在床上睡得正香，却被一个国外客户的电话吵醒了。跟那客户谈完后，我睡不着了，睡懒觉不是我的天性。我躺在床上看闹钟不停地闪着"七点钟"，想起我 18 岁时的暑假打工经历。那时，我上夜班。每个礼拜六清晨，我一看闹钟闪过"七点钟"，到了下班时间，我肚子就饿了！然后在回家的路上，想象着冒热气的热香饼、香喷喷的香肠、脆脆的薯饼和冰镇的橙汁，我就忍不住去麦当劳吃早饭。你可能会想："麦当劳那么好吃？"不是的。但是，我才 18 岁，钱不多，所以要去适应，去学习怎么享受生活中简单的事物。我回忆着我年轻的时候，看着窗外，意识到现在还很早，除了麦当劳 24 小时营业以外，在周六，上海的大多数面包店、饭店都还没开门。虽然快餐店的食物也都是垃圾食品，但因为那天我对中国路边的小吃，那些垃圾食品：千层饼、油条、手抓饼，没有胃口，我没有其他的办法。当然，我自己也可以做早饭，可这不是重点：尽管我长大了，但我还是非常喜欢吃垃圾食品，没关系！

One Saturday morning I was sleeping soundly in my bed when I was awoken by a phone call from a client overseas at six o'clock. After we finished talking, I was unable to fall back asleep. It just wasn't my nature. Lying in bed watching my clock flash seven o'clock, I thought of my summer job when I was eighteen years old. At the time, I was working the graveyard shift and every Saturday morning as soon as I saw the work clock flash seven o'clock, ending my shift, my stomach woke-up hungry! On the way home from work, imagining steaming pancakes, fragrant sausage, crisp hash browns and cold orange juice, I couldn't resist going to McDonald's for breakfast. And, if you are thinking, "McDonald's is that good?" It isn't. But I was an eighteen-year-old boy with little money. So you adapt and learn to appreciate the simple things in life. Still recalling my younger years, I looked out the window and realizing it was still very early, besides McDonald's and its twenty-four hour service, on a Saturday most of Shanghai's bakeries and its restaurants wouldn't have opened yet. And even though fast food is all junk food, because I had no appetite for Chinese street food, another form of junk food: thousand-layer cakes, fried oil sticks or Taiwanese breakfast wraps that day, I didn't have any other choice. And, sure, I could have cooked for myself, but that wasn't the point: even though I've grown-up, the adult me still loved to eat junk food so it was no problem!

走到麦当劳的服务台时，我把报纸夹在手臂下，对服务员说："你好，我想点一份两片热香饼的套餐。"它包括热香饼，一块圆圆的香肠，一块薯饼和一杯橙汁。我拿了我的早饭，找了一个小桌子，就坐了下来。我旁边坐着两位聋哑人，一个男的和一个女的，他们正在用手语交流。

Walking up to the McDonald's customer counter, with a newspaper tucked under my arm, I said to the service girl, "Hi, I'd like to order your two-piece pancake set meal." It included pancakes, a round sausage patty, a hash brown and a glass of orange juice. After receiving my order, I took my breakfast over to a small table and sat down. Sitting next to me were two deaf people, a guy and a girl who were using sign language to communicate.

每次吃麦当劳的热香饼之前，我都要进行一个比较复杂的"仪式"。临开始得准备一下，我的右眼看着我的食物，左眼偷偷看看那个男聋哑人。那样是不是有点不礼貌？为什么那样偷偷看他？因为他也在偷偷看我，或者至少一直注意着我的一举一动。反正，我开始了我的"仪式"：首先用塑料叉子把香肠叉到早餐盒子的一边；然后把两块黄油抹在热香饼上，每一片热香饼抹一块黄油；黄油平均分配了以后，把热香饼从上到下，从左到右切开；最后把甜甜的枫糖浆倒在饼上。因为饼已经切开了，糖浆可以流到饼里去，确保每一块，无论是上面或者下面，都会吸收到糖浆。剩下的一些糖浆我就倒在那根香肠上。准备好以后，我转头看了看他。似乎是想肯定自己已完成研究或者赞成我的做法，他对我点了一下头。

Before eating McDonald's pancakes, I have to perform a fairly complex ritual each and every time. Before I began the preparation, my right eye on my food, my left eye was spying on the deaf people. And wasn't that a little rude? Why was I spying like that? Well, it was because he was also spying on me or at least he was continually watching my every move. Anyways, I began the ritual: first using the plastic fork I put the sausage onto the inside of the breakfast set's lid, and then I spread two butter tabs on to the pancakes, spreading one butter tab on each pancake. After the butter was spread evenly, I would cut the pancake into strips from the top to the bottom, then from left to right. Finally I would take the sweet maple syrup and pour it over the pancakes. Because the pancakes were already cut, the syrup would run inside, ensuring that every piece, top and bottom, would have absorbed a little of the syrup. And I'd pour the remaining syrup over the top of the sausage. After everything was prepared, I turned to the left and looked at him. As if to confirm that his research was complete or that he had approved of my method, he nodded at me once.

我惬意地一边享用早饭一边看报纸，几乎忘记了他们的存在。过了几分钟，从眼角的余光，我看到他拿着和我刚才点的一样的套餐到我旁边的桌子来了。我不想那么明显，但还是有点好奇，我又偷偷看看他准备怎么做。他首先用塑料叉子把香肠拿到早餐盒的一边；然后他把黄油抹在热香饼上，每一片热香饼抹一块黄油；黄油平均分配后，他把热香饼从上到下，从左到右切开；最后他把甜甜的枫糖浆倒在饼上，他也把剩下的糖浆倒在那块香肠上。

Happily enjoying my breakfast while reading the newspaper, I almost forgot they were still there. After a few minutes, from the corner of my eye I saw him taking over the same set meal that I had just ordered to the table next to me. Not wanting to be too obvious, but still a little curious, I again spied on him to see how he would prepare things. First, using the plastic fork he put the sausage onto the inside of the breakfast set's lid, and then he spread two butter tabs on to the pancakes, spreading one butter tab on each pancake. After the butter was spread evenly, he cut the pancake into strips from the top to the bottom, then from left to right. Finally he took the sweet maple syrup and poured it over the pancakes. And he also poured the remaining syrup over the top of the sausage.

我再次转向他们，脸上露出抑制不住的笑容，我伸出大拇指站起来，用我唯一知道的手语说："很棒！"

I again turned in their direction, and unable to restrain from smiling, I gave him the thumb's up, using the only sign language I knew: "Perfect!"

我们一起笑了。

We smiled together.

很久前，孔子曾经说过："三人行必有我师。"可如果能让我改动一下，就更适合上面的情况："三人坐，必有我厨师！"

Long ago, Confucius once said, "When three are walking, one can be my teacher." But if I can change it a little, even more fitting to the above situation would be, "When three are sitting, one can be my chef!"

Chapter 14

三个婚礼：文化地雷
The Triple Wedding: A Cultural Landmine

第一个婚礼：在红印章下！
WEDDING NUMBER 1: BENEATH THE RED STAMP

"什么？！不要让你自己的母亲参加你们的婚礼是什么意思？！你疯了？！我是你妈妈，当然要受邀参加！！！我抚养你长大，这是我的权利！！！"在地球的另一端，我的母亲在电话里喊叫着，就好像我要亲手把我们母子之间的联结给剪断一样。缓缓出了一口气，将被背叛后的愤怒情绪暂时控制住后，她用那种母性的语气，一半威胁一半恐吓地一字一字地叫出我全名："史密斯·麦肯科恩·凯文，你最好是在开玩笑。"

"WHAT?! What do you mean by not wanting your own mother to attend the wedding ceremony?! I'm your mother, and of course I expect an invite!!! I raised you and this is my right!!!" halfway around the world my mom screamed into the other end of the line, acting as if I was trying to sever the tie that binds a child to his mother. Slightly out of breath, her feelings of betrayal and anger temporarily under control, she finished with that motherly tone that every mother possesses, one part threatening, one part daring a child to continue speaking, using my full name, emphasizing each and every word,

177

she continued, "You had better be joking, Kevin McKeon Smith."

　　站在上海市的美国领事馆前，我手里拿着刚刚被公证人证实的单身证明，意识到无论我以什么方式告诉母亲："嘿妈，我，呃，要告诉你一些事。但是，你发火之前，我无意以任何方式、方法或形式让你误解我们不要你参加婚礼，或者我们两个在没有你的见证下结婚——"她都会歇斯底里地打断我。所以，在母亲叫出我全名时——这可以理解为："孩子，你自己马上解释一下……这是对你的最后警告……准备迎接死亡！"——我竭力道："妈，请让我说完吧：我们要结婚，但是在中国这仅仅是一个规定，基本上只是结婚登记而已。"我故意避开任何听起来太官方的词句，希望我能淡化这件事的严重性："只是上交一份证件，好让相关部门有事可做罢了……"我相信接下来母亲又会发出更多质问。其实，对于一个一点也不熟悉中国的结婚登记系统的母亲来说，这样的反应再正常不过。在中国，真正的婚礼仪式可能在领取结婚证后几个月，甚至几个年之后才举行。

Standing outside of the US consulate in Shanghai, my recently notarized Single Status Certificate in hand, I already knew that no matter how I told my mom, "Hi, Mom, I, uh, have to tell you something. And, before you get upset, I don't want you to think in any way, shape or form that we don't want you to attend or that we are getting married without you—" I could predict the results—I would be interrupted by my mom going into hysterics. So, under a mother's use-of-the-full-name threat, which meant, "Boy, you better explain yourself immediately…this is your last warning…prepare to die!" I did my best, "Mom, let me finish. We are getting married, but it is just a formality in China, basically just registering to get married and nothing more." I was intentionally avoiding any words that included 'official' and doing my best to downplay the seriousness of it, "just a certificate to hand to the bureaucrats so they will have something to do." I believe this followed with a few more "WHAT?!" And, this was a completely normal reaction for a mother not familiar with the marriage registration system in China, where a ceremony can follow months and even years later.

我没打电话告诉她,我们即将结婚,因为父母知道我们已经订婚,所以迟早会结婚。我们打算在十二月二十五日,圣诞节,去中国的民政部门登记结婚。我却不敢对母亲说我要"结婚"。首先,我应该告诉我的读者们为什么我要在结婚上打引号。对普通的美国人来说,婚礼仪式基本上有两类:第一,在法院里登记结婚,意思是不要任何婚礼仪式,由一位称作"太平绅士"的法官为他们证婚,一个朋友或者亲戚担任他们的证婚人,然后马上收到结婚证;第二,在教堂、犹太教会堂,或者其他比较特别的地方,比如沙滩、房屋的后院等,举办传统的婚礼,由一个神父、牧师、拉比或者任何能主持婚礼仪式并具有法律效力的人*来证婚,然后与亲戚朋友们一起庆祝。但是几乎没有夫

*根据美国法律,不但太平绅士有权代替登记与签发结婚证,任何经认证的神

妻会同时举办这两类婚礼——非此即彼，不会先去法院登记结婚，再办传统的婚礼仪式。即使我知道在中国结婚登记是法律程序的第一步（也是唯一的法律步骤），大约几个月之后再举行第二步：婚礼仪式。因此，在中国第一步和第二步是分得比较开的。但是在美国，结婚登记证明和婚礼仪式是同时生效并具有同等效力的，所以登记后就不需要再举行婚礼。在美国的法院登记主要是为了避免因家庭分歧而发生私奔、再婚的情况，或者方便那些反对传统的婚礼仪式，想节约婚礼仪式费用的人。因此这种法官登记结婚的情况并不多见，我担心我母亲不能明白。最后母亲允许我向她解释，使我少受些听力损伤。我们的想法一致，她释然了。

  The call wasn't to tell her we were getting married as we already got engaged and they knew we'd get married someday. It was to notify her that we were going to the Chinese marriage bureau on December 25th, Christmas, to register, and I didn't dare say "get married." First, I should tell you, my readers, why I put the term "get married" in quotation marks: for the average American, in regards to the marriage process, you basically have two choices: a courthouse ceremony, which means you forgo an actual wedding ceremony and just get married at the court house by a judge, called a justice of the peace, with either a friend or family member acting as a witness, and you will receive the wedding certificate then and there; or a traditional wedding

---

职人员，例如神父（天主教）、牧师（基督教）、拉比（犹太人）、伊玛目（穆斯林）等，都有这项权利。因此人家没有必要去做法官登记或者"结婚"。

that is held in churches, temples and/or other unique settings such as on the beach, in a home's backyard, etc. with a priest, minister, rabbi and/or basically anyone who is legally certified to officiate a wedding ceremony, celebrating with family and friends. Hardly any couples would do both, as it is one or the other, and you won't first go to the courthouse to register your marriage and then have a traditional ceremony. So, while I understood that it was only the first step in the legal marriage registration process in China, and legally speaking, the only step, holding the actual wedding ceremony months later, in the USA marriage registration and the wedding ceremony happens simultaneously, thus in the USA it eliminates the need for a proper traditional ceremony—where both registration/certification take place more or less simultaneously. American courthouse weddings are typically reserved for those who elope to avoid some family disagreement, second or third marriages and/or people who don't agree with traditional ceremonies and the costs generally associated with them. But, as courthouse weddings are few, I worried my mom wouldn't understand. Eventually, after my mom allowed me to finish explaining to her, she calmed down, and minus a bit of hearing loss on my part, we were on the same page.

在那年的圣诞节，我跟我的新娘拜访了婚姻的"幸福"部门，在一位面无表情的、最多二十五岁的女公务员的对面坐下。虽然没有任何需要担心的理由，但是我一开始感觉有点紧张：她会提出什么问题？我们又该如何回答？她是否会拒绝我们的结婚请求？幸运的是，这些都是瞎操心。她向我们俩提了几个问题："您贵姓？""您有没有文件 A、B、C？"还有其他一些标准的问题。然后指向隔壁的办公室，示意说："请去那边合拍结婚照。"最后，在官印发出轻轻的"砰"的一声后，我听到那位公务员说："好吧，给你们。"很有可能只是我的想象，但是在她嘴角我瞬间捕捉到了一点变化，有可能是一个微不可见的笑。她继续说："祝贺你们。"也许在美国法庭里办理登记也是一样的无动于衷和官僚主义吧。

On that Christmas Day, the bride-to-be and I visited the Bureau of marital bliss, and we took a seat across from an emotionless pencil pusher who looked to be twenty-five at the most. Even though there was no reason to worry, I was a bit nervous about what she may ask and if she could refuse our desire to get married based on the answers we provided. Thankfully it was needless worrying. She asked us a few questions such as, "What is your family name?" "Do you have documents A, B, C?" and a few other standard questions. After, nodding to the room next door, she said, "Please go there to take a wedding photo." And finally, below the soft thud of stamps, handing us some documents, I heard the civil servant say, "okay, here you are." Possibly it was a figment of my imagination, but I believe I saw a little bit of movement at the corners of her mouth, that representing a smile, as she said, "Congratulations." Perhaps it is the same at an American courthouse, cold, official, bureaucratic.

那天下午，因为我的新娘要去办一些事情，我花了大半天陪我的岳父在杭州西湖边散步聊天。如果我们不是一天之前才第一次见面，如果我不是他认识的第一个外国人，如果我的中文水平不是那么低……或许也就不成问题了。但是，他是我的岳父，我要留给他一个非常深刻、美好的印象，并使他放心他女儿的老公不是一个白痴。可能是因为我们两个都感觉比较紧张，那时候岳父不太喜欢说话。而我与他完全相反，仿佛嘴巴自动发出了声音似的说个不停："您看，这些圣诞红花有毒。但是在美国有些狗会吃它们，结果是狗死了。所以我们不要吃它们。"这些话一脱口而出，我就想给自己一巴掌！见鬼！怎么会那样说？他看了我一眼，不知道他听不懂还是开始怀疑他的女婿是一个十足的白痴。后来，我们分享了一盒饼干，上面用英文印着 TRUE LOVE 的字样，我们两个陷入了沉默，我猜他和我一样在想他的女儿，我的新娘，什么时候能回来。

That afternoon, as my new wife had to go to the hospital to take care of some things, I spent half a day walking around the West Lake in Hangzhou with my new father-in-law as we got to know one another. If I hadn't just met him the day before, or that I wasn't the first foreigner he had ever met, or my Chinese level wasn't so low, this wouldn't be a big problem at all. But, this was my new father-in-law, and I wanted to give him a good and deep impression, and certainly didn't want him to worry that his daughter was marrying an idiot. And not sure if it was because we were both fairly nervous, but he didn't want to say much, and I was the complete opposite, and as if my mouth had a voice of its own, I continually rambled nonsense, perhaps fearing uncomfortable silence, seemingly wanting to avoid at all costs, at one point I even hearing myself speak out, "Look, these poinsettias are poisonous. But in American some dogs will eat them and they die. So we don't want to eat them." I wanted to smack myself as soon as those words left my mouth.

Why the heck would I say that? Looking at me, I wasn't quite sure if he didn't understand or began to suspect that his son-in-law was a complete fool. At one point, we shared a box of cookies with the English print on the box "True Love." Lapsing into silence, I'm guessing we both were wondering what was taking our daughter/wife so long.

　　那天晚上，我们在一家日本饭店吃饭，我开始向他解释——也许说胡说八道更合适——为什么我坚持跟他分享这个特别的日子。因为我知道，在中国，有父母会陪孩子们去领结婚证。由于一天之前我才第一次跟他见面，因此没有机会使他有时间认识我或赞成我跟他女儿的婚姻，因此我要表达歉意。我特别紧张，全身不断地出汗，我试图说明为什么要尊重新娘的父母，因为我爱他们的女儿，我将用这辈子永远尊敬并珍惜她。虽然已经和他女儿领取了结婚证，我还是希望能得到他的认可，允许我娶他女儿。正如各位想象的，就算用自己的母语也很难表达清楚这种心情，更别提是用第二语言。在这样的情况下，我花了近半个小时，讲得结结巴巴，然后我的岳父把他的酒杯举起来，简单有力地说："我在。"

That night, at a Japanese restaurant, I began to explain, perhaps more nervous blathering than explaining, why I wanted him to be with us on this special day, as I know Chinese parents rarely accompany their child when dealing with wedding registration. As we had only met for the first time a day before, he didn't have the opportunity to get to know me or approve of a marriage to his daughter, feeling apologetic, nervous and sweating profusely, I attempted to say why I wanted to respect my bride's parents, hoping to express my love for her, how I'll spend my entire life respecting and cherishing her. And even though our marriage had already been certified, I still hoped to receive his permission to marry his daughter. As you can imagine, this is difficult to express in your native language, let alone in a second language, especially under these circumstances. After stumbling over my words for about thirty minutes, he lifted his beer glass and simply said, "I'm here."

我猜你不可能听到一个比这更好的回答了。

I don't believe you could hear a more perfect response.

第二个婚礼：在上帝的眼睛下！
WEDDING NUMBER TWO: BENEATH THE EYES OF GOD

"我该穿什么样的婚纱？西方白还是中国红？礼服还是旗袍？谁会盘我的头发，给我化新娘妆？这是什么传统？那是什么风俗？谁愿意……哪里可以买到……什么时候要通知……为什么新娘要……？"以及一千个其他跟美国婚礼有关的问题和无数压力，使我可怜的老婆筋疲力尽。对美国姑娘来说，这些问题都不存在，因为从小她们就参加了很多婚礼。此外如果她们不知道，想听听别人的建议，她们可以询问母亲、阿姨们、姐妹或女朋友们等。但是我老婆没有这些关系，而且她母亲更不理解西方人的风俗。我母亲着手帮助她。我嫂子也说我新娘有任何问题她都可以帮忙。但是她们都住在美国，一点也不方便谈论、沟通这些事情。不幸的是她只有我。更糟糕的是，作为一个男人，对于这些婚礼风俗我从来没注意过，只能提供一些没用的回答："哦，对于那些事我不太明白。"她问起"有旧、有新、有借、有蓝"的婚礼习俗时，我只能回道："这是中国传统？"很不幸，我们两个这才意识到我真是一无所知。

"What kind of wedding dress should I wear? Western white or Chinese red? Traditional or qipao? Who will do my hair and makeup? What tradition is this? What custom is that? Who is willing to…? Where can I buy…? When do we notify…? Why does the bride…?" Alongside 1,000 other questions related to American weddings and an equal amount of pressure, my poor wife was exhausted. To American girls, these questions weren't necessary, as from a young age they had been immersed in images of marriage. Furthermore, if they don't know or want to get another's opinion, they could rely on their own mothers, aunties, sisters, girlfriends and the like. But my wife didn't have these relationships, and her mother knew even less about western customs. My mother had already begun helping her, and my sister-in-laws said she could asks about anything, but they all lived in the USA, not the most convenient for discussing these matters. Unfortunately, she only had me. Even worse, as a man, I had never paid much attention to marriage customs, and could only offer useless answers such as, "Oh, I don't know much about those things." When she brought up the custom of "something old, something new, something borrowed, something blue", I had to ask, "Is this a Chinese tradition?" Sadly, both of us were discovering just how clueless I was.

由于我是天主教徒，所以我们准备在教堂里结婚。让我们了解下教堂的规矩。首先，我不想毁灭很多中国女士们的不太切合实际的幻想，比如某一天她们能在大教堂里，充满浪漫的气氛下，拍摄结婚照。但是能在一座天主教（不知道基督教是否也有这种规定）的教堂里结婚，你和你的伴侣两人中的一个必须是教徒。同时你也必须是那座教堂的会员。总之，在教堂里结婚的意义远不止于拍照，而是精神灵魂的体验，在传统与仪式中感受心心相印的旅程。

As I was raised Catholic and we planned on getting married in the church, let us jump to the church and some of its related rules. First off, not to dispel the somewhat unrealistic notion of many young Chinese ladies, wanting to one day get married in a church, where the ultimate wedding pictures take place under a romanticized ideal. But to be married in a Catholic church (don't know if Christina churches have this rule), you, or at least one of you must first be Catholic. Second, you must be a member of the particular church you will be married in. Anyways, getting married is much more than a photo shoot, as it is a spiritual experience, one that is wrapped in tradition and ceremony.

刚刚说过我成长于一个天主教家庭，受过洗礼，获得了一个天主教的名字。虽然我仍然质疑教堂的一些信仰和规定，但是我本人是一个有灵魂的人，而且相信传统。很有可能，住在国外那么多年，我也希望能重拾一些被我遗忘的传统。

As I already stated I was raised Catholic, have been baptized and received a Catholic name, and while I question many of the church's beliefs and rules, I like to think I'm a spiritual person and also believe in tradition. And, perhaps, having lived overseas for so many years, I was hoping to re-capture some of the traditions I've left behind.

之所以要成为教会的一员，是因为每一对夫妇必须通过一种灵性辅导形式，即 PRE-CANON。这种辅导需要大约几个月，教父将评估一对夫妇是否合适，而且更重要的是，这种咨询会给他／她一些启示，增进夫妻双方的相互理解。最终，订婚夫妇可据此判断婚姻是否是他们的正确选择。因此我们遇到了一些问题：第一，在中国居住，我们没时间完全参与这种结婚咨询。而且很显然的，我们不是在美国住，所以我们不属于任何美国教堂的教会。

One reason you must belong to the church is that every couple must go through a form of spiritual guidance called PRE-CANON. This kind of counseling takes approximately a few months, and the priest will work with the couple to see if they are a good match, and if done right, it will provide the couple some food for thought and perhaps a greater awareness of one another. The engaged couple can then finally decide if marriage is the right decision. Therefore we came up against a few problems: first, as we live in China, we couldn't afford the time required for going through the marriage counseling. And, I don't need to point out, we don't live in the USA, so we are not members of any church there.

幸运的是，人情并不仅仅是中国的特有产物，在美国有时候也是很实用的。因为我嫂子的父亲本来就是一位神父，通过努力，他找到了一个愿意给我们证婚的神父，他的姓是"开始"。他已经退休了，因而不太受教堂的约束。而且因为他的心态比较灵活、开放，认为幸福比传统更重要，因此他愿意主持婚礼，并且为我们证婚。我们的 PRE-CANON 咨询花了半个小时，然后他带我们参观了教堂——位于克利夫兰市的一座有一百多年历史的教堂——彩色玻璃窗、主厅的拱顶天花板和华丽的祭坛，都体现出优美与经典的建筑设计风格。里面的大理石塑像都是在爱尔兰雕刻完成，然后运到美国的，每一个角度都特别绝妙。花了大约十分钟彩排后，神父告知我们两人在婚礼上的任务：我们应该站在哪里，坐在哪里，诸如此类。我想我目睹过好多婚礼，也当过我哥哥的伴郎，这能有多困难呢？但是我的新娘呢？当然一点也不容易，除了一些美国电影里的婚礼，我的新娘从来没参加过一个西方婚礼。

Fortunately, personal connections aren't limited to only Chinese society and they can sometimes be pretty useful in the USA as well. Because my sister-in-law's father was a former priest, he knew a few priests, and was able to find one willing to marry us. The priest, surnamed "Begin", had already retired, and thus wasn't overly bound to church regulations. Furthermore, having a flexible and open attitude, believing happiness is more important than tradition, therefore he was willing to preside over the wedding and provide us with a wedding certification. Pre-Canon consultation lasted for about thirty minutes, after which he walked us through the church: one of

Cleveland's hundred year old churches: the architecture and design of its interior, from the stained glass windows to the main hall's vaulted ceiling and the splendid altar, were both elegant and classical; its marbled features and statues all hand-carved in Ireland, then shipped to the USA, exquisite in all aspects. Father Begin spent about ten minutes explaining what our duties would be, where we should stand, sit, etc. during the actual ceremony. I felt that I've witnessed plenty of weddings and was the best man at my older brother's wedding, so how hard could it be? But, for my bride? Of course it wouldn't be easy at all, as outside of seeing weddings on TV, she had never attended an actual western wedding.

由于很多读者们跟我的新娘一样，对天主教婚礼的典型仪式不太熟悉，我来给你们做个介绍：所有的来宾，包括亲戚和朋友都会被伴郎团接待。根据他们是新娘方还是新郎方的亲戚朋友，按照传统的女方左边、男方右边的规矩入座。所有的来宾们坐好之后，新娘和神父站在祭坛的前面，伴郎们在她左边，伴娘们在她右边，略远一点，风琴手将开始演奏婚礼进行曲——最出名、优美的旋律《新娘来了》。在那旋律"吨吨哒吨"的响声下，宾客们都转向教堂的后门，注视新娘与她父亲（这次我的父亲代替她父亲）步入教堂，然后慢慢并肩走入耳堂。在那一刻，站在祭坛前，我的心就像跳进了喉咙口一般卡住了。新娘穿着传统的浅蓝和白色花纹的旗袍，美丽的传统发式还原了上海 20 世纪二三十年代的经典，我被这景象深深地迷住了。

For those of you as unfamiliar as my wife was on that day with how a Catholic wedding typically takes place, allow me to introduce how it typically unfolds: the guests, both family and friends, are received by groomsmen and according to tradition, depending on if they are family or friends of the bride or groom, they are led to either the bride's, the left side, or the groom's, the right side, for seating. Once everyone is seated, the priest and the groom standing before the altar, his groomsmen to his left, the bridesmaids a bit to the right, the organist begins to play a wedding's most well known piece, the graceful melody to "Here Comes the Bride." Under the sounds of 'Dun, dun, de dun, dun, dun, de dun,' the audience turns to the back of the church to witness the bride and her father (this time my father stood in for hers) enter, walking side by side down the aisle. At that moment, standing at the altar, my heart leapt into my throat, my entire being was captivated by my bride and the traditional sky-blue and white floral patterned Chinese qipao she wore— we had agreed early on that she should embrace its beauty and fashion—her hairdo reminiscent of the roaring thirties.

圣经的片段被朗诵着，婚姻的神圣被逐一呈现；许下婚礼的诺言，互换婚戒，在上帝的见证下，婚礼在这对情侣的互吻中圆满完成。天堂里，我的爷爷奶奶、外公外婆都向我们两个以微笑表示赞成，因为我愿意在教堂里结婚，而且我选了一个好伴侣。同时，虽然我对教堂的规矩有些看法，作为一个尊重传统的男人，我爱上了教堂带来的庄重气氛。根据风俗，那天晚上，我们在一家翻新的农舍办喜宴，那里有一个大餐厅、两层酒吧、私人后院。我们的宴席持续了六个小时，晚餐有烤猪、露天篝火、幽默又感动的结婚祝词、敬酒祝福、音乐……一切都是精彩的记忆！

Bible passages were read, the sanctity of marriage brought forth, as wedding vows were said, rings were exchanged and the couple's marriage was sealed with a kiss beneath the eyes of god. My grandparents smiled down from the heavens, expressing their approval at our marrying in the church as well as having chosen a great partner. And again, even though the church's regulations and I are often at odds, as a man who respects tradition, I loved the ceremonial atmosphere it brought with it. And as with custom, tradition continued into the evening: we had our reception in a renovated farmhouse, including a large dining room, an upstairs and downstairs bar and a private backyard, the six hour affair had roast pig, an outdoor fire, humorous and touching speeches, toasts, music and wonderful memories!

第三个婚礼：在中国文化的怀抱里！
WEDDING NUMBER THREE: WITHIN THE EMBRACE OF TRADITIONAL CHINA

老婆："爸爸，哪里能找到一个传统的木轿子？"

我岳父："轿子？那不行！新娘必须从我们家带到新郎的房子！要我们带你到美国？！"

老婆："能让阿文坐在轿子里吗？"

岳父吃惊地回答："天啊！想让大家看我们的笑话吗？"他自言自语地说下去："让女婿坐在轿子里，真丢脸。"

老婆："哦，好吧。我们找个游行乐队怎么样？"

岳父："舞蹈团怎么样？但是里面都是老大妈，也有点贵，二十分钟两千块！"

老婆："哦，啊，一匹——？"她觉得还是不要问是否能找一匹马来让我骑了。

岳父："婚宴要在什么地方举行？什么酒店？"

老婆："我们可以在家里举办。"

岳父有点紧张地问："什么意思？要准备多少桌子？多少顿饭？什么样的主持人？"

老婆："我们对那些事没兴趣，爸，也不要主持人。我们想要一个简单的婚礼。"

岳父快失去耐心了，接着说："简单的婚礼？你说的是什么话？不要主持人？如果没有的话，我们怎么知道怎么做？邻居们会怎么想？我的面子呢？"

老婆："我老公跟我不在意有没有面子。"

叹了一口气，岳父泄气地说："但是我在意！跟外国人结婚好烦，如果跟本地人结婚，哪儿有这么麻烦。"

老婆生气了："爸！"

Wife, "Where can we find a traditional wooden sedan?"

Father-in-law, "A What? No good! A wife must be carried to the husband's home! Shall we carry you to the USA?!"

Wife, "Can we let Kevin sit inside the sedan?"

Father-in-law responding in shock, "My god! Do you want us to be the laughing stocks of the town?!" Muttering to himself, "Allow my son-in-law to sit inside the sedan, talk about no face."

Wife, "Oh, okay. Can we find a marching band?"

Father-in-law, "How about a dance troop? But they are old aunties and it's a little expensive, two thousand renminbi for twenty minutes!!"

Wife, "Uh, how about a—?" My wife decided it was best to not ask about a horse that I could ride in on.

Father-in-law, "Where should we have the reception, which hotel?"

Wife, "How about at home?"

Father-in-law answered anxiously, "What kind of talk is that? And how many tables? How many meals? What kind of emcee?"

Wife, "We aren't worried about all that, father, and we don't want an emcee. We want a simple wedding."

Quickly losing his patience, father-in-law replied, "A simple wedding? What are you talking about? No emcee? If we don't have one, how will we know what to do? What will the neighbor's think? What about face?"

Wife, "My husband and I don't care about that."

Feeling dejected, father-in-law sighed and said, "But I do! Getting married to a foreigner really is a lot of trouble. Can't you just get married to a local guy?"

The wife answered angrily, "Dad!"

中国传统往往倾向于男方家，而我与我的父母都不是中国人，再加上他们只要飞过来参加婚礼，大多数中国传统婚礼风俗都不合适。最终，那些文化礼仪都被简单化了。第一，因为我们两个不想设置接待厅，我们决定举行一个家居婚礼，能让人感到更温暖、亲近。幸运的是，她父母在乡下有一个大房子。因为我不像中国人那么在意婚礼司仪——在美国婚礼，司仪的角色很小，主要给大家做一些简短的指示，比如："贵宾们，请站起来欢迎新婚夫妇——史密斯先生和太太！"总共差不多出场十分钟左右。但与美国相比，在中国一个我们都不认识的婚礼司仪会花半天絮絮叨叨，从主持到戏剧表演到游戏节目，因此我们没有雇用司仪，而是由我的小姨子担任这个角色，让婚礼更简单、亲切，一举两得。

Now as most traditions in China lean heavily towards the male's side of the family, and as neither my parents or I are Chinese, coupled with the fact they were only flying in for the wedding, a large amount of the Chinese traditions weren't suitable. In the end, the cultural aspects that remained were simplified. First, as the two of us wanted to avoid a reception hall, we opted on a home-style ceremony & reception, which would make it feel warmer and more personal. We were fortunate that her parents had a large home in the countryside. And as I am not a big fan of the wedding emcees found in China—in the USA, a wedding emcee's role is quite small, and outside of making a few announcements such as, "Dear guests, please rise in welcoming the newlyweds: Mr. & Mrs. Smith!" totaling approximately ten minutes, as compared to those in China who we don't know, seemingly does all of the talking, from announcements to comedy acts to game shows, it should be no surprise that we passed on hiring one. Killing two birds with one stone, my sister-in-law was kind enough to take the honor, making it both simple and intimate.

举行婚礼的那一天，由于交通有些拥堵，加上我母亲前一天喝过白酒后有些身体不适，我们差点迟到。一到新娘家，我看到一个充气的婚礼大红门，上面贴着我们俩的名字"阿文和阿文太太"，我立刻把新娘推进去。为什么要推我的新娘呢？举行婚礼四天之前，她的脚踝骨折了。她坐在一个轮椅上——尽管这没有让一位中国公主梦中的传统轿子变成现实——我尽力给新娘一种"王室"的待遇。在外面的酒桌间跟新娘敬酒，一个劝酒，另外一个敬酒，欢迎吃吃喝喝的宾客们。至少我把他们当作是我们的宾客，因为除了我的新娘，我谁都不认识。我站在布置精美的红色花环下跟亲戚拍了无数张照片：我岳父的伯伯、伯母、叔叔、婶母、姑妈、姑丈和岳母的舅舅、舅母、阿姨、姨丈……我简直跟不上，真想知道谁能记得住那么多头衔，特别是因为在美国称呼这些亲戚们并不是那么复杂，只需要叫他们阿姨或者叔叔就行了！至于堂哥、堂嫂、表姐、表姐夫之类，在我的国家都拥有同一个头衔：COUSIN。最后我已经放弃去记这么多称谓了，只能不好意思地对剩下的亲戚们再三笑着说："谢谢！"

The day of the wedding, due to some logistic challenges and my mom suffering a serious baijiu-induced hangover, we were somewhat late to our own wedding. Arriving at her home, I quickly pushed my wife beneath inflated red wedding arches, the Chinese characters for "Kevin & Mrs. Kevin" tacked to the front. And why was I pushing my wife? Four days prior to the wedding, she broke her ankle. And while not meeting a Chinese princess's dream of a traditional sedan, seated in a wheel chair, I did my best to give her the royal treatment. Pushing and rolling my wife through the many tables out front, one pushing, one rolling, we welcomed guests as they ate and drank. At least I assume they were guests as I didn't know anyone outside of my wife. After standing amongst delicate red decorations taking a few hundred pictures with relatives: my father-in-law's elder brother and that elder brother's wife, father-in-law's younger brother, and that younger brother's wife, father-in-law's sister and her husband and her husband, mother-in-law's brother, mother-in-law's younger brother and his wife, mother-in-law's sister and that sister's husband…I simply couldn't keep up, wondering how could anyone remember all of these titles, especially as addressing relatives in the USA isn't nearly as complicated as you basically call everyone either aunt or uncle! By the time we reached the older paternal male cousin and his wife, the younger maternal female cousin and her husband, and the likes, knowing back home that they are all called the same thing: cousin, I threw in the towel and embarrassingly just smiled and repeated "Thank you!" to the remaining relatives.

我跳进一个空房间里，希望自己能从一位典型的与中国传统仪式不相称的西方家伙变身为具备某些文化意识的新郎和女婿，我急忙穿上我的服装。我真不想变得像很多婚纱照片里看到的那样：可怜的新郎被逼着穿上不合身的、用廉价聚酯面料做的西装——那味道闻起来就像被几千个人穿过后留下的狐臭——像历史剧里戴着劣质的假发、穿着唐朝服装的西方演员那样格格不入；新婚夫妇脸上被拍上一层厚粉，在至少三位摄影师的大声指挥下 45° 角仰望天堂，摆出各种夸张的姿势和空洞乏味的表情，巴不得赶紧完成这场噩梦。尽管我没化妆，也没有一帮摄影师对我喊叫，然而就像一般的西方人穿上中国传统服装那样看起来不和谐，我知道圆满完成这样的拍摄一点也不容易！

I jumped into an empty room, and hoping to make the transition from average out-of-place-looking western-dude-at-traditional-Chinese-ceremony to somewhat-culturally-aware husband and son-in-law, I quickly slipped into my costume. I really wanted to avoid looking like one of those poor grooms you see in countless wedding photos: forced to wear poor-fitting outfits made of a cheap nylon and smelling of a thousand other fellas, looking completely out of his element like those western actors in time period dramas sporting awful wigs and Tang Dynasty apparel; slapped with a layer of makeup, while being shouted at by no less than three photographers to pose in the most ridiculously sappy fashion, as the newlyweds looked off to the heavens in feigned longing typically completing the nightmare. And even though I wasn't wearing any makeup and didn't have a gang of photographers shouting at me, knowing that the average westerner just didn't look right in traditional Chinese clothes, I knew it wouldn't be easy to pull it off.

　　我提醒着自己，收拾好外表是为了讨岳母的欢心，毕竟在婚礼当天新郎似乎跟新娘的钱包没两样，只是另外一个配件而已。我开始穿衣服：一件定做的米色中山装，从肩膀处向下系着一条红绸带，中间是一朵巨大的人造红花。我把那个和西瓜一样大的红花挂在我胸部上，在后面打结；然后我把一个中国古代驸马爷戴的、旁边悬着两条螺旋桨似的长片的红帽子戴在自己头上。我的两只手神经质地抚弄着服装，走入了客厅的聚光灯下。楼梯上下、一半的客厅都被挤满了人。许多来宾穿着看上去是要去户外野餐的休闲服装，围成了一堵 T 恤和牛仔裤的墙。美国婚礼基本上要求正式着装，但是现在大家都露出善良又热情的微笑，令我感觉轻松了点。我坐在一块红色的缎子幕布前，醒目的"囍"字点缀在幕布的中心。我父母坐在右边，父亲身穿西装外套，戴着一条红领带，母亲身穿一件非常优美的裙子。在他们左边，我岳父头发梳得服帖帅气，在他身边是我的岳母——我最担心能否给她留下好印象。

Reminding myself, this is for my mother-in-law's happiness, and that at the end of the day, the groom is nothing more than a girl's handbag, just another accessory for the bride, I began to dress: already wearing a tailored beige tunic, I pulled a red sash over my shoulder, a massive red artificial flower attached to its center, adjusting the watermelon-sized flower until it hung slightly loose and tied it in the back; then I put on the red hat worn by the emperor's son-in-laws in ancient China, two propellers sticking out from behind. Nervously fidgeting at my outfit, I stepped into the front room and the spotlight. Guests filled the stairs from top to bottom and half of the living room. And it didn't matter that they were dressed as if they were going for a picnic in the countryside, a wall of T-shirts and jeans—American weddings generally require formal dress—everyone revealed kind and welcoming smiles, putting me slightly at ease. Sitting before a red satin curtain, the character "double happiness" hanging prominently at the center, sat my parents to the right, my father dressed formally in dress slacks, a sports jacket, sporting a red tie, my mother in a very elegant dress. Sitting to their left was my father-in-law, his hair stylishly slicked back. Next to him was the person I was most worried about making a deep impression on: my mother-in-law.

有可能只是我自己的感觉，自从我们来到岳父母家，岳母就一直注视着我，打量着我的一举一动，评估我是否确实配得上她生的第一个孩子，仿佛一只母鸡看着一只偷偷溜进她鸡窝里的狐狸，充满怀疑地眯起了眼睛。我诚惶诚恐地向她看了一眼：她包裹在一件豪华、合身，但还是保守的紫色旗袍里，领口被几个中式纽扣紧紧地系好，头发一丝不苟地梳向脑后，姿态比陆军中士更笔直。我不得不开始质疑自己的服装不够体面。突然我开始焦虑自己中山装的纽扣是否都扣好了，担心那个巨大的人造红花是否下垂了。感觉驸马爷红帽子里面的订书钉固定在我的头顶上，我肯定自己比她以前看到过的任何小丑都要更加搞笑。我把帽子上的螺旋桨调整了很多次，终于敢和我的岳母进行眼神交流了：她仿佛打消了疑虑，用一双水汪汪、亮晶晶的眼睛朝我看了一眼，露出一个喜气洋洋的笑容。她似乎全身散发出喜悦和骄傲，向我点了点头表示赞许。那一刻使我明白，无论我感觉自己的样子是多么愚蠢，我的岳母对我可笑的尝试都非常认可，而且欢迎我成为她们家庭的一员。

Perhaps it was only perceived, but since we had arrived in their hometown, as a hen would eye a fox sneaking into its hen house, eyes narrowed with suspicion, she kept close watch of me, evaluating my every move, sizing me up to see if I was truly worthy of her first born. I looked in her direction with trepidation. Wrapped in a luxurious, slim-fitting, yet modest purple qipao, the neck fastened tight with Chinese-style frog buttons, hair pulled sharply back, posture stiffer than an army sergeant, I couldn't help but begin to question whether I was dressed respectably enough. Suddenly, I was wondering if I had buttoned up my tunic properly, felt that the giant artificial flower drooped too low, and started to feel the staples inside the imperial red hat, a paper mache cap, pressing into the top of my head. I most certainly looked sillier than any clown she had ever seen before. Adjusting the propellers on my cap for the umpteenth time, I finally dared to make eye contact with my mother-in-law: as if all doubt had been removed, she looked at me with eyes sparkling, and showing a jubilant smile, beaming with pride and joy, nodding her head at me in approval. At that moment, I understood that no matter how foolish I felt I looked like, my mother-in-law appreciated my clumsy attempt and was welcoming me into her family.

我将双手放在新娘的细腰上，扶着她。她戴着金黄的凤冠头饰，站在我的正对面，优雅而美丽，一双眼睛注视着我。我觉得我是世界上最幸福的新郎。我们为双方父母奉茶，一拜天地，二拜高堂，夫妻对拜；

燃放鞭炮，吃吃喝喝，吸了雪茄，唱了卡拉 OK，度过了一天。据我所知，我们的仪式尊重了风俗和传统。

With both of my hands on her small waist, supporting my bride and her broken ankle, her beautiful features looking up at me beneath a tiny golden tiara, standing before my one and only, and feeling as any man would in such a situation, I felt I was the luckiest man in the world. We served tea to our respective parents, bowed respectably to the heavens and earth, parents and each other, lit fireworks, ate and drank liberally, smoked cigars, sang karaoke and eventually finished the day, and as far as I know, without overly offending any deities or local customs.

Chapter 15

怎么跟老外搞好关系?
How to Develop a Relationship With a "Laowai"?

在 MSN(社交网络)上跟一位中国销售代表的对话结尾是:

The tail-end of a conversation on MSN (a social network) with a Chinese sales representative:

销售代表(男生)发给我一个玫瑰的表情符号。

Sales rep (male) sent me a rose emoticon.

我:"不好意思,应该给你一个专业的建议:送玫瑰给另外一个人不太合适,特别是男对男。"

Me: "Excuse me, I should give you a piece of professional advice: sending a rose to another person isn't very appropriate, especially man to man."

销售代表立刻回答:"我不是同性恋!"

Sales rep immediately responded with: "I'm not gay!"

我："好的，我没说你是。只想建议一下。"

Me: "Okay, I didn't say you were. It was just a suggestion."

销售代表："我的女朋友比你的更漂亮！"

Sales rep: "My girlfriend is prettier than yours!"

（那天是我第一次跟他合作，而且我没给他看过我女朋友的照片。）

(That day was our first time to begin cooperating with one another, in addition, I hadn't even shown him a picture of my girlfriend.)

我："好的。"

Me: "Okay."

销售代表："你不懂中国人！"

Sales rep: "You don't understand Chinese people!"

我：BLOCKED / 屏蔽了（不敢跟他合作）。

Me: BLOCKED. (Wouldn't dare work with someone like that).

为什么他反应那么敏感呢？我不知道。如果他只回答"哦，好的"或"不好意思，可能这是文化差异"就没问题。送给我玫瑰没事，可送后的反应，才真的有事。刚开始，他就因为行为不专业而丢了一个潜在客户。因为没有人是一个天生的园艺家，当种养植物的时候，是不是该考虑一下买什么样的化肥和营养，给它浇多少水，放在阳光中还是阴凉处，对它唱什么歌？我们的客户就是我们的植物：化肥和营养是你的产品，水是你的工作态度，阳光或阴影是你的社交技巧，你的歌声能让我们听出你的个性。

Why such a sensitive reaction? I don't know. If he had just answered, "Oh, okay," or "Sorry, perhaps it's a cultural difference," it wouldn't be a problem. Sending me a rose wasn't a problem, but the reaction that followed, that was what really mattered. We had just started, but because of his unprofessional behavior, he already lost a potential customer. As no one is born a natural gardener, when cultivating plants, shouldn't you first consider which kinds of fertilizer and nutrients to buy? How much water should you give it to drink? Whether to place it in the sun or the shade? What song should you sing to it? Well, our customers are our plants: fertilizer and nutrients are your products, water your attitude, the sunlight or shade is your social skills and your singing voice allows us to see your personality.

在下面我写了一些"Do's & Don'ts"：有些很搞笑，有些你可以试试，另外一些请你别用。

Down below I wrote some "Do's & Don'ts": some are quite funny, some you should try, while others, well, please don't.

第一，不要说："Hello Dear."
1: Don't say, "Hello Dear."

写正式的电子邮件或信件的开头会常常先写"亲爱的客户"。这是正常的，很尊敬的。然后，你不能再用包含 dear 的单词。比如，在

MSN、QQ、SKYPE 这类的软件上，你不要说："你好，亲爱的。是的，亲爱的。谢谢你，亲爱的。好的，亲爱的。"因为这样频繁使用 dear 这个单词，是比较亲密的，像男朋友对女朋友、老公对老婆之间讲话一样那么甜蜜。而且有点像在调情。开头能用，后面不要再用，除非你真的想培养更特别的"关系"。如果客户是色狼或比较天真，会误会你的意思，然后一个尴尬的情况就出现了。

When writing a professional email or letter the heading often begins with: "Dear customer." This is common and very respectful. After that, you cannot use the word "dear" again. For example, on MSN, QQ, SKYPE and others like this, you don't want to say, "Hello Dear. Yes, dear. Thank you, dear. Okay, my dear." Frequently using the word "dear" like this is fairly intimate, similar to something sweet shared between a boyfriend and girlfriend or wife and husband. In addition, it's also a bit like flirting. You can use it at the beginning, but after that you don't want to use it again, unless of course you want to develop a special "relationship". Some customers are perverts, others are naive and can misunderstand your meaning which could allow embarrassing situations to arise.

第二，除非你是客户的老妈，否则不要说："相信我。"

2: Unless you are the customer's mother, you don't want to say, "Trust me."

第一次跟供应商联系，我总听到对方说："相信我。"可是，为什么要相信呢？特别是没合作过的公司，多半你不是买方的家人或老朋友，因此他怎么会那么快就相信你？所以你会问："好的，那我该说什么？"我的答案非常简单：什么都不用说。要赢得别人的信任，必须让你的职业精神、产品的质量和检测报告代表你的"信服力"和工厂的"能力"。我找新供应商的时候，根据这三个方面来寻找，我称之为3P：Product/产品（最重要的是要符合客户的要求）、Price／价格（如果产品好可是价格不好，怎么买？）和 People／人（就是供应商的职业精神）。根据这些方面，我能够越来越信任我的供应商。相合性和可靠性也能培养信任。希望你某一天能变成客户的老妈！因为在那天，你被客人寄予信任了。

The first time I contact a supplier, I always hear, "Trust me." But, why do I want to trust them? Especially with a company I've never worked with before? More than likely you aren't the customer's family or an old friend, therefore how could he trust you that quickly? So you ask, "Okay, what should I say?" My answer is quite simple: you don't need to say anything. If you want to win someone's confidence, you must allow your professionalism, your product's quality and test reports represent your "trust" and the factory's "ability". When I'm looking for a new supplier, I search according to three aspects, which I call The Three P's: Product (this is important as it must match the customer's requirements), Price (if the product is good, but the price isn't, how will they purchase it?) and People (this is the supplier's professionalism). According to these aspects, I am capable of trusting my suppliers more and more. Consistency and reliability can also cultivate trust.

And I hope someday you can become the customer's mother! Because on that day, trust has been given.

第三，不要尽说："我知道。没问题。有。"
3: You don't want to just say, "I know. No problem. We have it."

我老是遇到第三种情况，供应商真的不知道，可就是回答没问题。比如："供应商，产品有 ABC 认证？"供应商回答："我知道，没问题，有。"几天后我再问："能把 ABC 的认证转发给我看吗？"供应商说："呃，呃，我不知道，有点问题，我们没有。"我的观点是，如果不清楚的话，必须问你的经理、技术员、工程师……我知道，有些人会想："如果我说不知道，客户可能认为我不太专业，不太了解自己的产品。"对，你有你的道理，可如果客户发现你们本来就没有而你说有，那时怎么办？信任度就破坏了。可是，如果你对买方说："我认为有，可是我想查一下。稍等，我一确认就告诉你，好吗？"对方肯定能接受。女生读者们，如果你们突然问老公："老公，你听到我刚才说了什么？"他就点了点头说："是呀。"如果你接着不耐烦地问："好的，那我刚才说了什么？"我估计他就回答："我不知道。我没有听清楚。"一旦被抓住，就无法逃跑了。

I often run into #3's situation, where the supplier really doesn't know, but they respond with "it's not a problem." For example, "Supplier, does the product have Certification ABC?" The supplier responds, "I know, no problem, we have it." A few days later I ask again, "Can you please forward me a copy of the certification?" The supplier says, "Uh, uh, I don't know, we have a problem, we don't have it." My point is, if you aren't clear, you need to ask your manager, technician, engineer, etc. I know, some are afraid and believe, "If I say I don't know, maybe the customer will think I'm not very professional, and don't know my own product very well." Yes, you have a point, but if the customer discovers that originally you didn't have it but you said you did, then what will you do? The trust is already broken. But, if you said to your buyer, " I believe so, but I would like to check. Just a moment please and as soon as I confirm, I will tell you, okay?" The buyer certainly will agree. Female readers, how many times do you suddenly ask your husbands, "Hubby, did you hear what I just said?" He'll nod his head and say, "Yes." If you continue to ask impatiently, "Okay, what did I just say?" I estimate he will respond with, "I don't know. I didn't hear clearly." Once you are caught, there's no way to escape.

第四，不要说："这是我们公司的机密。"
4: Don't say, "This is our company secret."

如果一位客户问你："供应商，请你提供这个材料的规格／报告。" 你不要回答："这是公司的机密。"因为买方将会这样解读这个回答： "我们没有报告或我不知道。因此，我不想告诉你。"客户当然需要调查基本信息、第三方验货公司的报告或公司的内部报告。如果没有的话，客户如何能看清楚工厂是否了解自己的产品和客户的要求，并保证这个产品就是他们说的产品？公司账户中有多少钱、老板的情妇是谁，这才是公司的秘密！

If a customer asks you, "Supplier, can you please supply the material specifications/test report?" You don't want do say, "This is a company secret." Because the buyer will translate that into this answer, "We don't have any report or we don't know. Therefore, I don't want to tell you." Of course the customer needs to inquire into at least the basic standards, a third party inspection company's test report or a company's in-house test report. If you don't have them, how can they clearly see the factory really understands their own product and the customer's requirements? And furthermore how can they guarantee that the product is the product they say it is? How much money is in the company's bank account, how do they keep up good relations with the local government officials and who is the boss's mistress…now those are company secrets!

第五，不要常常用"表情符号"。难道你刚从幼儿园毕业吗？

5: Don't always use "emoticons". Did you just graduate from kindergarten?

笑脸、愁容或竖起大拇指的表情符号，都可以用，它们能表示你的感情，令人有轻松的感觉，可是请你学会控制。有一次在 MSN 上跟一个销售代表聊天的时候，我看不清她写了什么，因为在对话框里有好多猪（卡通图）飞来飞去，心（也是卡通图）跳来跳去，到处有闪烁的星星。我真头晕。如果遇到一些问题，要把项目推迟一下，请你直接说出来。即使你读的本科专业是动画，也不要让一只用小绿爪把额头上流下来的汗水擦掉的乌龟卡通图代表你的回答。

A smiley face, sad face or a thumbs up, they are all alright to use, can express your emotions, let people relax, but please exercise control. One time on MSN when discussing business with a sales representative, I couldn't read clearly what she was writing because the dialogue box had many pigs (cartoons) flying back and forth, hearts (also cartoons) bouncing all over and flashing stars everywhere. My head was spinning. If for example you ran into some trouble and the project needs to be delayed, please just say it. Even if you majored in animation, you shouldn't use a cartoon of a turtle using its little green hand to wipe away sweat from its forehead to act as your answer.

第六，穿什么衣服？第一印象至关重要。
6: What to wear? First impression is everything.

第一次接待客户，应该穿比较正式的衣服。我的意思不是穿名牌或很贵的衣服或该马上去外面买一套西装，而是不要穿 T 恤、运动鞋或一条有破洞（就算那比较时尚）的牛仔裤。第二次可以放松一点，因为第一次跟客户见过面，很有可能他对你的专业已经有信心了（这就是 3P 理论中的第三个 P！）如果站在你前面的人穿着一件有米老鼠图案的衬衫，以及后面有两个兔子尾巴挂着的鞋子，你想买她的产品吗？还是想问："小孩儿，你迷路了吗？你妈妈在哪里？"

When meeting a client for the first time, you should wear relatively formal clothes. I don't mean famous name brands or very expensive clothes or that you should immediately go out and buy a suit, you just don't want to wear a t-shirt, sneakers or a pair of jeans with holes in them (even if that's fairly fashionable). The second time you can dress a little more relaxed because you've already met the customer for the first time and he's probably already made up his mind about your professionalism (this is the third P!) If the person standing in front of you was wearing a shirt with Mickey Mouse on the front and hanging from the back of her shoes were bunny tails, would you want to buy her products or would you like to ask, "Little child, have you lost your way? Where's your mommy?"

第七，点什么菜？
7: What to order?

老外喜欢吃什么？这方面有点复杂，因为我们老外从各种各样的地方来到中国。中国老板想给客人面子，让自己也有面子，所以对客人挺礼貌。他们的做法之一是给客人介绍本地的特色，越贵越好。可是，如果客户不喜欢吃那些菜（比如：有些不喜欢吃内脏，另外一些不敢吃肉或是有其他的宗教信仰），那老板会丢脸，客户也会挨饿。那么怎么解决这个问题呢？一个很简单的建议是先问客户："有什么菜你不喜欢或不能吃的？"或"你想吃什么？"如果他说随便，就带客户去一家什么都有的饭馆，然后可以让客户选几样，自己也选几样。这样双方都可以愉快地享受一下了！服务员，一份鸡爪和一份比萨！好平衡。

What do foreigners want to eat? This aspect is a little complex because what does "foreigners" actually mean? We foreigners come from all kinds of places to China. A Chinese boss would like to give their customers face, while also giving him or herself face by treating the customer politely. And one way of doing this is by introducing some local specialties—the more expensive, the better. But, if the customer doesn't like those dishes (for example, some don't like eating the innards, others won't dare to eat meat and others have religious beliefs they must follow), the boss will lose face and the customer will starve. So how to decide? One easy suggestion is, first ask the customer, "What dishes don't you like or cannot eat?" or "What would you like to eat?" If they say it's up to you, just take the customer to a restaurant that displays their options. Than you can allow the customer to select a few and the supplier can select a few. That way everyone can happily enjoy the meal. Waiter, a plate of chicken feet and one pizza, please! Now that's balance!

第八，帮助客户，可别忘了，他们不是小孩。
8: Help a customer, but don't forget, they aren't children.

中国供应商对客户非常礼貌，很想照顾他们，比如想帮他们买火车票、泡茶、订房间等。当然都可以，可是告诉客户怎么吃/喝，怎么去想，这不太好了。有一次供应商说我该喝一瓶可口可乐，因为我是美国人。但是，我不喜欢喝可乐。我说啤酒就好。他不理我，坚持要我喝可乐。

我说喝茶也好。他说不行，你要可乐。我老板发火了，说："你是谁？别强制他喝什么！"如果连客户要喝什么的要求都不听，客户怎么能相信他听从对产品的要求？

Chinese suppliers are very polite to customers and really take care of them, for example assisting them with buying train tickets, preparing tea, booking hotel rooms, etc. Of course this is fine, but telling him how to eat/drink, how to think, this isn't very good. Once a supplier told me I should drink a bottle of Coca-Cola because I'm American. But, I don't like cola. I said beer was fine. He ignored me and insisted I drink cola. I said tea was also okay. He said no, you want cola. My boss lost his temper and said, "Who are you? Don't force him to drink something!" If you don't know how to listen to what a customer's requirements are for what he wants to drink, how can a customer believe that you will listen to the requirements of his product?

第九，明天面子会再回来的！别哭，别发火。

9: Tomorrow your face will grow back! Don't cry, don't lose your temper.

在中国，面子非常重要，可对客户来说，生产出好产品，还有按时交货最重要。如果工厂做错了，可又不想承认是自己的错，交货时间已经过了，客户当然要发火了。供应商该做什么？该让客户发泄一下。如果你感觉自己被冒犯了，无所谓，那是私人的问题，不是生意的问题。为什么呢？就是因为你是他们的联系人，你相当于公司的脸面，你必须咬牙忍受。你下班就告诉你老婆 / 老公，但不要对客户哭泣、发火，或者撒谎等。比如你在餐厅发现服务员上错菜或菜不好吃，被你批评过后，服务员会哭或者把菜往你的脸上扔吗？不，他只会说："不好意思。"我们都体会过不好受的感觉。不是说你要习惯这种感受，而要学习怎么控制自己的反应。

In China face is very important, but to the customer, producing a good product and following production time is most important. If the factory makes a mistake, but won't admit its own mistake, and the production time is already past due, of course the customer will lose his temper. What should the supplier do? You should allow the customer to vent. If you feel the customer has offended you, it doesn't matter, that's a personal problem, not a business problem. Why? It's because you are their contact, you are the face of your company and you must grin and bear it. After work you can tell your wife/husband, but you don't want to cry or lose your temper with your customer, lie, etc. If you discover in a restaurant that the waitress sent the wrong dish or the dish is no good, after receiving your criticism, will the waitress cry or throw the food back on your face? No, he or she should only say, "Sorry." We should all experience how it feels to feel bad. And I don't want to say you should get used to the feeling, rather you should learn to control your reactions.

第十，学习 small talk 是什么意思。

10: Study the meaning of small talk.

这个是比较重要的，而且不太容易学习。如果跟客户开车到工厂或在一起吃饭，应该知道怎么跟他们闲聊一下。没有人喜欢令人不安的沉默。可以谈论的事情有：天气、时事、文化、美食、家人、运动、旅行或者任何其他比较"轻松"的话题。不要谈论政策、宗教或其他比较有争议的话题。如果客户快飞到了，先看一看那天的新闻或者写下一个话题单子。跟客户一起吃饭而没人说话时，不要低头假装看手机消息，这十分不礼貌，你可以偷看一下话题单子（把单子记在心里最好）再提出新的话题。更重要的是，该留意他回答些什么，用你的眼睛看一下，耳朵听一下，用嘴巴确认一下：不要只回答"嗯"。

This is fairly important, but also not easy to study. If driving with the customer to the factory or eating together, you should know how to make small talk with them. Nobody likes uncomfortable silences. You could discuss: the weather, current events, culture, cuisine, family, sports, travel or any other relatively "relaxed" topics. You don't want to discuss politics, religion or other fairly controversial topics. If a customer will fly over soon, take a look at that day's news or you could write down a list of topics. If when eating with your customers and no one is speaking, don't look down and pretend to look at messages on your mobile phone, its really rude, just sneak a peek at your list (memorizing your list is best) and bring up a new topic/question. Be mindful of what he says, use your eyes to watch, ears to listen and mouth to confirm: and this doesn't mean the "um" response.

第十一，更加酒，更加好。

11: Add alcohol, Add good.

如果其他所有的方法都失败，就加酒。老板、经理都知道：为了生意，牺牲肝脏！（只是开玩笑，请适量饮酒）

If all other methods fail, just add alcohol. The bosses, managers all know this: for business, one must sacrifice their livers! (only joking, please drink in moderation.)

最后要说：中国人的特色就是接待客户时，对客户礼貌，给面子。这是中国文化的其中一个方面。而且我敢说好客就是中国人的理念。但是由于好多公司的销售代表是年轻人，专业是英文，而不是产品（特别是产品的技术方面），他们不太熟悉怎么跟别人做生意，就要从老板、销售经理和老客户那里学习怎么做，慢慢学。加上他们专业性的缺乏，人生阅历的有限，不是很容易理解这种理念。反正，不管是在你的工作中，还是社会中或家庭中，上面的观点都可以考虑一下吧！

Finally I want to say: A Chinese specialty is receiving customers, treating customers very politely and giving face. It is an aspect of Chinese culture. Furthermore I dare say hospitality is a Chinese concept. But due to the fact that many young people are the company's sales representatives, and their majors were English, they aren't very familiar with how to conduct business with others, They can only gradually learn from their bosses and managers how to deal with old customers. And combined with limited professional and life experience, the concept isn't easy to grasp. Anyways, no matter if in work, society or your home life, the above viewpoints can all be considered!

Chapter 16

谁杀死了小孔子和小老子？
——中国侦探故事
Who Killed Little Confucius and Little Laozi?
—A Chinese Detective Story

在 2004 年夏季，我发现，有时候安全感只是一座海市蜃楼。

During the summer of 2004, I discovered that sometimes a feeling of safety is merely a mirage.

在我的天真被打破了的那天，我的当地朋友邀请我陪他去一个海鲜饭馆吃饭。他说要跟一个最近参军的朋友和那朋友的战友们一起吃饭，想介绍我们认识一下。老实说，听说他们都是军人以后，我是有点紧张的。我不知道其他国家的年轻士兵会对我怎么样，我没参过军，没有军人的生活经验，我更不想指出如此明显的差异：我们的国家不一样。但不幸的是，根据自然规律：哪里有两个国家，两个男人，哪里就有冲突：

一山不容二虎。我希望不会发生这种情况，但我禁不住想，他们会欺负我吗？会问我为什么美国跟阿富汗、伊拉克打仗吗？我不是政客，维护本国的对外政策很累，而且本国的对外政策我也不太懂，有些也不太接受。我实在不喜欢谈论那些话题。反正正忧虑着，我们走进包房，看到了八个非常热情的年轻人。他们都是干净整洁的样子，平头的军人发型，可是都没穿军装。所以，除了军人发型和看上去很健康以外，他们的样子跟其他小伙子没有区别，看不出来是士兵。有几个正玩着我不太知道的划拳喝酒的游戏，只知道谁输了，谁罚酒了；有几个很快乐地吃饭，嘴里吐出鸡骨头。士兵的脸色都被酒染红了。看起来他们都比我小七八岁左右。他们都热情地跟我打了招呼，非常欢迎我跟他们一起坐下。我一看到这里的环境后，就意识到这并不是一个一山不容二虎的情形，而是像我跟普通朋友见面一样：大家都喜欢大声地说话，开玩笑，随便说，随便做。所以我开始放松了下来。

On the day that my innocence was shattered, my local friend invited me to accompany him to a seafood restaurant. He said we were going to eat with a friend of his who recently joined the People's Liberation Army and that friend's fellow soldiers, and that he wanted to introduce me. Honestly, after hearing that they were all soldiers, I was a bit nervous. I didn't know how another country's soldiers would treat me, I've never been in the military, had no military experience and I really don't want to point out the obvious difference: we come from different countries. I'm a lover, not a fighter, but unfortunately, according to a law of nature, where there are two countries, two men, there will be conflict: if two men ride on a horse, one must ride behind. I really hoped not, but couldn't help but wonder, will they gang up on me? Will they question me on why America attacked Afghanistan and Iraq? I'm not a politician or a country, defending one's government's foreign policies is really tiring, furthermore I don't really understand or support some of my government's foreign policies. I really don't like to discuss these topics. In any event, feeling anxious, we walked into the private room and I saw eight very boisterous young guys. They were all clean-shaven, sporting the military flattops, but no one was wearing military uniforms. So, besides the military haircuts and that they looked quite fit, they didn't look different than any other dude and you couldn't tell they were soldiers. Some were playing a finger counting drinking game that I wasn't too familiar with and I only knew that the loser had to drink as punishment. Some were happily eating, spitting out chicken bones. All of their faces were flush from alcohol. They looked like they were all younger than me by about seven to eight years. They greeted me enthusiastically and welcomed me to sit down with them. As soon as I saw the environment, I immediately realized that this wasn't a case of "who will ride behind who", but that it was just like meeting regular friends: everyone speaking loudly, joking, and saying and doing as they pleased. I finally began to relax.

　　我们坐下后，他朋友站起来，举起自己的杯子对我说："美国好不好？"

　　After sitting down, his friend stood and lifting his glass, he said to me, "America, good or bad?"

一听到这个问题，我的担心好像就快变为现实了：男人间的对峙又来了。因为不知道是否是一种测验、挑战或友好的戏弄，我不愿意反对自己的国家，就有点不好意思地回答："好。"我露出微笑跟着问："中国好不好？"

As soon as I heard this question, it seemed my worries immediately became reality: another confrontation between men. Not knowing whether or not it was some kind of test, a challenge or a friendly jest, unwilling to oppose my own country, a little embarrassed I answered, "Good." I released a smile and followed with, "China, good or bad?"

他笑着回答："好！"

Smiling he answered, "Good!"

我们一起干了一杯啤酒。大家都欢笑着拍手。

We downed a glass of beer together. Everyone had a laugh and clapped.

我还不清楚这是不是一种测验、挑战或友好的戏弄，我也不在乎，反正我都能接受，特别是最后一种。

Still not sure if this was a test, a challenge or a friendly jest, I also really didn't care, I could accept them all, especially the last.

坐在他旁边的一个有点胖的士兵站起来也问道："美国，好不好？"

A pudgy soldier sitting next to him stood up and asked, "America, good or bad?"

这次有了心理准备，我笑着回答："好。中国好不好？"

This time prepared, smiling, I answered, "Good. China, good or bad?"

他按了按大肚子骄傲地回答："当然好！"

Rubbing his belly he said proudly, "Of course good!"

我们一起又干了一杯啤酒。大家都欢笑着拍手。

Once again we downed another glass of beer together. Everyone had a laugh and clapped.

第三个很瘦的士兵站起来说得含糊不清："美国？"我说："好！中国？"他先敬礼再说："好！"又干了杯酒。

A third skinny soldier stood and said not very clearly, "America?" Me, "Good! China?" First saluting, he said, "Good!" And another glass was drunk.

第四个，我："好！"他："好！"直到第五个、第六、第七、第八个！不需要再回答和喝什么了。

The fourth, I, "Good!" Him, "Good!" Fifth, sixth, seventh, eighth! No need to repeat our answers and what we drank.

喝完一轮后，我已经有点醉了，不是因为喝得太多，而是喝得太快！我的朋友有点不好意思地对我说："阿文，如果你喝不了，就别喝了，没问题的。他们是士兵，很强壮的。"但是，我怎么办呢？我不想当男子汉吗？放弃或拒绝的话，如何维护自己的形象？而且哪怕是友好的戏弄，国家也在指望我守护它的名誉！再说外交官应该友好，并且可靠！我知道自己的弱点，可面子有时候能代替智慧。不幸的是本性难移，男孩子到底是男孩子。为了面子、国家和交新朋友，一定要喝下去！

After the first round, I was already a little drunk, not because I drank a lot but because I drank so quickly! My friend, a little embarrassed, said, "Kevin, if you can't drink, you don't have to, it's not a problem. They are soldiers and are very strong." But, what could I do? I didn't want to be a real man? If I gave up and refused, how could I maintain my image? Furthermore, no matter if a friendly jest, my country still expected me to uphold its reputation! Moreover, diplomats should be friendly as well as reliable! I knew my weaknesses, but sometimes pride replaces wisdom. Unfortunately you can't change who you are and boys will be boys. For pride, for country and for making new friends, I most certainly would continue drinking!

第二轮开始了："好不好？""好！""好不好？""好！"

The second round began, "Good or bad?" "Good!" "Good or bad?" "Good!"

在很短的时间内，打嗝、摔瓶子、大笑、呕吐和叫着"好！干杯！"的气氛中，像一个漩涡一样，那个晚上不断地往下沉：谈过什么，吃过什么，我都记不住了。喝到第三轮，那八个人已经变成十六个人，地球开始在我的脑子里转来转去……

Within a very short period of time, beneath the sounds of belching, broken bottles, hearty laughing, spitting and shouting, "Good! Bottoms up!" as if in a whirlpool, the evening continued spinning downwards: what we had discussed, what we had eaten, I could remember none of it. Drinking into the third round, the eight had already turned into sixteen, and the world had begun to spin within my head...

突然我醒了。

Suddenly I woke-up.

这非常奇怪，因为如果没睡觉，自己怎么可能醒来呢？不过紧接着，我躺在自己的床上用差点睁不开的眼睛看到窗外又是白天了，原因很明显：那晚已经过去了，现在已经是第二天的早上了！

But this was really strange because if one hadn't slept, how could one wake up? But, immediately after, lying on my own bed, using eyes that would hardly open I saw through the window that it was daytime again and the reason was clear: the evening had already passed and it was the second day's morning!

谁送我回家，几点钟回的，怎么回家的，我一点也记不起来！我头疼得快裂开了。感觉昨晚我几乎喝光了一个湖的湖水。膀胱要爆炸了，我真的需要上厕所！快忍不住了，我赶快翻身从床上滚下来。我要吃两片止痛片，尽快上洗手间！我还没清醒，摸索着蹒跚走出卧室。站在马桶的前面，我感觉身体像是一大桶水，我大约耗费了半天的时间上厕所。根据科学家的说法，人类的身体百分之六十由水构成，但看来我的是百分之百！突然口中一个又大又充满海鲜臭味的嗝飞出来了。我知道北海是一个海边城市，但是昨晚吃的海鲜味道怎么会那么重，还留在嘴巴里。我不断吐口水，试图用舌头把味道从牙齿上擦掉，真恶心。上了厕所后，感觉好点了，我手里拿着两片止痛片，走去了客厅。

Who sent me home, for that matter, what time did I return home? How did I return home? I couldn't remember a thing! My head was ready to split open and it was throbbing. I felt like I had nearly drunk a lake dry last night. My bladder was ready to explode and I really had to use the restroom. Fearful I would no longer be able to bear it, I quickly flipped over and rolled off the bed. I needed two aspirin and the bathroom ASAP! Still groggy, I stumbled blindly out of the bedroom. Standing in front of the toilet, as if my body was a big barrel of water, I wasted what seemed like half the day going to the bathroom. According to scientists, sixty percent of the human body is made up of water but it would seem I was one hundred percent water! Suddenly a large, seafood-laced belch came flying out of my mouth. I knew Beihai was a seaside city, but how could the flavor of the seafood we ate last night be that strong and still remain in my mouth? I tried to use my tongue to scrape the flavor off my teeth. It was disgusting. After finishing in the bathroom, feeling much better, holding the two aspirin in my hand, I walked towards the living room.

在瓷砖地上，我赤着脚发出响亮的拍击声。才走过一半，我居然踩到一件又湿又软的东西。我想，这是什么东西？抬起脚，我一低下头就发现了一件很可怕的事！在一束阳光的照射下，我的两条金鱼——小孔子和小老子静静地躺在又冷又硬的地板上。它们两个都被杀掉了！

My bare feet slapped loudly against the tiled floor. Halfway across, I unexpectedly stepped onto something wet and soft. I thought, what was this? Lifting up that foot, I lowered my head and discovered a very frightening scene! In a beam of sunlight, my two goldfish, Little Confucius and Little Laozi lay still on the cold, hard tiled floor. They had been murdered!

把它们拾起来，我温柔地摸了摸它们的小尸体。它们的原色，很迷人的金黄色，已经褪去了。

Picking them up, I tenderly stroked their lifeless little bodies. Their former color, an attractive gold, had already faded.

发生了什么事？必须有一个符合逻辑的解释。我的意思是，这两条鱼真的很友好，谁会伤害它们？我看了看电视机，鱼缸还在上面放着。可非常奇怪，鱼缸里面的水早就没了！也许是自杀？不会，我是好好照顾它们的，而且谁听说过鱼能自杀？那不是自杀，而是谋杀！绕着走到鱼缸的那边，我仔细地检查了一下鱼缸和里面的东西。鱼缸里的彩色小石头还在下面，一座小泥土做的桥还在小石头上。这怎么可能？也许鱼缸有洞，小孔子和小老子从洞口漏出来了？我把鱼缸举起来，看了看下面，没有洞！不过鱼缸里没有水，电视机上和地板上都是干的。除了我的可怜的小宠物，什么地方都没有湿。

What had happened? There must be a logical explanation. What I meant was, they were really friendly, who would want to harm them? I looked at the top of the TV and the fish bowl was still sitting there. But what was really strange was that the fish bowl's water was gone! Perhaps it was a suicide? No way, I really took good care of them and whoever heard of fish committing suicide? It wasn't a suicide, but murder! Walking around the fish bowl I examined the fish bowl and its contents closely. The fish bowl's small colored pebbles remained in the bottom. A small clay bridge was still on top of the small pebbles. How was that possible? Perhaps there was a hole in the fish bowl and Little Confucius and Little Laozi leaked out? I picked up the fish bowl and looked underneath, but there was no hole! And even though the fish bowl had no water, the top of the TV and the floor were dry. Other than my two little pitiful pets, nowhere else was wet.

我看了下沙发后的墙上，那里挂着阴间钟馗捉鬼的画卷。"钟馗，昨晚有鬼飞进来了吗？你为什么没保护我的小朋友？"我半真半假地问它。

I looked at the wall behind my sofa. A scroll of the underworld ghost fighter Zhong Kui hung there. "Zhong Kui, did a ghost enter in the middle of the night? Why didn't you protect my little friends?" I asked, half serious, half skeptical.

我坐在地板上回忆了一下这整件事是如何发生的：昨天我跟我的朋友和他的士兵朋友喝了很多酒，可是然后呢？到底谁送我回的家？谁送我回家后会杀死那么没有防备的动物？我的朋友？不会吧，他十分善良。那些士兵们？也不会，他们没有动机。我的打扫阿姨呢？也不会，她下午才来家里打扫，现在还是早上。老板呢？她也有房子的钥匙，虽然有时候我让她生气，可她总是原谅找。莫非君子报仇十年不晚？肯定也不是，老板喜欢睡懒觉。小偷？我已经检查过门锁，没被弄坏。我向钟馗看了一眼，鬼杀？还是自杀？

Sitting on the floor I recalled the situation and how things may have happened: yesterday I was drinking a lot with my friend and his solder friends, but what about after? In the end, who had sent me home? Could whoever sent me home have murdered two very innocent pets? My friend? No way, he was too kind. The soldiers? Also no way, they had no motive. My cleaning lady? Also no way, she comes to clean in the afternoon and it was still early. My boss? She also had the apartment key, but even though I sometimes made her angry, she always forgave me. What about revenge being a dish best served cold? No, certainly not, the boss likes to sleep in. A thief? I already inspected the door's lock, and it wasn't broken. Glancing at Zhong Kui, I thought, murder by ghost? Or was it suicide?

最后我去卫生间把可怜的它们海葬了。

Finally I went to the bathroom and gave the two pitiful fish a sea burial.

"尘归尘，土归土，鱼归海，一路走好，阿门！" 我祈祷说，然后就冲水了。

"Ashes to ashes, dust to dust, fish to sea, bon voyage, amen! " I prayed and then flushed the toilet.

读者们，你能找到那个凶手吗？

Readers, can you find the killer?

Chapter 17

哪里、哪里：塞了谦虚的派
Where? Where? A Slice of Humble Pie

见到她极有吸引力的女儿之后，我对我们英语培训的厨师，一个不太喜欢微笑，仿佛面部是被水泥筑成的严厉的老大妈说："阿姨，你的女儿真漂亮。"

Afer meeting her stunningly attractive daughter, I said to our school's cook, a tough old woman who didn't take to smiling and seemed to be made of cement. "Ayi, your daughter is quite beautiful."

她向女儿不屑的点头，笑着说："哈！哪里漂亮？她没什么好看，"摇了摇头，她接着说下去，"谁会要她？"

With a dismissive nod towards her daughter, she shook her head and chortled, "Ha! Where's the beauty in that? She's nothing to look at." And she finished with, "Who would want her? "

我张口结舌。首先，从头顶到脚下她女儿都很美。其次，一个母亲怎么能对她亲女儿那样说？女儿不会受打击？她脆弱的信心会不会像一支盛开的花朵被一块无情的砖块打破？预计看到一滩眼泪，我向她女儿看了一眼，但根据她的脸色，她似乎不在意母亲的话，只是脸朝地板害羞的笑。

I was at a loss for words. To begin, from head to toe she was exquisite in all the right places. Second, how could a mother say that about her daughter? Wouldn't the daughter be traumatized? Her gentle confidence crushed like a budding flower beneath a heartless brick? I glanced at her daughter expecting a puddle of tears, but instead saw that she didn't seem bothered by her mother's comment and simply smiled shyly, her face pointed downwards.

我的助理翻译后用英文说："哈哈，中国母亲，真搞笑。"

My assistant finished translating and said, "Haha, Chinese mothers, very funny."

午餐时，我吃着平常吃的半只炸鸡，抓了抓头，惊讶地自言自语道："哪里是漂亮？她没什么好看？谁会要她？那有什么好笑？"

Over my daily lunch, a fried half-chicken, I scratched my head and repeated in shock, "Where's the beauty in that? She's nothing to look at? Who would want her? What's funny about that?"

那是我第一次接触中国人的谦虚：用谦让的能力——无论多么小，来拒绝恭维，即便那看上去是以牺牲自己的或者周围人的面子为代价。

And that is how I first came across the face of Chinese humility: the ability to be self-effacing and rejecting another's compliments no matter how small, even if seemingly at the expense of themselves or those close to them.

在我过去多年的中国生活中，我经常碰到这种谦虚，一个我渐渐开始了解、接受乃至欣赏的特点：受邀去朋友家，他们称准备的食物没有味道，质量很差，数量不多——虽然每一份食物都很美味，品质超出预期，或者桌子上几乎全部被各种各样的菜覆盖；因为礼数不周而向顾客抱歉等。在主人抱歉的同时，他们那些尊贵的客人们却享受着名贵的好茶，嘴里塞满了好吃的橘子和进口的巧克力；用英文给自己介绍，有时使用完美无瑕的语法，而拥有一种让我羡慕的古雅的英式英语口音。这些都是以对自己蹩脚的英文抱歉为开头或者结尾而说的话。另外，父母回绝老师们给他们的孩子们的赞美："不，他真笨，不值得您的过奖"；在路上碰到的陌生人好像想代表整个国家的谦卑的个性："我们没有你们那么强壮。"或者"中国人没有信心。"也经常替其他有点没礼貌的人说："中国人的素质太差，没有你们那么礼貌。"

And over my years in China I would regularly come across this form of humility, a trait that I slowly began to understand, accept and even admire: invitations to friends' homes where they would declare the food as being tasteless, of poor quality and always lacking in quantity – while the food was exploding with taste, the quality above and beyond and the tables spilling over with various dishes; apologizing for their hospitality while at the same time drowning their honored guest who certainly didn't deserve the attention in expensive teas and stuffing their mouth with auspicious mandarin oranges and imported chocolates; introductions made in English, sometimes said with impeccable grammar and a rather quaint British accent that I'd be happy to have that always began or ended with apologies towards the speakers so-called poor grasp of the language; to parents rejecting compliments given to their children often as, "No, he's quite stupid, he doesn't deserve your compliments"; to complete strangers on the street whom seem to want to represent an entire nation's humble nature with comments such as, "We (Chinese) aren't as strong as you (USA)," or "Chinese have no confidence," or often said for those that were impolite, "Chinese lack class and aren't as polite as you."

这有可能是因为信心不够，也会令不太理解这种中国文化的人误解成是一个弱点。但是，我认为这反映了谦逊，在中国它可以被视为一种艺术形式。

Perhaps it is a lack of confidence, and it can be misunderstood as a weakness by those whom don't understand this aspect of Chinese culture, something I know I have often misunderstood, but I believe it is more a reflection of humility, something that could pass as an art form in China.

我之前的中文老师教了我一个常用的说法："哪里、哪里"是什么意思和怎么用，比如听到中国人说："您的中文很棒！"（外国人只不过说了非常简单的一段话，例如"你好"，我们就将听到中国人那样赞美）我们应该接着说："哪里、哪里。"例如："我中文好？具体哪个地方？哪里？哪里？"老师教过我，假如某些方面被过奖了，或者不值得赞赏，受到表扬的人可以使用这种礼貌的方式拒绝表扬，可以回答："哪里、哪里。"尽管，好像只有外国人会那样说，因为直到现在，除了课本里或者其他的外国人以外，我从来没听说过中国人说出这两个字："哪里"。可能是由于很多包括我在内的不以汉语为母语的人，缺乏语言能力或者不够谦逊，才说"哪里哪里"，然而中国人已经掌握不出风头的行为的艺术，没有必要使用如此简单的方法，因为他们拥有一套很聪明的办法来拒绝表扬，同时却偷偷地享受它。

I was taught early on by my Chinese teacher the common Chinese phrase nali nali and how to use it, as in: "Your Chinese is quite good," (often said by a Chinese person after a foreigner has uttered nothing more than a "Ni Hao"), which should then be followed by a "Nali? Nali?" as in, "What is good about my Chinese? Where exactly? Where?" Basically, I was taught by my teacher that this is the polite way for someone who receives a compliment to dismiss the praise, as in pretending that whatever was complimented doesn't exist, or isn't worthy of the praise, thus can't be found and you utter, "Where? Where?" Though it would seem this is only something foreigners say as I have only heard foreigners say it and have yet to have ever heard a Chinese person utter this phrase. Perhaps that is because many of us non-native speakers lack the linguistic skill or the required humility to say more than nali nali where as most Chinese have mastered the act of self-effacing behavior and do not need to resort to such simplicity when they have an arsenal of clever ways to reject a compliment, while perhaps secretly enjoying it.

也许，您在想："他到底说了什么？中国人已经掌握了不出风头的行为的艺术？有一套很聪明的办法来拒绝表扬，同时又偷偷地享受？什么意思？我怎么不懂？"所以，在此请让我给你解释一下为什么西方人，特别是美国人，表现得那么明显。

And perhaps you are reading this and thinking, "What is he talking about? Chinese have mastered the act of self-effacing behavior? An arsenal of clever ways to reject a compliment, while perhaps secretly enjoying it?" So, at this point I think I should explain why it appears so obvious and somewhat misunderstood by many westerners, especially Americans.

作为美国人，自出生时我们就享受着百般赞美，周围的父母、老师们、亲戚都给予我们鼓励与称赞，没有嘲笑或者言语侮辱。当我们说错话的时候，老师们、父母会回答："嘿，几乎……尝试得好……将近……下次好运吧。"相反的，中国人的处理方式很直接："不，这不对。您要更加努力学习。"所以，这并不令人惊奇，我们美国人几乎不懂谦虚。我们受的教育就是抬头走路，显示自信，即使我们没有拥有任何自信。我们被教育错误不是失败，是走向成功过程的必要步骤。我们被鼓励用眼睛直视世界，说："我们什么都不怕面对！来吧！"

As an American, we are showered with praise from birth, where parents and teachers offer encouragement and compliments over ridicule and what many of us would consider verbal abuse, where we are told after getting an answer wrong, "Well, almost…good try…pretty close…better luck next time," as opposed to the Chinese direct method of, "No, that is wrong. You should have studied harder." So, it shouldn't come as a surprise that we rather lack humility. We are taught to walk tall, head held high and show confidence even when it may not exist. We are taught that a mistake isn't failure, yet a necessary step towards success. We are expected to look the world in the eye and say "I'm not afraid! Bring it on!"

我曾听中国人说过："美国人拥有一种所谓的'敢作敢为'的态度，不怕丢脸或失败，而且遇到不熟悉的情况，无论会不会挣扎，他们都会跳进去继续。"虽然自信很重要，但如果没有谦虚作为制衡，骄傲很容易变成傲慢。现在每次听到同胞们高呼"美国！美国！美国！"或者再三喊叫"我们第一！"虽然跟运动比赛有关，我还是忍不住有点畏缩。我经常听人说美国人有侵略性。当我回国的时候我留意了下，美国人，特别是美国男人，与中国人相比，相对有侵略性。比如，在中国，如果不小心碰到别人，无论是谁的错，双方都不会说什么。可是，在美国，别人会误会这是一种挑战。

And, I've been told by Chinese, "Americans possess a 'Can-do' attitude and without fear of losing face or failure, they jump right in and no matter if they flounder or not, they press on!" And while that confidence is important, without humility to act as a counterweight, it is easy to go from proud to arrogant. I now cannot help but cringe when I hear my fellow countrymen chanting "USA! USA! USA!" or shouting "We're #1!" even if it is only in relation to sports. I've been told that Americans can be aggressive and whenever I return home I notice this, especially amongst males. For example, if I accidentally walk into someone in China, both parties don't really say anything and just continue on, regardless of whose error it was. While in the USA an accident can often be misconstrued as a challenge.

上面的现象跟国家的人口有关？也许。作为地球上人口最多的国家，如果每次不小心碰到别人，中国人得花半辈子不断地说："对不起。"在私人场合没有问题，但在公共场合，大家都必须分享有限的空间，碰到别人就像走路一样是正常的。也许，感觉自己更像茫茫人海中的一滴水，在人海中，私人空间是一种负担不起的奢侈，这本身就令人感到谦卑。但是，美国人口是中国的五分之一，为何会产生"一山不容二虎"的想法？这可能是因为我们太有空间了，所以我们更应该注意其他人的私人空间。通常，因为美国人对私人空间这个概念非常重视，如果不小心入侵了别人的空间，我们要马上道歉。同时，因为高度重视私人空间，如果这个空间被侵入了——我觉得用这个常用的动词"侵入"来描述这种行动会让读者们更理解西方人怎么强调私人空间的重要性——很容易彼此误解，会被以为这是故意的轻视或者一种挑战。如果任何一方表现出那个负面的观点——一山不容二虎——就会采取消极的行动。此时，尊敬变成了一种自我防护，然后又变成了一种傲慢，不幸的是，还会变成侵略。

Is the above phenomenon related to the size of the population by chance? Perhaps. As the world's most populated nation, if every time someone accidentally bumped into someone they'd spend half their life saying, "Excuse me." In an environment where personal space has no choice but to become public space, people are forced to share limited space, and bumping into one another becomes as common as walking. Perhaps feeling as if you are nothing but a drop of water in a vast sea of humanity, where personal space is a luxury that most don't have, this in and of itself must be very humbling. But as America's population is only a fifth of China's, why do so many go around with the attitude that "this town isn't big enough for the two of us"? It could be that we have the space, and thus should be aware of other's personal space. And more often then not, if we accidentally invade another's personal space, as we have high regard for this concept, we are quick to apologize. Yet, at the same time, because personal space is so highly valued, if that space is invaded – I believe using the common verb used to describe such an act "invade" will help the reader to better understand how westerners emphasize the importance of personal space—it is easy to misperceive it as in intentional slight or challenge and act rather negatively to the situation, thus the negative view that "this town isn't big enough for the two of us."At this point, respect has turned to protection, which becomes arrogance and unfortunately can transform into aggression.

而尽管什么事都得有时间和特点，这两个风格是很受欢迎的：当漫不经心地撞到别人或者当别人侵入您的私人空间时，表示消极的反应应少一点。

While there is a time and a place for everything, a little less of both styles: mindlessly walking into others or displaying such negative reactions when someone does "invade" your personal space should be welcomed in each of our respective societies.

在英文中，有一句流行的俗语："Eat humble pie."直译是"吃塞了谦虚的派"或者更准确的翻译是忍辱含垢。这句俗语的基本意思是，有时候，当一个人太骄傲时，某件事情将发生，以使他谦卑。举个例子，我永远忘不了有一天我从美国一家加油站的公共厕所走出来，一打开门，就撞到了一个脸比我大两倍的人身上。那时刻，我觉得自己不该低声下气，但是他站在面前：从头到脚裹在黑色皮革里，脖子和胳膊上都有纹身，很明显的迹象表明，他属于一个摩托党帮派，得离他远点儿，外面很可能还有一辆巨大的哈雷戴维森摩托车停在那，确实得忍着点。我抬头看了看他，开始咕哝着想道歉时，从他差点被蓬乱茂密的胡子掩藏的那张巨人的嘴巴里露出了一个微笑，他打断我说："没问题，每个男人时不时都要挨点打。"很有可能这个例子不像孔子的教导那样诗意或者深刻，但是它明确提醒我们：时不时的，大家都需要吃一片谦虚的派，无论我们多大或多强，多聪明或多能干，如果头长得太大，需要有人走过来拉一下我们大头上的耳朵，释放下里面的热气，让我们回归脚踏实地，表现出更多的谦逊。在我看来，美国人太过傲慢，太过自信，可是另一方面，中国人太过谦虚，因此而缺少信心。对于后者，当您学习第二语言（这种逻辑适用于开会／对话中），如果缺乏信心或者怕丢脸，以为更好的方法是什么都不要说，因为害怕说错，这会变成交流的障碍。同样的，如果前者学习怎么多用耳朵、少用嘴巴，很有可能会更加理解对方，在这个过程中，自己也会谦卑一点。希望有一天中国会把一个耳朵借给美国听，而美国将交换一个嘴巴给中国说。

In English we have a popular saying, "Eat humble pie," the literal translation being a "pie filled with humility" or a more accurate translation would be putting aside one's pride. And, this saying basically means, that from time to time, when someone is too proud, something comes along and humbles them. For example, I will never forget the time when I was exiting a public restroom in a gas station in the USA when I threw open the door and struck a man twice my size in the face. Not that I needed humbling, but standing before someone dressed head to toe in black leather, tattoos covering his neck and arms, obvious signs that he belonged to a motorcycle gang and best to steer clear of, a monstrous Harley Davidson more than likely parked outside, was humbling indeed. As I looked up to the giant and stuttered an apology, the giant revealed a smile nearly concealed beneath a shaggy beard and interrupted me by saying, "Not a problem, every man needs a smack in the face from time to time." While perhaps not as poetic or deep as the teachings of Confucius, we're reminded: we all need a slice of "humble pie" from time to time to remind us that no matter how big or strong we are, how intelligent or capable we are, if our heads grow too big, someone needs to come along and pull on our ear to release a bit of the hot air and bring us back down to earth where we will display a bit more humility. And from my perspective, perhaps Americans lean a little too much towards arrogance, having a little too much confidence, where as Chinese lean a little too much towards a lack of confidence due to too much humility. And, in regards to the latter, it can act as quite a handicap when speaking a second language (this same logic can be applied to meetings/conversations in general) if you lack the confidence or fear losing face and decide it is better to say nothing over saying something with the fear of being wrong. Though, on the other hand, it would also help if the former could learn to use more of our ears and less of our mouths, we may better understand others and humble ourselves along the way. And I hope someday China could lend one of its ears to America for listening and America could lend one of its lips to China for speaking.

也许我经常受到的表扬不是一种证明，从另外的角度看它们是另外一种谦逊。慷慨地给予表扬，无论是否合适（比如我受过的表扬都很夸张！）这表示提出表扬的人想加强对方的信心，同时说出他们的印象。

And, maybe the compliments I regularly receive though rarely warrant, are humility seen in another light. Giving compliments generously, whether fitting or not (the above are certainly exaggerated), may show that people offer them not only to boost another's confidence, but also to show how they are impressed.

在另外一个国家生活时，就会自然而然地接纳了一些东道国的特点：现在我更喜欢喝温水，至少室温水比冷水更好喝；喝茶而不是喝咖啡，不过说实话，我一直都不喜欢喝咖啡；无论是西餐还是中餐，更喜欢分享菜品；还有一种像试图穿上一件被烘干机收缩了而非常紧的衬衫那样，我开始欣赏但还做不好的特点——为人谦逊、行为谦让。在我用"不是，还是很差" 或者"只能说一点点"来回应"你的汉语很好"时，我取笑自己比赞美自己更多一点——美国人真的非常善于取笑自己，前面说的谦虚离我还是非常远的，我还没找到骄傲和傲慢的平衡点。

When living in another country it is only natural to take on some of the hosts characteristics: I now prefer warm or at least room-temperature water now as opposed to cold; tea over coffee, though in all fairness I never drank coffee; communal sharing of dishes, no matter if Chinese or "Western"; And, one trait that I've come to appreciate, one that was hard to put on and still doesn't fit very well, like an under-sized t-shirt shrank in the dryer, is that of being humble or the act of humility. While I regularly find myself responding to comments such as, "Your Chinese is quite good" with, "No, its quite poor," or "I only speak a little," and insulting myself more than praising myself – Americans are actually quite good at laughing at themselves, I have a long way to go before showing the level of humility required to find a balance between pride and arrogance.

从今天起，每当我表现出傲慢时，我要马上来到那个我称之为脑海里的空空的黑板前，默写一千遍这个词："哪里、哪里……"

From this day forth, whenever my arrogance shows it face, I will visit the big blank blackboard that I call my mind and write the phrase nali nali one thousand times…

Chapter 18

一个老外的春节回忆

A Foreigner's Recollection of Spring Festival

回到前线，飞过来的碎片，红、蓝、黄色的夜光弹从头上射过来，鼻孔被呛得辛辣，眼睛被火药灼伤了，穿过夜空的尖叫声和雷鸣般的爆炸接二连三地一再击打着耳膜，路面都被红色覆盖了！

Returning to the front lines, shrapnel flying by, red, blue and yellow tracers shooting overhead, nostrils choked by an acrid scent, eyes burnt by gunpowder, in every direction the night sky's filled with prolonged shrieks and thunderous explosions, one after another assaulting the eardrums, the roads covered in red!

这是一名军人的前线报告？听起来像，但绝对不是！这就是中国每年最刺激、最兴奋的晚上：春节除夕夜！

Was this a soldier's report from the front lines? It sure sounds like it is, but it most definitely is not! It's just China's most thrilling, most exciting evening of the year: Spring Festival Eve!

　　这一天从我的两个"室友"开始——在两只固执己见、挺烦的公鸡的喔喔叫声中，我醒得很早。因为我是早起的人，想早点开始新的一天。我跳下了床，向它们的门轻轻地走去，准备祝福它们早上好。我一开门，就吃惊地发现它们两只虽然个头很小，但是具有非常强的破坏力。我立即后悔昨晚的仁慈：为使它们那孩子似的哭叫平静下来，我把拴着它们那又脏又糙的脚的绳子剪断了。因为怕留在阳台上它们会自杀，我放任它们在一间没有家具的空房间里活动。让我沮丧的是，从黄昏到黎明它们俩设法利用粪便把全部的地板都给装饰了！根本不听话，满屋子都是羽毛，它们一定是想被斧子咔嚓掉！如果能时光倒流到昨天，我会对我朋友说："我不知道为什么你的汽车后备厢里有两只鸡，但是我一定不要这该死的东西！"

My day began early as my two roommates, two opinionated and troublesome roosters, cock-a-doodle-doo'ed their morning alarm. Because I'm an early bird and wanting to start the new day, I jumped out of bed and walked lightly over to their door. Ready to wish them a good morning, I opened the door and to my surprise discovered that although they were very small, chickens could be quite destructive. I immediately regretted the previous evening's moment of weakness: to silence their childlike cries, I had cut the strings that had held their dirty, gnarly feet together. And, because I was worried that they'd accidentally commit suicide if left on the balcony, I let them loose in a room without furniture. And to my dismay, from dusk to dawn they made the best use of their excrement to decorate the entire floor. Totally disobedient, with a brain full of feathers, it seemed they were itching for the ax—WHACK! If I could have turned the clock back to yesterday, I would have told my friend, "I don't know why you have two chickens in the trunk of your car, but I certainly don't want the damn things!"

为了庆祝这个重大的日子，中国的神话创造者，盘古，已经准备好很完美的天气：灿烂的阳光照耀在头上，温度是很让人满足的24度。洗好穿好以后我出了门，在卖鞭炮和烟花的小摊子之间转来转去，装满了各种各样的火药：从小型的爆竹等物品，包括给小孩子玩的火柴炮，到给成人玩的三尺长的礼花炮和冲天炮。

To celebrate the big day, China's mythological creator, Pangu, already prepared the perfect weather: a brilliant sun shining overhead, with the temperature a satisfying twenty-four degrees. After washing and getting dressed I headed out and sped back and forth amongst the firework and firecracker stands, filled with any and all kinds of explosives: from small-sized firecrackers, including ladyfingers for children to play with, to three-foot long mortars and bottle rockets for the grown-ups.

把三种"炸药"卸在今晚的主人的房子外后，我飞奔回家去接那两只鸡。下午刚开始，就已经能听到人们的热切期盼在广西壮族自治区的海滨城市——北海市，蔓延开来了。每一条街道，每一条马路都被噼噼啪啪声充满了。换骑了本地的"公共交通"——一辆摩托车，我和两只鸡坐在司机的后面。好像怕自己会掉下去似的，我的腿夹紧前面的司机，那两只鸡粗糙的脚也被我抓得很紧，我们开始向今晚的目的地开去了。鸡的羽毛被风吹得翻飞起来，我对司机喊了好几次"慢一点"。仿佛明白自己的命运似的，那两只鸡几次试图飞跑，可每一次都失败了，它们用翅膀攻击着我俩，不是撞到我的肩膀，就是司机的头盔上。司机并不高兴。十分钟后，穿过无数硝烟弥漫的枪林弹雨，我们在伤痕累累中总算安全到达了。一把将那两只鸡送给那晚的主人后，我就跟我的羽毛朋友永别了。但我没有流泪。

After unloading three loads of "explosives" outside this evening's host home, I flew home to fetch the two chickens. The afternoon had only just begun and I could already hear eager anticipation spreading throughout Guangxi's coastal city, Beihai, as every street and every alley was brimming with cracks, booms and bangs. Trading my electric bike for "public transportation", a motorbike, I hopped on behind the driver with my two chickens in hand. Legs pressing tight against the driver's, fearing I'd fall off, clutching the two chickens gnarly feet tightly, we began to drive towards the evening's destination. Feathers flying from the blowing winds, my regular shouts of "SLOW DOWN!" filled the driver's ears. As if they knew their imminent fate, the birds made regular attempts to fly away, but they failed to escape every time, only managing to strike the two of us with their wings, either crashing into my shoulder or the back of the driver's helmet. The driver was none too pleased. After ten minutes, having passed through countless clouds of smoke and crossfire, riddled with firecracker shot, we arrived safely.

As soon as I handed the chickens over to the evening's host, I was separated from my feathered friends forever. No tears were shed.

　　我的朋友们，包括我朋友的父亲——这户人家的主人，一个家里的朋友，我们称之为"叔叔"，以及另外两个英文老师都围聚在电视机旁一边吃橙子，一边看一个我只能看而听不懂的春晚表演。几个孩子们坐在地板上高兴地吃糖果，都在等着最重要的事情：除夕晚餐。主人的太太和她的姐姐，我们称她大姐，都在厨房里一边八卦，一边努力准备又香又漂亮的菜：煮虾、炸沙虫、糖醋鱼、锅包肉（我们的主人来自东北）、泡香肠……别忘记了，也包括我的两位羽毛朋友：它们在阿姨的手艺下变成了白斩鸡。你可以想象，大家都围着桌子坐好，开始把那些菜来回传递，客厅沉浸在欢乐的气氛之中。

　　My local friends, including my friend's father—our host, a family friend, who was addressed as "uncle" and two English teachers sat around the television eating oranges and watching the Chinese New Year's Eve Gala which I couldn't understand a word of. A few children sat on the ground happily eating candy, all waiting for the main event: the Chinese New Year's Eve dinner. The host's wife and her sister, we called her "Big Sister", were in the kitchen gossiping while working hard to prepare many fragrant, attractive dishes: boiled shrimp, deep-fried sand worms, sweet and sour fish, sweet and sour pork (our host is originally from the Northeast), preserved sausage and let's not forget to mention, it also included my two feathered friends—crafted beneath the aunty's hand—sliced cold chicken. As you can imagine, once everyone was seated around the table and we began to pass the dishes back and forth, the living room was brimming with a festive atmosphere.

　　为了敬酒，主人站起来，举起一小杯白酒，说了几句听起来像中国的古诗，他读得抑扬顿挫，却很好听，但是我听不懂。那不是我第一次喝中国白酒，但是第一杯酒还是好不容易干了。后来，大家都随意地互相敬酒，祝身体健康、万事如意这类的。主人的太太教过我怎么说，结果这变成我最喜欢的祝福："一醉方休。"女士们举起可乐，我们其余都举起酒杯，碰在一起说："一醉方休！"肉吃饱了，酒喝足了，我们就像小孩子似的，对主人、他太太和阿姨说："谢谢你，叔叔；谢谢你，阿姨，很好吃。"他太太看出了我们的迫不及待，说："去吧，我们自己打扫，你们去外面玩儿。"她才说完，我们六个人——三个中国人，三个美国人，就每人拿着烟火与鞭炮跑出门去了。到了海边，在沙滩上把鞋子脱了，很凉快的沙子贴在赤裸的脚下，我们开始准备我们的烟花盛宴。

　　For the toast, the host stood up, lifting a small glass of a Chinese white spirit. Making use of a voice reminiscent of ancient China, stressing each and every tone, he recited some poetry that sounded quite nice but which I couldn't understand. It wasn't the first time I had drank the Chinese white spirit, but the first glass was always a bit difficult to drain. Afterwards, everyone toasted as they liked, sometimes toasting for good health, for wishes to come true, and similar such wishes. The host's wife taught me how to say what became my favorite toast, "Let's get good and drunk." The females lifted their colas, the rest of us our glasses of spirit and together we quickly said, "Let's get good and drunk!" Stuffed with meat, sated with drink, acting like children, fidgeting as if we had ants in our pants, we said to the aunty and our host: "Thank you, uncle; thank you, aunty, It was delicious." Apparently we were as transparent as the white spirit because the hostess said, "Go on, we'll clean up, you all head out and have fun." She didn't need to say it twice and the six of us—three Chinese and three foreigners, all Americans—grabbed the fireworks and firecrackers and ran outside. Reaching the seaside, kicking off our shoes on the beach, the cool sands sticking to the bottom of our bare feet, we began to prepare our firework extravaganza.

一个又一个礼花炮在夜空的衬托下爆炸了：轮番闪耀的有黄花，蓝星，红、绿、紫色的烟花，璀璨了整个夜空。扔进大海里的鞭炮炸出的水花像莲花，埋进沙滩里的鞭炮将小小的沙粒炸得四处飞扬，震耳欲聋。有些火柴炮在朋友的手里发射，打中了另一个人的屁股。有些导火线实在太短了，焰火距离脸上没几个英寸就爆炸了，让点着它们的人差点毁了容；有些导火线太长，却又让大家很失望，没反应，只是哑弹一发。

Against the backdrop of the night sky, one after another the mortar shells exploded: one by one their explosions flashed yellow flowers, blue stars, reds, greens and purples, illuminating the entire sky. Thrown into the sea, firecrackers exploded as if they were erupting water lilies, sending water spraying upwards. Exploding firecrackers placed beneath the sand brought grains of sand raining down, leaving our ears ringing from the noise. A few smaller bottle rockets were shot from the hands of a friend only to strike the backside of another. Some of the fuses were really short, nearly allowing the one doing the lighting to lose his good looks as the fireworks exploded inches from their face, while some fuses were too long, letting everyone down, with zero reaction, nothing but a dud.

最后剩下的是最大的焰火：那个箱子和小冰箱一样大，里面有一百发礼炮。跪在箱子边，我的伙伴们的顽皮的脸被一根点燃了的火柴照亮了。导火线被点燃了，他笑着说："都点燃了。" 我问："都？" 他疯狂地叫："跑！"我们六个都飞快离开焰火大约十米左右。我们都非常兴奋，一起抬起头看着天上，准备欣赏眼花缭乱的表演。我们先听到一个小鞭炮发出小小的爆炸声。很奇怪，那个声音是从大箱子的下面发出来的。然后我们就听到一个听起来有点像一个很重的盒子掉到沙滩上的"砰"的声音。我们低头紧张地看向那个大箱子和它的导火线，线在灼灼燃烧。 那个箱子包括里面全部的一百发礼炮都打翻了，全都直接指着我们！在我们旁边，我听见我朋友说："这可不在我的计划之内。"我："什么计划？"他赶紧给我解释原来他把一个小鞭炮放在大箱子下，他的想法是……我不知道他的想法是什么！那个大箱子一定被那个小爆炸给打翻了。六双眼睛看着箱子的发射口，看到又一条导火线被烧着了。

The last one was the largest of the fireworks: the box the size of a small refrigerator, it contained one hundred rockets. Kneeling beside the box, my fishing buddy's mischievous face glowed behind the lit match. Once the fuse was ignited, he smiled and said, "They are both lit." A little confused, I asked, "Both?" And then he shouted madly, "RUN!" The six of us quickly ran about ten meters from the fireworks. All excited, impatiently looking upwards readying to enjoy a dazzling performance, we heard what sounded like a heavy box falling onto the sand with a thud. Lowering our heads, we glanced nervously towards the big box and its burning fuse. The box had fallen over and currently the fireworks, including all one hundred rockets were pointing directly at us! I heard my friend who had just lit the fuse say, "This wasn't part of my plan." And I said, "What plan?" He quickly explained how he had secretly placed a smaller firework under the large box. His thinking was… I don't know WHAT his thinking was! The smaller explosion must have pushed the box over. Six sets of eyes took another look at the barrels of the rocket's openings, then at the burning fuse.

因为都是成年人，大家都想保持淡定，但是我们真的太恐慌了。外国人吃惊地喊出："啊啊啊啊啊啊啊啊啊啊啊！"中国人大声喊叫："呀呀呀呀呀呀呀呀呀！"刹那间，一束礼花从圆形的黑色弹筒里射了出来，接着源源不断地：一些在我们的头上爆炸了，其他的像地雷一样在我们的脚下引爆了。急于逃跑的我们像在一个可怕的游乐园里成了碰碰车，向四面八方乱跑，却总是撞到另一个。看着周围，现场像一个恐怖的舞池：每一次烟花爆炸，在闪光中，人影似乎被时间抓住了，我们六个漆黑的侧影都暂时冻结了，定格在狂奔中。感觉像是过了一个小时，但可能只过了三分钟。最后一束礼花终于射出去了。我呼吸急促，拍了拍整个身体，才确认没受伤。大家都数了一下手指是不是完整。数到十，我才放心地松了一口气。

Because we were all adults, no one wanted to panic, but we had reason to and we did: terrified, the foreigners shouted in surprise: "Ahhhhh!" The Chinese screamed loudly, "Yaaaaa!" In a flash, a rocket shot out from the dark round hole, followed by a steady stream: some exploded over our heads, others were like land mines, detonating below our feet. Wanting to escape, it was like we had become bumper cars in some kind of ghastly amusement park, people racing madly in all directions, only colliding into each other. Looking around, the scene resembled a macabre dance: every time a rocket exploded, within the bright flash, as if stuck in time, our six black silhouettes were temporarily frozen, fixed in a mad dash. What felt like an hour was more than likely really only three minutes. The final rocket was eventually spent. Panting hard, I began to pat down my entire body, and only then was I able to confirm there were no wounds. Everyone counted to make sure their hands still had all of its fingers. Counting an even number, I sighed with relief.

过了一会儿，我坐在沙滩上，手里拿着一瓶啤酒，好朋友坐在我的周围，感觉非常惬意，我跟他们一起向天上看：在夜空中，从西边到东边都能看到无穷无尽的烟花爆炸，给我留下了深刻的印象。

A few moments later, sitting on the sand, holding a beer in one hand, surrounded by good friends, feeling rather content, I looked up with them: in the night sky, from the east to the west an endless line of fireworks exploded, leaving an unforgettable impression.

回到朋友家里，找到主人、太太和阿姨，他们衣服上都沾上了面粉，正卷了袖子，站在饭桌旁：一个用木勺子搅拌一大碗碎猪肉和切碎的白菜，另外一个在把一堆面团擀平。"包饺子吧！"阿姨开玩笑地命令我们。在她的指导下，我们开始包饺子。没有阿姨包得那么完美，但在我看来，不管包成什么样子，饺子的命运没有差别。我瞥见太太偷偷地把几枚硬币放在饺子里面。她小声地说："如果孩子吃到了，就给他们红包吧！"我想，他们的牙齿怎么办？有可能也需要准备一个红包送给他们牙医啊！十二点钟到了，水饺、蒸饺和锅贴都尝试过了。孩子们疯狂地把饺子装进嘴里，有时喊叫："我找到了！阿姨，恭喜发财，红包拿来！"我从来没吃过那么多饺子。令人庆幸的是，我没吃到硬币；我可没有牙医保险。好像那晚，阿姨的箴言是："多吃一点！"我实在吃撑了，再多吃一个饺子的话恐怕自己就会变成鞭炮爆炸了！

Returning to our friend's home, we found the host, his wife and the aunty, clothes covered in flour, sleeves rolled up, standing around the dining room table: one was using a wooden spoon to mix a big bowl of minced pork and chopped cabbage together. Another was rolling a big ball of dough flat. "Let's make dumplings!" the aunty ordered jokingly. Under her training, we began to make dumplings. They didn't look as perfect as the aunty's, but in my opinion, it didn't matter how good they looked as the dumplings' destination were all the same, so who cares. I caught a glimpse of the wife secretly slipping a few coins into the dumplings. She whispered, "If a child gets one, they'll get a red envelope!" I wondered, and what about their teeth? Perhaps they should also prepare a red envelope for the dentist! At midnight, we sampled boiled dumplings, steamed dumplings and pan-friend dumplings. The kids stuffed the dumplings into their mouths madly, sometimes shouting, "I found one! Aunty, good fortunes for you, and a red envelope for me!" I had never eaten so many dumplings before. Thankfully, I hadn't found a coin; I didn't have dental insurance. It seemed that night, the aunty's motto was, "Eat more!" Totally stuffed, I feared that if I ate one more dumpling I'd turn into a firecracker and explode!

几个小时以后，我朋友一家都睡着了，朋友们都回到自己的家。我在阳台上，坐在我最喜欢的竹摇椅上，沙子还留在我脚趾间。远处，黎明在沉睡中张开一点眼睛，让一片青色中流露出一点红黄色的曙光。我的手指被火药弄黑了，食指上有点烧伤。我回忆起一个人，不是孔子、老子、庄子或其他同样很深奥的思想家。他并不是那么聪明，他曾经说过一个比较奇怪的成语：指失事知。意思是：尽管丢失了一根手指，一部分肢体之类的，但你得到了一个故事，一分知识，一种经验。打了一个混有白酒和白菜味道的响嗝，我想，老文，有时候你真能胡说八道。带着满面笑容，老凯文终于醉倒了。

After a few hours, while my friend's family slept soundly and my friends having returned to their own homes, I sat on my balcony in my favorite customized bamboo rocking chair, sand still between my toes. In the distance, emerging from its slumber, dawn opened its eye, allowing a day break of green, red and yellow. Fingertips still black from gunpowder, the index finger slightly burnt, I recalled one's; not Confucius, nor Laozi or Zhuangzi or any other similarly profound philosopher, as he really wasn't that clever, who once said a rather strange proverb: A finger lost, is a story gained. What it meant was, even though one has lost a finger, limb, etc. you have gained a story, intellect, experience. Releasing a belch, laden with a white spirit and cabbage, I thought, Old Wen, sometimes you really could talk nonsense. Smiling from ear to ear, Old Wen finally passed out.

Chapter 19

为了一份报纸，就牺牲了自己的尊严？
Sacrificing Self-respect for a Newspaper?

喇叭里传出机长的欢迎广播："飞机已经在一万英尺高空平稳飞行。地面管制部门刚刚通知我们今天的飞行路线风平浪静。请您放松坐好，好好享受今天的航班。"各位乘客都舒舒服服地坐在他们的座位上。有些睡觉了，有些跟坐在他们旁边的人小声地聊天。一个高个子、中等身材、三围符合中国航空公司严格规定的空姐推着报纸手推车从走廊中走过来。飞机里的气氛非常正常。

The speaker broadcasted the captain's welcoming message, "The plane has already stabilized at 10,000 feet. Ground control has just informed us that today's flight path will be smooth sailing. Please sit back, relax and enjoy today's flight." All of the passengers were sitting comfortably in their seats. Some were sleeping, others were speaking quietly with those sitting next to them. A tall flight attendant, neither thin nor fat, bust, waist and hips meeting

China Airline's strict regulations, was pushing her newspaper cart down the aisle. The atmosphere inside the plane was relatively normal.

谁能猜到我们快要体验到末日来临的感觉？

Who would have guessed that we were about to experience Armageddon?

我还是坐得很直。因为我个子比较高，有189厘米。我能理解腿部空间的重要性，为了尊重后面的乘客，我没把我的座椅靠背向后调整。我右边坐着一个估计是做生意的男人，他穿着西装，把笔记本包放在大腿上，在睡觉。他的头靠在窗上，面部表情像一个小孩一样无忧无虑。我真是太羡慕他了。我看了一眼窗外：我们在白白的云海上飞行着。

I was still sitting up straight. Because I'm quite tall, 189 centimeters, I understood the importance of legroom and in order to respect the legroom of the customer behind me, I hadn't reclined my seat. On my right was what I guessed to be a businessman, dressed in a suit, his laptop bag on his lap, sleeping. His head rest against the window, his facial expression similar to that of a carefree child's. I was green with envy. I glanced out the window: we were flying above a white sea of clouds.

空姐用温柔、礼貌的声音问前面的乘客们："先生，想看什么报纸？"我欣赏她温柔、迷人的声音，听起来像飞机场广播发出的声音一样，又"治愈"又轻柔。听到这样的声音，人们会情不自禁地放松下来。我开始想，中国机场是想利用这点令紧张的或者烦躁的乘客冷静一点吗？

In a tender, respectful voice, the flight attendant asked the passengers up front, "Sir, what newspaper would you like?" I was appreciating her warm and charming voice. It was similar to the voice heard overhead in the airports, soothing and soft. Hearing this kind of voice, people couldn't help but loosen up a bit. I started to think, was this why Chinese airports wanted to use it, to calm overly anxious or frustrated passengers?

"先生，《环球时报》还是……"她离我还有四排座位。

"Sir, *Global Times* or……" four more rows.

她穿着中国航空公司的制服：合身的褐红色的裙子和小背心，围着一条彩色的领巾。她的头发被盘成一个很紧的发髻，头顶上戴着一顶很可爱的小帽子，有点像小丑喜欢戴的那种，但并不滑稽。当她再次说："先生，想看报纸吗？"我开始想象她的话只对我说，没有其他人。在她甜蜜的声音和飞机发动机的持续轰鸣中，我的眼睛渐渐地闭上了。

She was wearing the China Airlines uniform: a form-fitting maroon-colored skirt and vest and a multi-colored scarf. She wore her hair in a tight bun. On the top of her head was a cute little cap, something like a clown enjoys wearing, but not as funny. I started to imagine her words were only for me as she repeated again and again, "Sir, would you like to read the newspaper?" Under her sweet song and the engine's steady roar, my eyes slowly began to close.

"先生，想看——"她没机会说完。

"Sir, would you like···" she didn't get the chance to finish.

　　突然，从眼角的余光中我看到一道光射出来！我立刻把眼睛完全睁开了。前面第二排靠窗的乘客，是一个穿着一套又旧又不合身的西装的男人。显然没有耐心等待轮到自己，他站了起来向空姐的手推车伸出手抓走了一份报纸。在走廊另外一边的另一名乘客，穿着颜色过于俗艳的衣服，戴着一副墨镜，一看到那位乘客不耐烦的行为，他的反应是立刻也这样做。他往空姐方向转身向前冲过去，也抓走了一份报纸。一下子，在那位空姐周围的人，甚至好像全部的乘客都被第一个乘客不文明的抢报纸行为感染了！就好像这些是地球上最后的报纸一样，他们都疯狂地争抢报纸。我不敢相信自己的眼睛，我僵在座位上想，他们在干什么？！怕报纸送完了？空姐喊道："先生们，马上就轮到你了啊……您……你们干什么呀？！"但是她力气不够，她被来自四面八方的好多只手"攻击"了！从座位后面和周边我听到一些安全带咔嚓咔嚓地解开了，然后几个乘客奔向那位空姐和她的报纸。在一群暴风雨般的挥动的手臂里，那位空姐的安全感被至少 20 个人破坏了 。

　　Suddenly, from out of the corner of my eye I saw a flash of light! I immediately opened my eyes wide. Two rows ahead from the seat next to the window, a man wearing an old, ill-fitting suit coat, apparently unable to patiently wait his turn, stood up and reached his arm towards the flight attendant's cart, grabbing a newspaper. Upon seeing the passenger's impatient behavior, another passenger sitting on the opposite side of the aisle, dressed in loud, garish clothing and wearing a pair of sunglasses, promptly reacted in the same way. He turned in the direction of the attendant and leapt forward, also grabbing a newspaper. All at once, around the attendant, two, three, four, five, until what seemed to be every one of the passengers had been infected by the first passenger's uncivil scramble for the paper! As if they were the last newpapers on the earth, they all madly grabbed for a newspaper. I couldn't believe my own eyes, and was frozen in my seat, thinking, what were they doing?! Were they afraid they were going to run out of newspapers? The attendant tried to shout, "Gentlemen, it will be your turn soon…you—hey, what are you all doing?!" But she wasn't strong enough, and was attacked by multiple hands from all directions! From behind my seat and around me I heard seatbelts clicking as they were released, followed by more passengers rushing towards the attendant and her newspapers. Within a storm of waving arms, the flight attendant's sense of security was destroyed by at least twenty people.

一个个表现得好像不是在抢报纸而是在抢一瓶金瓶五粮液白酒，他们带着胜利回到自己的座位上。一张在混乱中被撕下的头版慢慢地飞到地上去了。我预测头版上将发表可怕的粗体大字标题"玛雅预测成真，末日到了！"

One by one, acting as if they weren't holding newspapers over their heads but gold bottles of Wuliangye liquor, they victoriously returned to their seats. A single front page, torn free during the melee, slowly fell onto the carpeted floor. I expected to see printed across the front page in bold face letters the terrifying headline, "THE MAYAN PREDICTION HAS COME

TRUE! THE END IS HERE!"

几秒钟过后，气氛又恢复常态了。空姐还站在手推车后面。她茫然地盯着前方。她的小帽子差点被碰落，以一个奇怪的角度挂着；一根发夹还勉强保持在原来的位置上，发髻解开了一半。手推车上仅存了一份报纸。

After a few minutes passed, the atmosphere returned to a state of normalcy. The flight attendant was still standing behind her cart. Her small hat had nearly been knocked off: it hung from the side of her head at an odd angle, a single pin keeping it in place. Her bun was half unraveled. On top of her cart remained a single newspaper.

坐在我前排的男人紧张地看看右边，然后往左边看了一眼。他似乎也忍不住了，像一只老鼠从小洞里着急地爬出来抓住一块被房屋主人掉落了的奶酪一样，他伸手把那份英文报纸拿走了。从前面的两个座位之间的缝隙我能偷看到：那只"老鼠"把那份"奶酪"压在他胸口上。

The man sitting in front of me nervously looked right, then he glanced left. As if he couldn't resist, like a mouse nervously crawling out of its hole to grab a piece of cheese dropped by the owners' of the house, he reached for and then grabbed the newspaper. I saw that it was an English newspaper. From the small gap between the two seats in front of me I sneaked a glimpse: the mouse was pressing his "cheese" to his chest.

这时，那位空姐镇定下来了。她把小帽子和发髻调整了一下。把小背心拉展后，她抬起头推着推车到我们这边。她用有限的权力重新分配了报纸，把那份英文报纸从前排男人紧紧搂住的怀抱中拽了出来认真地说："这是你后面的外国人的。"

By that time, the flight attendant had regained her composure. She adjusted her little hat and hair bun. After straightening her vest, she lifted her head and pushed her cart towards us. With her limited authority refreshed, she yanked the newspaper from his tight embrace and said in earnest, "This is for the foreigner sitting behind you."

我转过来往后看。没有其他的老外。感觉有点不好意思，因为那份报纸好像就是我的，可是我并没预定。但是，我能了解她的想法：我是老外，老外看不懂中文，只能看英文报纸。那只"小老鼠"哭出来了，说："可我没有报纸。"

I turned around and looked behind me. There weren't any other foreigners. I felt a little embarrassed because it seemed that newspaper was mine, but that I certainly hadn't reserved one. Though, I could understand her thinking: I'm a foreigner and foreigners can't read Chinese. The foreigner had no choice and could only read an English newspaper. The little mouse cried out, "But I don't have one."

坐在他旁边的人，估计是他的朋友，讽刺地说："英文你看不懂！"

The person sitting next to him, guessing it was a friend, said sarcastically, "You can't read English!"

他坚持："可是，我没有报纸。"

He insisted, "But, I don't have one."

朋友又说："哎呀，没用，你不懂英文。"

His friend said again, "Come on, what's the point, you can't read English."

他几乎要放弃了，说："可，我没有报纸。"

Almost giving up, he said, "But, I don't have one."

我期待她将报纸拿给我并说："亲爱的，这是你的。"但是，好像她精神没有我那么兴奋，她只拿给我，什么都没说。谁能怪她呢？难道她没看见刚才文明几乎完全陨落？难道她没看见刚才男人都成了动物？

I was happily waiting for her to hand me the paper and say, "Dear, this is yours." But, it seemed her spirit wasn't as excited as mine, and she just handed me the newspaper and didn't say anything. And who could blame her? Hadn't she just seen a near total collapse of civilization? Had she not witnessed man transform into an animal before her very eyes?

我看着推车过去了，推车的小轮子和空姐的鞋子都嘎吱嘎吱地响，踩到那份掉在地上的报纸上面。在一篇印着鞋印的文章里提出："根据最近的研究，科学家认可过去的研究——人的思考能力使人异于动物。"

Watching the cart go by, the small wheels and the flight attendant's shoes crunched as they rode over the newspaper that had fallen to the floor.

In the imprint of a shoe an article stood out: "According to recent studies, scientists have reconfirmed past research: Man's cognitive thinking is what sets us apart from animal."

可是发生了刚才那样的事情后，我想听到另外的观点。

After what had just happened, I'd like to hear a second opinion.

Chapter 20

珠峰，谁在高原病倒了？
Mt. Qomolangma, Who Would Succumb to Altitude Sickness?

我费力地发出一个很长的呼哧呼哧的声音。

我吸入一个更长的呼哧呼哧的声音。

又发出……

又吸入……

I struggled to exhale a long wheeze.
I inhaled an even longer one.
Exhaling…
Inhaling…

在四条令人浑身发痒的单薄的羊毛毯子下，我穿着一套保暖内衣，一条牛仔裤，一件羊毛作为里衬的夹克，一件外套，戴着针织帽和一双手套，在一个不够长的、只能保持零度的睡袋里裹得很紧。我又试图呼吸一下。好像一座山，不是普通的山，而是世界上最高的山——珠穆朗玛峰的重量全部压在我的胸膛上，我又发出一个呼哧呼哧的声音。

Beneath four itchy, threadbare wool blankets, wedged tightly within a sleeping bag that was too short, but could withstand temperatures of zero degrees, wearing a complete set of long-underwear, a pair of jeans, a jacket lined with sheep's wool, a coat, a knit cap and a pair of gloves, I tried to breath again. As if a mountain, and not a normal mountain, but the weight of the world's highest mountain—Mt. Qomolangma—had been placed on my chest, I once again exhaled a very harsh wheeze.

我比那些可怜的，永远在珠峰的冰冷怀抱里睡觉的登山者包得更紧，全身都动不了一下，只能往上看。卧室太黑了，天花板都看不见。即使能往右看看室友，一定也看不见。屏住了自己的呼吸，我想听一下他是否还活着。我听到他发出很平和的鼾声。谢天谢地，他还没对高原病屈服。搞不好是我先走一步。

Wrapped tighter than the pitiful climbers who were forever trapped in Mt. Qomolangma's freezing embrace, my entire body unable to move, I could only look up. The room was too dark and I couldn't see the ceiling. Even if I could look to my right at my roommate, surely I also couldn't see him. Holding my breath, I wanted to hear whether or not he was still alive. I could hear a mild snore. Thank god he had yet to have surrendered to the altitude sickness. It looked as if I would be be the first.

呼哧呼哧……

Wheezing…

　　高原的寒冷的手指慢慢地又滑进我的胸膛里，我的胸腔又缩小了，剩下的空间不足以让我的肺再扩大一下。我听说如果人得了高原病，为了生存，让他恢复一下，必须立刻把那个人移到海拔较低的地方。如果没其他办法的话，那个人可能就死了。我想到地板，如果从床上滚下地板，能算是降低了海拔吗？估计不行。我头疼欲裂，晕晕乎乎。

The high altitude's frigid fingers slowly slid within my chest, my chest contracting, leaving little room for my lungs to expand. I have heard that if people get altitude sickness, in order to survive, to recover, you must immediately move that person to a lower altitude. And if there were no other options, the person would cease to be. I thought about the floor. If I could roll from the bed onto the floor, would it count as a lower altitude? I figured it wouldn't. My head was pounding and I was dizzy.

　　呼哧呼哧……

Wheezing…

　　我需要氧气。我又骂自己，为什么在拉萨市没买？本地的西藏导游没推荐？认为自己是真正的男子汉？我忍不住骂自己是笨蛋，为了面子，就一点氧气都没了。可是我的室友，那个土耳其人也没买过。虽然在我头顶靠着的墙的另一边有好多氧气瓶，不幸的是，那些氧气瓶都是被几个人保护着的。更不幸的是，几个小时之前，我变成了那些人的敌人……

I needed oxygen. I cursed myself. Why didn't I buy any in Lhasa? Hadn't the local Tibetan guide suggested it? Thought you were a real man, didn't you? Oaf, in the name of pride, you don't have any oxygen! My roommate, a Turk, hadn't bought any either. Although, on the other side of the wall that my head rested up against was a lot of oxygen tanks. Unfortunately, those tanks were all protected by a few. And even more unfortunate, a few hours before, I had become their enemy.

七个小时之前：

Seven hours earlier:

当旅行大巴的轮胎在冰路面上还没完全停止转动的时候，我就跳下车去了。爬山的鞋子一落到珠穆朗玛峰的大本营上，我就像一个过于亢奋的少年第一次有机会给喜欢的小姑娘一个吻一样，暂时失去了理智。我疯狂地向一座小山跑去。到了小山顶上，站在一层又硬又脆的雪上，无数多彩的西藏经幡围绕着我，我突然看到黑色的星星在我眼前开始爆炸了。我忘记了，在海拔 5200 米的地方氧气不足，人不能很快地行动。我的身体和脑子受不了了。我晕倒了。虽然小星星还在我眼前跳舞，但我开始欣赏这个世界上最伟大的美女：珠穆朗玛峰。她坐落在我面前。我想使用"她"称呼珠峰是因为只有女性才能展示出真正的外在美。

Before the tour bus's tires had completely stopped turning, I jumped down from the passenger seat. And as soon as my hiking shoes landed on Qomolangma Base Camp, like an over-excited adolescent boy and his first chance at kissing a girl, temporarily losing my mind, I rushed frantically up a small hill. Reaching the hill's summit, standing on a thick, crunchy layer of snow, countless colorful Tibetan prayer flags surrounding me, black stars suddenly began to explode in front of me. I forgot, at 5,200 meters above sea level the oxygen wasn't enough, and you don't want to move too quickly, as your body and mind can't take it. I fell down. Lying on my side, the little stars still dancing before my eyes, I began to appreciate the world's greatest beauty: Mt. Qomolangma. She sat before me. I felt I should address Qomolangma as a "she" because only a female could emit such genuine physical beauty.

蓝宝石般的天空成了大自然创造的最纯洁的背景。雪峰上的雪旋转起来了，像她的头发被北风吹来吹去。即使她穿的冰雪做的白长袍已经被强烈的阳光晒得破破烂烂，暴露出里面岩石构成的深褐色的皮肤，我也不敢批评珠峰的表现方式。她具有自然美，那种美丽，即便是缺点也能让她更夺目。因为一直处在强光下，她的北面被晒得裸露出来。好比一个仁慈又残酷的皇后被艰难困苦折磨而形成的一样，在恶劣的环境下珠峰长得非同一般。不知道是不是因为北风从背面吹过来或者是我的脑子还在被高原病影响，但是我几乎能听到她用那很吸引人的声音呼唤着说："过来吧，只要爬一下山就能尝到我拥有怎样神秘的味道……我永远等着……过来吧。"她要人类，她需要人类挑战一下，征服她的美。但是，同时我能听见好多被她致命的亲吻杀掉的登山者警告说："小心……"

A rich sapphire blue sky acted as a backdrop for Mother Nature's purest creation. As if her hair was being blown around by the northern wind, the dusted peak's snow swirled. Even though the robe she wore, one made of ice and snow, was already ragged beneath the intense sun's rays, exposing her skin, the dark brown rock beneath, I didn't dare criticize her manifestation. She possessed a natural beauty, the kind of beauty where even a shortcoming added to its splendor. Overexposed to the sun's powerful rays, her north face was left bare. Like a benevolent, but at the same time cruel empress, shaped beneath hardship and torment, under a harsh environment, Qomolangma has grown into something extraordinary. I didn't know if it was from the northern wind blowing from behind or my mind was still affected by the high altitude, but I could almost hear her seductive voice calling out, "Come here, you only need to climb a little to sample the mysterious tastes I possess…I will wait forever…come here." She wanted men, she needed men to challenge her, to conquer her beauty. But, at the same time I could hear the warnings of many climbers who were killed by her lethal kiss, "Beware…"

旅行大巴按了喇叭，打破了她的咒语，让我又回到现实生活里了。手指都已经冷得麻木僵硬了，我用拳头慢慢地把身体从下面的冻土上剥出了一些，发出一个撕裂的声音。整个身体都快冻僵了，我跌跌撞撞走在小山上。我和珠峰在一起的时光不够，真想多待一会儿。但是，不管她怎么迷人，人类都不敢逗留太久！必须敬畏珠峰，同时也必须注意气温，特别是冬天零下三十度的时候！我们要回到自己的旅馆，地球上最高的旅馆：绒布旅馆（在绒布寺的对面）。在回到旅馆的路上，蜷缩在车里的暖气中，我的身体很快就暖和了许多。大本营离旅馆有五公里左右，还剩下两公里，我问西藏导游我们可不可以下车走回去，我还想在大自然的壮丽中晒一会儿。导游的脸颊被强烈的太阳晒红了，皮肤很黑，本地口音很重，他用英文笑着说："当然可以，但是不要走得太慢，天快黑了！"在我们的旅行团中，有五个人想晒一下：一个很幽默的苏格兰老人和他的女儿、一个年轻的法国男孩儿、一个跟我一样大的土耳其男生和我。其他人都没说话，只想留在车里享受车里的暖气。

The tour bus blew its horn. Breaking its spell, I once again returned to reality. Fingers already numbed and hardening from the cold, I used my fists to peel my body from the frozen earth beneath, releasing a ripping sound. My entire body nearly frozen stiff, I half walked, half crawled down the small hill. Our time together wasn't enough and I really wanted to share more time with Qomolangma. But no matter how enchanting, no man dared to stay for too long! I had to respect Qomolangma, while at the same time I had to respect the temperature, especially the winter's thirty degrees below zero! We had to return to our hostel, the Earth's highest hostel: the Rongbu Hostel (across from the Rongbu Monastery). On the bus returning to the hostel, huddled over the heater, my body quickly warmed up. Qomolangma Base Camp was five kilometers from the hostel. With two kilometers remaining, I asked our Tibetan tour guide if we could get down and walk back. I still wanted to bask a little longer in Mother Nature's magnificence. The guide's cheeks sun-kissed red by the intense sun, skin very dark, his local accent thick, smiled and said in English, "Of course it's okay, but you don't want to walk too slowly, darkness is approaching!" Out of our tour group, five wanted to bask: one old, humorous Scotsman, his no-nonsense daughter, a young French boy and a Turk who was the same age as I. The others didn't say anything and just wanted to stay on the bus and enjoy the tour bus's heat.

在世界屋脊上很慢地走着，珠峰压到我的背上，四面八方有大大小小的山，感觉有点像是在另一个星球上，我又一次觉得特别满足。此时此刻，就算手指麻木或脚趾在鞋子里蜷缩着躲避潜在的冻伤，对我来说又算什么？这难道不是一种冒险？无论是把一本从没读过的书打开，还是第一次吃一种没尝试过的食物，或者飞到新地方探险一下，生命的目标之一不就是探究世界的神秘吗？我高兴极了！

Walking slowly across the "roof of the world", Qomolangma pressing down from behind, hills and mountains in every direction, feeling as if we were on another planet, I realized once again how content I was. Who cares that I once again couldn't feel my fingers, or that my toes were curling up inside of my shoes, hiding from potential frostbite. Wasn't this a kind of adventure? No matter if it's opening a book you've never read, your first time to eat or drink something you've never tasted before or flying somewhere new to explore, isn't one of life's goals to investigate all of the world's mysteries? I was ecstatic!

走到绒布寺的旅馆，我发现那七个不想下车跟我们步行的旅客们还没下车。我们的西藏导游名叫丹增，他说他们都不愿住在这里，因为没有热水，也没有暖气。我吃惊地回答道："热水和暖气？当然没有！这又不是五星级大酒店！"下车后，我感觉到他们七个人都在看着我，因为我敢反对他们。我想，行程上难道没说这家寺庙是非常粗陋的吗？没说该带自己的睡袋过来因为晚上非常冷吗？我下了车找到了与我一同晒太阳的旅客。两个苏格兰人说："他们竟然想去找有热水、有暖气的地方？太搞笑了！"他们在苏格兰的高地长大，对他们来说这里的冬天跟家乡的冬天没有区别。那个土耳其人因为从旅程开始到现在什么都没说，我猜他可能是哑巴，但是他突然小声但特别认真地说："我们有机会天天住在珠峰的影子中吗？能天天早上起床面对那么伟大的东西吗？不可能！"我看着他橄榄色的脸庞，在他非常丰满的黑眉毛下，一双平静的棕色眼睛也看着我，没有任何一点表情。他说完了，又变成旅行团中沉默的雕像。他们都是爱冒险的人，肯定要尊敬祖先的风俗。我们的想法一模一样。虽然有点冷，但是因为一天不能洗澡就要牺牲这个一生一次的机会，就想放世上第一美人的鸽子？不行！当我问法国人的时候，他笑着说："随便吧。"根据历史规律，法国人又不知道怎么站队了。

Reaching the Rongbuk Hostel, I discovered that the seven other tourists who hadn't wanted to get off the bus and walk with us still hadn't exited the bus. Our Tibetan tour guide, his name was Danzig, said that they didn't want to stay here because there was no hot water and no heating. Surprised, I asked, "Hot water and heating? Of course there isn't any! This wasn't a five star hotel!" Getting on the bus, it felt as if all seven were staring at me, daring me to go against them. I thought, didn't the original travel plans state that this monastery was really coarse and crude? Didn't it say you should bring your own sleeping bag because it would get really cold at night? I got off the bus and found my fellow sun-basking travelers. The Scottish duo said, "No way! Where do they want to go for hot water and heat? Ridiculous!" They were raised on the highlands of Scotland, and to them the winter here was no different than the one back home. Because he hadn't spoken since the trip began, I kind of thought the Turk may have been a mute, but suddenly he said quietly, but quite seriously, "Do we have the opportunity to live in Qomolangma's shadow every day? Can we wake up every day and come face to face with something so great? No way." I looked at his olive skin. Below full, black eyebrows, a pair of serene brown eyes looked at me. He was expressionless. After he finished, he once again became the tour group's silent statue. Their characters were those of explorers, and they certainly wanted to respect their ancestor's custom. Our thinking was one in the same. Because of a little cold, and the fact that you can't shower for a day, you are willing to sacrifice a once in a lifetime opportunity, and want to stand up the world's greatest beauty? No way! When I got to the Frenchman, he said smiling, "Whatever." Based on history, the French once again didn't know how to pick a side.

回到旅行车上，我们的导游站在外面，我问道："其他的旅馆有热水和暖气吗？"

Returning to the tour bus, the guide standing outside, I asked, "Does the other hostel have hot water and heating?"

他说："估计没有。"

He said, "I'm guessing not."

我接着问："那边也能看得见珠峰？"

I continued to ask, "Can we also see Qomolangma from there?"

他笑着说："那可看不到。"

Laughing he said, "Certainly not."

我说："现在已经是晚上七点钟，已经太晚了，没时间去别的地方了。我要住在这里。"我上了车提起背包。

I said, "It's already seven o'clock at night, already too late, and there is no time to go somewhere else. I want to stay here." I got back on the bus and picked up my backpack.

导游跟着我上车说："旅行团不能分开，别忘记了，我们是紧紧粘在一起的'饭团'！凯文说我们住在这里，我们就在这里住。"

Following me onto the bus, the tour guide got on the bus and said, "The tour group cannot split up, don't forget, we are sticky rice! Kevin said we will stay here. So we will stay here."

我感到有点意外和惭愧，不想让自己听起来那么自私，于是我小声地说："不是我，是我们要住。"

Unexpectedly, feeling a little ashamed, not wanting to sound so selfish, I said quietly, "Not me, but WE want to stay."

对他们七个来说，这没有什么区别。他们在座位上，都穿着几层厚厚的衣服，像棉花糖一样，又胖又圆。他们都看着我：一对希腊夫妻，在氧气瓶的后面慢慢地吸气、呼气，丈夫很累地看了看我，妻子瞪出了眼睛；一个长得像圣诞老人，但是脾气很大，年纪也很大的德国人和他的美国胖女儿都怒视着我；一个尼泊尔裔英国女孩也生气地看着我，她那眼白跟周围黑色皮肤形成鲜明的对比的眼睛，挑战着我的决定。虽然她很漂亮，但是愤怒让她的外表变得难看了。还有一个很友好的泰国女人和她的旅伴——一个印度尼西亚的男人，像两根棒冰，都不停地发着抖。我感觉有点内疚，过了一段时间又重新审视我们的决定。当然，我们五个有点自私，但是我们的梦想才刚刚实现，不要那么快就让那个梦破灭！让我们牺牲这个梦想，就因为他们有点冷，要洗澡，这不是同样自私吗？从这家只有一层的石头造的旅馆顶上我又看到了珠峰的面孔。明早必须再一次对她表示敬意。算了，我告诉自己。我转身下了车。

But to the seven, there was no difference. From their seats, all wearing layers of thick clothing, akin to Marshmallows, fat and round, they all stared at me: a couple from Greece, from behind an oxygen tank, inhaling and exhaling slowly, the husband looked at me with tired eyes, the wife staring blankly; one who looked like Santa Claus, but with a strong temper, a middle aged German and his chubby American daughter both glared at me; a Nepalese-English girl also looked angrily at me, her eyes, the whites a stark contrast to the surrounding dark skin, challenged my decision. Unfortunately, while she was really pretty, her appearance was distorted by her wrath; and one very friendly Thai woman and her traveling companion, an Indonesian man, had no choice, and looking as if they were a pair of popsicles, they couldn't stop shaking. Feeling a twinge of guilt, I spent a few moments reconsidering our decision. Sure, the five of us were acting a little selfish, but our dream had only just been realized, and we didn't want to allow that dream to so quickly leave our side! And, wanting us to sacrifice our dreams because they were a little cold, and wanted to take a shower, wasn't this equally selfish? From the window, above the stone rooftop of the hostel I once again saw the face of Qomolangma. Tomorrow morning we must pay homage to her once again. Forget about it, I told myself. I turned around and began to get off the bus.

虽然不是故意的，但是我意识到自己刚刚成了他们七个人的敌人，而在我的背上一个比珠峰更宽的目标出现了。我提起背包下了车。

I realized, it wasn't intentional, but I had just become the seven's enemy, and on my back a target wider than Mt. Qomolangma had formed. I hoisted my backpack and got off the bus.

呼哧呼哧……

Wheezing…

难以呼吸，我想，有可能是因为身体在睡袋里，为了让自己放松，我试图慢慢地活动身体。但是，我动不了。有几次我试着让整个身体跳动一下，但是效果一样，我还是被困在我的睡袋里。我有点惊慌了，我全身疯狂地翻来覆去。终于，睡袋的态度软化了，暂时放开了它的受害者，让我把左手拿出来了。尽管减小了压力，但我浪费了宝贵的氧气。

我像刚跑过一个马拉松那样气喘吁吁。我往右边看，但是看不见人，室友没问我需不需要帮助，因为他还在发出那种很平和的鼾声。

Difficult to breath, I thought, perhaps it was because my body was too tightly wrapped in the sleeping bag. In order to loosen up a bit, I slowly moved my body back and forth. But, I couldn't move. I tried a few more times making my body hop lightly. But the results were the same: I was trapped within my sleeping bag. Panicking, my entire body began to thrash back and forth. And finally the sleeping bag relented, temporarily releasing its victim, allowing me to pull my left hand out. While relieving some of the pressure, I had wasted precious oxygen. I was left gasping for air as if I had just run a marathon uphill. I looked to my right. I couldn't see him, but my roommate hadn't asked, "What's wrong? Need my help?" He continued to sing out a peaceful snore.

六个小时之前：

Six hours earlier:

按照西藏的风俗，烧木头的火炉都放在房间的中央。房间里到处弥漫着牦牛奶制黄油和烟雾的香味。里面有点暗。可以说，除了几个临终的灯泡和火炉里烧着的橘黄色的木炭以外，没亮着的东西了。尽管旅馆很传统的藏式客厅比外面暖和，我却无法享受藏式盛情了，因为感觉自己像是刚刚走进了敌人的领土：圣诞老人、他那位胖女儿、尼泊尔裔英国女牛，三双眼睛都在喷火！坐在他们旁边的那对希腊人互相抱得很紧，男的低着头在看地上，可能是因为他知道自己的坏习惯——吸烟，才是影响他健康的罪魁祸首，而不是我们留下的决定。

According to Tibetan customs, the wood-burning stove sat in the center of the room. The smell of yak butter and smoke hung everywhere. It was fairly dark inside, you could say, outside of a few aging light bulbs and the glow from the smoldering flames-orange coals within the stove, there wasn't much light. And even though the hotel's traditional Tibetan-style main room was warmer than outside, I was unable to appreciate the Tibetan hospitality, as it felt like I had just walked into enemy territory: Santa Claus, his chubby daughter, the small Nepalese-English woman, three pairs of eyes breathed their own dark, smoldering fire of hate. Sitting next to them, the Greek couple held each other tightly. The man lowered his head and looked at the ground, perhaps because he knew that his own bad habit: smoking, and not our decision to stay was what was affecting his health.

他的老婆冲我做了个表情，像是在说："不好意思，我们两个真的很想支持你，但是你看看，我们太弱了，没法站在你这一边。"在火炉的另外一边，泰国人和印尼人，牙齿不停地咔嚓咔嚓打战，挨挨挤挤，互相拥作一团。我非常不好意思地把手套脱下来递给泰国人说："对不起。"他们的眼里没有憎恨，只有苦恼。这就是佛教徒的天性。我想表示我的歉意，我善意地对大家说："今晚，我请你们喝酒！"

His wife gave me an expression that said: sorry, the two of us would like to support you, but take a look, we are too weak, and can't join your side. On the other side of the stove, the Thai and the Indonesia, their teeth chattering non-stop, huddled together as one. Really embarrassed I handed over my gloves to the Thai and said, "Sorry." Their eyes held no anger, only misery. And that was the nature of a Buddhist disciple. Wanting to express my apologies to everyone I said with good intentions, "Tonight, drinks are on me!"

圣诞老人发出低沉的咆哮声。他生气地说："先让我冻死，然后再用酒杀死我？"

Santa Claus let loose a muffled roar. And he said angrily, "First you want me to freeze to death, then you want to kill me with alcohol?!"

我忘记了，很多人曾告诫我说：不要喝酒，喝酒会加重高原病的病情。

I had forgotten, many warnings said: don't drink alcohol as it will increase the conditions of altitude sickness.

除了圣诞老人，其他人都没回答。

Besides Santa, no one else responded.

我看了看四周。火炉的周围没有空地。就算有的话，我也不受欢迎。

I looked around. There was no room around the stove. And if there was, I wasn't welcomed to it.

丹增用一把铁锨把又硬又小的圆圆的牦牛粪铲入火炉，用中文笑着说："你要小心，阿文。"

Using a shovel, Danzig fed small, hard pieces of round yak dung into the stove. Smiling he said in Chinese, "Looks like you'd better be careful, Kevin."

像一个小男孩儿从学校蹦蹦跳跳地回家那样，那个法国人跳进客厅里说："大家好！"

Like a little boy skipping home from elementary school, the Frenchman hopped into the room and said, "Hi everyone!"

胖女孩看了看我，向他安慰地说："过来吧，法国人，跟我们一起坐。"

Glaring at me, the fat girl said comfortingly, "Come here, France, sit with us."

法国人跳到他们中间去，说："好的呀！"

Hopping in between them, the Frenchman said, "Alright!"

背信弃义！我们五个又少了一个！

Treachery! The five of us became four!

不知道该怎么做，我选了一个离火炉有点远，在阴影中的桌子坐下来，自我放松一下。

Not sure what to do, I selected a seat at a table a little far away, in the shadows, and relaxed a little.

老苏格兰走进来说："终于找到暖和点的地方了，太好了！"他的心情一点也没被温度影响。这不足为奇，因为在冬天苏格兰男人曾经穿过苏格兰短裙，而且里面不穿内裤！

The Scotsman walked in and said, "Finally found some warmth, great!" His attitude hadn't been affected by the temperature in the slightest. This was no surprise as the Scotsman used to wear their kilts in the winter without aid of underwear!

"嘿，你为什么坐在这里？"他问我。我快速解释了一下目前的情况。

"Hey, why are you sitting here?" he asked me. I quickly explained to him the current situation.

他拍了拍我的肩膀，笑着说："哈哈，你深陷困境！"

Patting my shoulder, he laughed and said, "Haha, you're in deep trouble!"

"不只是我！你呢？"我小声地说。

"Not only me! What about you?" I said quietly.

"我？我老了，谁会搭理我？哈哈哈！"

"What about me? I'm old, who'd pay attention to me? Hahaha!"

这时，他女儿走进来大声地说："嘿，为什么没有人喝酒？阿文呢？"

At that moment, his daughter walked in and said loudly, "Hey, why isn't anyone drinking? Kevin?"

她老爸告诉她我们的情况。她像苏格兰的英雄威廉·华莱士面对英国军队那样，向其他的人挥了挥手说："我们喝酒吧！"

Her father told her about our situation. As if she were Scotland's hero, William Wallace, facing the English army, she waved her hand in the direction of the others and said, "Ba! We drink!"

看着她周身散发着活力，我忍不住佩服她比苏格兰高地更健壮的体格！虽然我没有从小被大自然的乳汁哺育，也没在一个那么冷的地方长大，但是我难道不是男人？我的祖先不也是从爱尔兰——另一个粗糙的地方过来的？我脸上不也蓄了七天的胡子吗？我一定要跟这个厉害的苏格兰女人一起，庆祝今天的珠穆朗玛峰！不喝一杯酒向珠峰表达尊敬，就像男人拒绝一个美女露出脸颊等他亲吻一样！干杯！一切都是值得的！年轻的男孩儿终于跟他最喜欢的小姑娘亲吻了。

Seeing her entirety exuding such vitality, I couldn't help but admire her robust physique, stronger than that of the Scottish highlands! Yep, I wasn't suckled from a young age by the nipple of Mother Nature, nor did I grow up in such a cold place, but wasn't I a man? Didn't my ancestors also hail from Ireland, another rough land? Had my face not sprouted seven days worth of whiskers? Certainly I must drink with this incredible woman and celebrate this day's Mt. Qomolangma together! Unwilling to drink a glass of alcohol in order to express your respect to Mt. Qomolangma, would be like a man refusing to kiss a beautiful woman's exposed cheek! Cheers! What a good feeling and totally worth it! The young boy finally gave the girl he liked best the appropriate kiss.

呼哧呼哧……

Wheezing…

我没办法把自己翻转过来，这时候我才意识到我的另一个当务之急。

我把大腿挤压在一起，又骂了自己：为什么临睡前敢喝啤酒？不仅快死了，而且非常想上厕所！花了半天我才从自己的茧里滑出来。

Unable to turn myself over, I realized at this moment that there was another matter of vital importance. Pressing my thighs together, I once again cursed myself: why did you dare to drink beer just before going to bed? Not only was I probably going to die soon, but I also had to use the bathroom! Spending what seemed like forever, I was eventually able to slide out of my cocoon.

在走廊中我穿过有氧气的房间。但是我不敢敲门或进去，里面的氧气被三个根本不想帮助我的人霸占着。走廊漆黑一片，除了自己的脸，我什么都感觉不到。

In the hallway, I passed the room with the oxygen. But I didn't dare knock on the door or enter, as the oxygen within was being guarded by the three people who really didn't want to help me. The hallway was pitch black, and besides my own face, I couldn't find a thing.

我就不告诉你厕所的细节了，简直太糟糕了：露出的屁股被冷风欺负了，脚就像踩在冰黄水坑上滑冰。我的呼吸放松了一点点。我觉得有可能是新鲜的空气让我感觉更舒服。此外，我在大城市工作，偶尔才能抓住机会享受夜晚的温柔。我把针织围巾拉紧了一些，手塞入外套口袋里，在兴奋的期待下，我大步跨进露天空地的庭院。那晚的夜空使我充满赞赏。我崇敬地说："谢谢，上帝。"

I won't tell you the details about the restroom, they were simply too terrible to describe: exposed bottom bullied by freezing winds and ice-skating across frozen yellow puddles. My breathing let up a little. I thought that perhaps the fresh air made me feel better. Furthermore, I work in the big city, seldom am I able to snatch an opportunity to really enjoy the gentle touch of the night. Pulling a knit scarf tighter, hands stuffed in my coat pockets, with excited anticipation, I strode out and into the open-aired courtyard. That night sky left me brimming with admiration. With reverence I said, "Thank you, Lord."

天上的星星很大，仿佛白色的苹果挂在一棵又黑又粗的看不见的树上，我把手伸出来试图摘下一颗。我们只有一个月亮，但是好像站在世界屋脊，每一颗星星都像我们的月球一样大，无数"月亮"挤满夜空。此处，在地球上，很少有地方能看清楚星系，看清楚银河的尾巴，跨过夜空，延伸数万里。像是有一个顽皮的星座，双子座或双鱼座，用白漆把那些星星喷涂在夜空很辽阔的黑色画布上。这样的景象我当然在书上读过，在电视上看过，但却从没有亲眼见证过。我整个心灵都被静谧而壮观的景象感动了。一滴眼泪流了下来。用手套擦掉眼泪，我想，自己好久没哭了，特别是被充满魅力的事物感动而哭。又擦了一下，我才意识到，我不是在哭，而是眼皮快冻住了！我的鼻涕已经变成两条冰柱，嘴唇麻木了，我动了动脚趾但是感觉不到它们。我在心里说：在一床天堂制造的壮丽的被子底下去世比在一间很黑、很冷漠的卧室里，在破破烂烂的被子底下去世是更美的结局。每次呼吸，我看着水汽凝结，在空气中被零下三十多度的气温冻结成缓慢移动的白色浓雾冰块。我的脑子说：不行，不要违反自然规律，必须回卧室去！

    As if white apples hung from the thick, black branches of an equally invisible tree, I stretched my hand outwards in an attempt to pick one of the large stars above. Our world only had one moon, but it seemed that night standing on the roof of the world, every star had become as large as our moon, countless "moons" completely filling the night sky. Here, on the earth, there were very few places that you could clearly see the tail of our galaxy, the Milky Way, stretched across the night sky, extending tens of thousands of miles. It looked as if a mischievous constellation, Gemini or Pisces had used white spray paint to graffiti the stars upon the night sky's vast black canvas. Of course I'd seen it in a book and on the television, but not with my very own eyes. My entire soul was stilled by the above and I was deeply moved by the spectacular scene. A single tear ran down my face. Using my gloves to wipe it away, I thought, it had been a long time since I had cried, especially because of something so fascinating. Wiping some more away, I realized, I wasn't crying, but my eyelids were about to freeze-up! My snot had already turned to two icicles, and lips numbed, I wiggled my toes but I couldn't feel them. My heart said: passing away beneath a glorious, heavenly-produced cover was a much more beautiful ending than passing away in a dark, cold and detached bedroom, beneath ragged blankets. After every breath, watching it condensate, turning into slow moving blocks of white fog beneath temperatures reaching thirty degrees below zero, my brain said: No way, you don't want to violate the laws of nature and you must return to your room!

五个小时之前：

Five hours earlier:

除了那两个苏格兰人和我，没人多说话。不知道什么时候，土耳其人也进来了。他一半坐在客厅的阴影中，一半隐在自己脸上的阴影里，我几乎看不见他。他怀疑地看着周围。我真想保持好心情，但是无法坚持了。在圣诞老人和他胖女儿谴责的目光下，像火炉的暖气一样，我的幸福感减少了。我的咖喱牦牛太老了，米饭太硬了，啤酒淡了，屁股冷了，心也凉了。今晚我们在珠峰附近过夜，但是我却无法享受。

Besides the two Scotsmen and myself, no one said much. Don't know when, but the Turk had also entered. Half sitting in the shadows, half obscured by his own gloomy face, I could barely see him as he eyed those around him with suspicion. I really wanted to maintain a good mood, but I couldn't persist. Under the condemning eyes of Santa Claus and his chubby daughter, like the stove's heat, my happiness had diminished. My curried yak was overcooked, the rice was hard, the beer weak, my bottom was cold and my heart was colder. Tonight, we were living in Qomolangma's dark shadow, but I couldn't enjoy it.

呼哧呼哧……

Wheezing...

在庭院里站着，我才能呼吸得顺畅。其实，我并不确定。可能那时候，在神奇的景色下，我已经忘记了自己是否能很顺畅地呼吸。但是，又回到睡袋里，我无法不提醒自己每一口呼吸我都需要不断挣扎。很多登山人被珠峰夺去了生命，但是如果仅仅是在寺庙里和旅店里呢？那将非常尴尬。我必须得忍住！目空一切，我吸了一口气，再吸一口气！

Standing in the courtyard, I was able to finally breath freely. Actually, I wasn't sure. Perhaps at that time, beneath the mystical display, I had forgotten whether or not I could breath freely. But, once again back in the sleeping bag, I couldn't help but remind myself that each breath was still a continuous struggle. Many mountain climbers have been carried away by Qomolangma, but in the monastery and its hostel? That would just be embarrassing. I had to persevere! Defiant, I took one breath after another!

四个小时之前：

Four hours earlier:

圣诞老人站起来，样子像一只暴躁的老狗，操着浓重的德语口音。他严峻地宣布："好了，我老了，心脏比较弱，估计今晚我要死了。"他转身面向我，接下来责怪般地说："谢谢你。"

Santa Claus stood up, and resembling a grumpy old dog, letting everyone hear, in his thick German accent, he announced grimly, "Okay, I'm old, my heart is fairly weak, and I estimate I will die tonight." He turned towards me and said accusingly, "Thank you."

紧接着父亲，胖女儿也站起来，盯着我，用眼睛说："谢谢你，你杀了我的老爸。"

Following her father, the chubby daughter stood, glared at me and said with her eyes, "Thank you, you killed my father."

呼哧呼哧……

Wheezing…

圣诞老人的话——要死了——有可能是他最后的话，在我的脑海里不停地回响。后来苏格兰人和其他人说了什么、我们又做了什么我都记不得了。我接下来吸了一口气，又吸了一口气。我想继续呼吸，但是觉得自己好累。我控制不住眼皮，闭上了眼睛，开始想象我跟世界上首次登顶珠峰的新西兰的埃德蒙·希拉里爵士和他最信任的搭档尼泊尔的夏尔巴人丹增·诺尔盖在一起。站在他们旁边，我想体会一下珠峰峰顶上的风景怎么样：白茫茫的雪海一直伸展到视线尽头。雪峰就像那海面上闪闪发光的雪海里的波涛。山谷是很平静的，让人类的担心有暂时歇息一会儿的地方，在大自然母亲的怀抱里漂着。我的眼皮越来越重。接着，珠峰顶上的一切渐渐变成了白色。

Santa Claus's words, perhaps his last words ever: WILL DIE, echoed over and over within my mind. Whatever Scotland and the others said afterwards, and whatever we did I couldn't remember. Then I took a breath, and then another breath. I wanted to continue, but I was so tired. Unable to control my eyelids, I closed my eyes. I began to imagine I was with the first climber to ever ascent Qomolangma: New Zealand's Sir Edmund Hillary and his trusted companion, Nepalese Sherpa Danzig Norguet. Standing next to them, I wanted to savor the view from Qomolangma's peak: a vast expense of a white snowy sea stretching endlessly towards the far reaches of sight. Snowy peaks were the sea's glittering waves. The valleys were tranquil, allowing mankind's worries to rest for a period within, floating within Mother Nature's bosom. My eyelids became heavier and heavier. Then, from Qomolangma's peak, everything gradually became white.

几个小时以后:

A few hours later:

身体比尸体还僵直,被包裹在自己的棺材中,我一瞬间以为自己去世了!但是,我的眼睛睁开了!我复活了!我往右边看去,土耳其人已经离开了房间。看了看窗外,我发现我在睡懒觉,已经七点钟了,我失去了亲眼看见珠峰的面纱被日出掀开的机会。起床后,我才回忆起圣诞老人临别时说的话:"要死了。" 我又看了看窗外,没有救护车的红蓝灯闪动,没有救援直升机的桨叶旋转,可能我没杀死圣诞老人!身体被冷气冻硬的我,像一个木偶般僵直地向庭院走去,我走到客厅里,没注意温度是零下多少度。在里面,靠火炉最近的是圣诞老人,我没杀死他!世界上的孩子们都不会恨我了!他回头看了我一眼,好像很失望我昨晚没去世。

Body more rigid than a corpse, wrapped within my own coffin, I thought for a split second that I had died! But, my eyes opened! I was resurrected! I looked to my right. The Turk had already left the room. Looking out the window, I discovered that I had slept in and it was already seven o'clock, I had lost the chance to witness with my own eyes the moment when Qomolangma's veil was lifted by the sunrise. Getting out of bed, I recalled Santa Claus parting words, "Will die." I looked back at the window and there wasn't an ambulance flashing red and blue lights! There wasn't a helicopter and its spinning blades! Maybe I hadn't killed Santa Claus! Body stiff from the cold, like a puppet, I rigidly walked through the courtyard, not paying attention to how much the temperature was below zero, and I walked into the sitting room. Inside, very close to the stove was Santa Claus! I hadn't killed him! The world's children wouldn't hate me! He turned around and glanced at me. It seemed he was disappointed to see that I hadn't passed away during the night.

大家都上了回市区的车，在寺庙的旁边我一边转动金色的转经筒，一边晒着西藏最美丽的阳光，说："上帝，请原谅我，昨天因为我的自私，一个人差点去世了。"

As everyone boarded the bus back to the city, alongside the monastery I spun the golden prayer wheels, basking in the ambiance of Tibet's beautiful sunshine and said, "Lord, please forgive me, yesterday I nearly allowed another to pass away due to my own selfishness."

我不知道是珠峰的风声，还是那个转经筒的吱吱声或者是上帝的话语声，但是我始终听见一个很小的声音说："阿文，近一点吧。"我离那些转经筒非常近，充满热情地把它们转动起来，我想着：您准备告诉我什么？我的未来？世界上最神秘的秘密？歌手猫王是不是真的死了？

我又忍不住把转经筒转动更快，又传来一个声音："你——"

I don't know if it was Mt. Qomolangma's wind, the spinning prayer wheel's squeaking or the Lord's voice, but I began to hear a very faint voice say, "Kevin, come closer." I got really close to the prayer wheels and spun them passionately as I thought: What do you plan on telling me? My future? The world's most mysterious secrets? Was Elvis really dead? I could hardly wait! Spinning the prayer wheels faster, a sound came forth: "You—"

叭叭叭！旅行大巴的喇叭再三发出响声。

Ba-ba-ba! The tour bus's horn blasted again and again.

转经筒停止转动了。就这样，时机错过了。我的未来，世界最神秘的秘密，猫王……

The prayer wheels stopped moving. The moment was lost. What about the Lord's pardon, my future, the world's most mysterious secrets? Elvis?

回到大巴车上，为纪念猫王和在绒布旅店度过的这个凄凉的黑夜，我戴上耳机放出《伤心旅店》这首歌……

Back on the bus, I put on my headphones and played "Heartbreak Hotel" in honor of Elvis and a desolate evening spent at the Rongbuk Hostel.

Chapter 21

一个老师的忏悔
A Teacher's Regret

想当一名好老师，必须遵守几个基本规则：

To be a good teacher, you must respect a few basic rules:

1. 准时

1. Always be on time.

2. 备好课

2. Be prepared.

3. 有开放的思想

3. Have an open mind.

4. 永远不要笑话学生

4. Never laugh at your students.

我不想承认我的失败，可如果您愿意充当天主教的神父——除了上帝以外，他们是唯一能赦免天主教徒的罪的人——我想讲给你们听我作为英语老师的那段最黑暗的日子。这是我的忏悔：我嘲笑了一名学生。

I don't want to admit my failure, but if you are willing to act as my Catholic priest, the only ones outside of God who can absolve a Catholic of their sins, I'd like to tell you about my darkest day as an English teacher. This is my confession: I laughed at a student.

我第一年来中国的时候，在广西壮族自治区北海市一所外语培训学校担任英语老师，我的职责很简单：周末教小孩子，周一、周三、周五教成人初学者。

In Beihai, Guangxi, during my first year as an English teacher for a foreign language training school in China, my responsibilities were quite simple: on the weekend I taught children and on Monday, Wednesday and Friday I taught adult beginners.

在成人初级班里，有十五个学生，其中有一个老先生。每节课开始的时候，为了把他们脑子里的英文部分唤醒，我让他们做课前的热身练习。学生们互相问对方一个已学过的英文句子，回答的人可以使用已学过的答案或提供自己的答案。比如，问问题的人可以问："你好吗？"回答的人会回答："我很好。"容易极了。

In the adult beginner class, I had fifteen students, only one of which was an older gentleman. At the beginning of every class, in order to wake the English side of their brains, I'd have them begin with a warm-up exercise. The students would ask each other questions using English sentences we had previously learned. The responder could use answers that we previously learned or create their own. For example, the one asking the question could ask, "How are you?" and the responder could respond with, "I'm fine." Easy as pie.

因为那节课只是我们这学期的第三次课，还有几个新来的学生。新学生基本上是非常害羞或不太了解这个活动的。因此，我让几个对这个活动已经很熟悉的学生先来。

Because this was only the third class of that semester's course, there were some new students. New students are typically very shy or don't really comprehend the activity. Therefore, I'd allow students who were already familiar with the activity to go first.

轮到老先生的时候，我用英文对他说："好的，你是甲（问问题的人）。"我挑了一个新学生当乙（回答的人）。我对那个头发挺长，有点像是要躲在她头发里那么害羞的女生，非常温和地说："你是乙。"她没点头，我不清楚她是否明白我的意思。我想确认一下，就轻声地用英文问道："你明白我的意思吗？"她的一双大眼睛紧张地盯着我。

When it was the older man's turn, I said to him in English, "Okay, you are Person A (the one asking the question)." I chose a new student to be Person B (the one responding). I spoke very gently to a woman who seemingly wanted to hide within her hair, she was that shy, "And you are Person B." She didn't nod her head, and I wasn't sure if she understood or not. Wanting to check, I asked softly in English, "Do you understand what I mean?" Two wide eyes stared at me nervously.

突然，从我背后，甲用英文大声问："你好吗你好吗你好吗？"他说得真快，差点听不清他说了什么。

Suddenly, from behind, Person A began to repeatedly shout in English, "Howareyouhowareyouhowareyou?" He spoke so quickly you could hardly comprehend what he was saying.

我提醒他："慢一点，好吗？"可是他还是不停地喊："你好吗你好吗？"听起来像机关枪一样快：哒哒哒哒！

I reminded him, "Slower, okay?" But he continued to shout out, "Howareyouhowareyou?" It sounded like a machine gun he was that quick: "ta-ta-ta-ta!"

我转身又请他说慢一点，一个词一个词地说，语速放慢，发音清晰："你——好——吗？"可他完全不理我。乙被吓到了。幸运的是，甲终于闭上了嘴。

I turned around and again asked him to speak slower, and to say it word by word, speaking slowly and enunciating clearly: "How-are-you?" But he ignored me completely. Person B was scared stiff. Fortunately, Person A finally shut his mouth.

然后我回到那个女士的面前安慰她说："没事，你可以回答：'我很好，谢谢。'好吗？"她快速地说出："Imfunsanyuok."因为太紧张，她说不清。

Then I returned to the woman and said comfortingly, "It's okay. You can answer: 'I'm fine, thank you.' Okay?" She quickly said, "Imfunsanyuok." Because she was so nervous, she couldn't say it clearly.

我耐心地说："No, no, no."她马上跟着说："Nonono."

I patiently said, "No, no, no." She immediately said, "Nonono."

坐在她旁边的学生对她用中文说："不，不是说这个。"她还没说完，乙就模仿她，也用中文打断叫："不不不！"

The student sitting next to her said in Chinese, "No, not that." But before she could finish, Person B interrupted her and copying her words in Chinese also said, "Nonono!"

我不知道怎么做，只好说："没事的。"乙又模仿我说："Itskayitskayitskay。"

Not knowing what I should do, I only said, "It's okay." Person B again copied me and said, "Itskayitskayitskay."

正当我以为没有比这种情况更糟糕的了时，甲改变了他的英文句子，突然不停地越问越快道："你叫什么名字你叫什么名字你叫什么名字？"我觉得他有点古怪，要么就是像女同学一样紧张。在教室里，我还没碰到过那么紧张的人，没想到在一学期中能碰上两个！

Just when I thought it couldn't get any worse, Person A changed his English sentence and suddenly started to say over and over, faster each time he asked, "Whatsyournamewhatsyournamewhatsyourname?" He seemed either a bit crazy or he was as nervous as she was. I hadn't run into such a nervous person before in an English classroom and never thought I'd run into two at the same time!

"你叫什么名字你叫什么名字？"甲继续道。

"Whatsyournamewhatsyourname?" Person A continued to say.

没有逗号，没有句号，只是一连串单词。在每一个句子之间也没吸一口气！机关枪又开了：哒哒哒哒！

No comma, no periods, a stream of words and nothing more. In between the sentences he didn't even take a breath! The machine gun continued to fire: ta-ta-ta-ta!

"Wadsyonamwadsyonamwadsyonam……"乙紧张地回应了。

"Wadsyounamwadsyounamwadsyonam…" Person B nervously echoed.

"请停一下。"我对他说。

"Please, stop," I said to him.

"Peasepeasepease。"乙嘟囔着说。

"Peasepeasepease." Person B stuttered.

"请你听老师说什么。"坐在她旁边的同学用中文说。

"Please listen to the teacher," the classmate sitting next to her said in Chinese.

乙只能吐出："请请请请请请。"

Person B could only spit out, "Pleasepleasepleasepleaseplease."

不管是甲、我或坐在乙旁边的同学对她说什么，不管是英文或中文，乙都模仿我们说话。

No matter what Person A, myself or the classmate sitting next to her said to her, if in English or Chinese, Person B copied everything we said.

至此，一半的学生笑着，一半生气地看着那位男同学。我必须帮助她，这是我的责任，不能让学生的信心被伤害了。

By this time, half the students were laughing, half were staring angrily at their male classmate. I had to help her. It was my responsibility to make sure that a student's confidence wasn't hurt.

我告诉甲，让他休息一下。他不理我，坚持说："你叫什么名字？"然后我也对乙说："休息一下。"当然她仍旧模仿我说话。

I told Person A to take a break. He ignored me and persisted in saying, "Whatsyourname?" Then I said to Person B, "Take a break." Of course she only mimicked my words.

我的脸越来越红，眼里已经有眼泪了，我真受不了了。我跑到黑板后，藏起……我的……

My face was turning redder and redder and my eyes had began to produce tears. I couldn't take it. I ran behind the black board, hiding…my…

……啊，我在开什么玩笑呢，我没有哭，反而捂着嘴偷偷大笑了起来，我失控了。

…ah, who was I kidding, it was quite the contrary: I didn't want to hide my crying, I wanted to muffle my laughter, as I'd lost control.

从黑板后我能听到一个英文水平比较好的女生问道："阿文老师，你在干什么？"

From behind the blackboard I could hear a female who's English level was higher than her classmates ask in English, "Kevin, what are you doing?"

我无法回答，因为我的肚子笑疼了，眼泪开始滑过脸颊。在黑板后，我批评自己说："不要笑学生。"可是，从那里还能听见甲和乙非常奇怪的舌战在黑板前继续着。

I couldn't respond because I was laughing so hard, tears running down my face. Behind the blackboard I chastised myself, "Don't laugh at students." But, from where I was, I could still hear Person A and Person B's totally bizarre war of words continuing on the other side.

那个英文水平较高的学生走到黑板后笑着对我说："老师不可以笑学生。"

The student with the high level of English walked around the blackboard and smiling said, "A teacher cannot laugh at students."

这就是我的忏悔。

And that is my confession.

我的神父——我亲爱的读者们，求求你们，告诉我怎么做才能赎我的罪过？

"告诉我告诉我告诉我告诉我！！！"

My priests, my dear readers, I beg of you: how can I atone for my sins?
"Tellmetellmetellmetellmetellmetellme！！！"

Chapter 22

老外在说什么?
The Foreigner Said What?

　　住在地球的另一头，特别是在一个文化完全不一样，语言一点也不熟悉的国家，常常说错（英文里说：把脚放在嘴里）、做错 （基本上做事不加考虑）或想错 （文化差异），这并不意外。可对我来说，该错的地方都错了，不该错的也错了。

Living on the other side of the world, especially in a country where the culture is completely different and the language is totally unfamiliar, often saying the wrong thing (in English we say: putting your foot in your mouth), doing the wrong thing (typically acting before thinking) or misunderstanding (a cultural difference) certainly isn't surprising. But for me, you could say that wherever there was a mistake to be made, I would make one.

"双皮（屁）眼的手术"
"Double Anus Surgery"

　　想说服一个 18 岁的小姑娘别把单眼皮割成双眼皮的时候，我想要给她介绍一个后悔把单眼皮做成双眼皮的朋友。当她们两个见面时，我把那两个中文字"眼皮"搞反了，把"皮"放在"眼"的前面，傻傻地说："这是我朋友，她想割双皮（屁）眼。"当然，她们都脸红了，一起惊讶地说："什么？"

　　When hoping to convince an eighteen-year old girl not to go ahead with double-eyelid surgery, I wanted to introduce her to a friend who regretted changing her single eyelids into double-eyelids. When they met, I mixed up the two Chinese characters "yan pi（eyelids）," putting the "pi" before the "yan" totally changing the meaning and foolishly said, "This is my friend, she wants double anus surgery." Of course their faces both turned red and said together in surprise, "What?"

"给你孩子。"
"Give you a baby."

　　我们住的楼盘老总请我老板、两个英文老师和我一起吃饭，因为想让他快要去加拿大留学的 19 岁女儿练习英文。晚饭我吃得很撑，胃发胀了。我拍了拍肚子，想暗示我像怀孕一样，开玩笑地说："我的baby。"大家都笑了。然后我转头对他女儿用我很烂的中文说："我可以给你孩子。"除了那两个明白我意思的英文老师外，没人笑，鸦雀无声。我老板和女孩的父亲盯着我看，她母亲则脸红了。我原本只是想说："多吃一点吧！"这样她的肚子就会像我的一样凸出。没想到大家误会我说：让她怀孕！

有些玩笑真的不能直译。

The owner of the complex where we were living invited our boss, two other English teachers and myself to dinner so his nineteen-year old daughter who planned to go abroad and study in Canada could practice her English. After dinner I was stuffed and my stomach was bloated. I patted my stomach, implying I was pregnant, and jokingly said, "My baby." Everyone laughed. Then I turned to his daughter and said in broken Chinese, "I can give you a baby." Besides the two English teachers who understood, no one laughed, and it was completely silent. My boss and her father glared at me, and her mother's face turned red. I only wanted to say, "Eat some more," and her belly would extend outwards like mine. I never thought they'd misinterpret it as: get her pregnant!

Some jokes really shouldn't be translated.

" 我 要 鸡 乳 房 。 "
"I want chicken breast."

站在德克士快餐厅的服务台前，我对年轻女服务员说："我要鸡乳房。"她看着我，不明白。我又慢一点说："鸡乳房。"我有点不好意地用手势比画一下我的胸部，又说："鸡乳房。"这时，她的脸色比煮熟的龙虾还要红，说："你的意思是鸡胸？"我才发现我错了。

在英文里，我们说鸡乳房，可在中文里……你们都知道。

Standing before the Dicos fast food restaurant counter, I said to the young waitress, "I want chicken breast." She stared at me and didn't understand. I said it again slower, "chicken breast." A bit embarrassed, I used my hands to gesture towards my chest and again said, "chicken breast." At this time, her face redder than a lobster's, she said, "Do you mean chicken chest?" I finally realized my mistake.

In English we say chicken breast, but in Chinese…well, you all know.

"玩纸钱是不吉利的！"
"You can't play with ghost money!"

在给小学生上英语购物课时，我不想给他们真正的钱练习买东西。所以，我准备了一些在一家卖香火的佛教商店里买的假币，我自己以为这是一个好主意，也非常实用！上课的时候，小学生小手里都是假币，老板在窗外看我上课。我以为她想进来恭喜我想出好方法，可是她进来就着急地说："你干什么呢？这是纸钱！烧给下界的！玩纸钱是不吉利的！"

我应该把那些为幼儿园上课用而买的纸娃娃、纸房子、纸车子，等等，退给那家卖香火的商店。

阿弥陀佛！

When giving elementary school students a lesson on shopping, I didn't want to give them real money to practice purchasing items. So, I prepared some fake money that I had bought from an incense store for Buddhists. I thought, what a great idea and how practical! While teaching them, their little hands full of the fake money, the boss decided at that moment to watch the class from the window. I thought she was going to come in and congratulate me on a great method, but she came in and said nervously, "What are you doing? This is ghost money! It is burned for the underworld! Playing with ghost money is bad luck!"

I should probably return the paper dolls, houses, cars, etc. that I had bought from that incense store to use in my kindergarten classes.

Amituofo.

"那是个很好的例子！"
"That was a very good example!"

在一个朋友的家里，我看到一本李阳疯狂英语的口袋书。我大声朗读那本书后面的文字："想要听起来像一个美国人，您需要把一切夸张一点！"感觉这话太荒唐了，我就把书向对面墙上扔过去叫道："胡说八道！"我的朋友笑着说："阿文，你现在就是一个很好的例子。谢谢。"我只能低声地抱怨。

Visiting a friend's home, I came across one of Li Yang's Crazy English pocketbooks. I read the back of the book out loud, "To sound like an American, you need to exaggerate everything!" Thinking it a ridiculous thing to say, I threw the book across the room and shouted, "What a load of garbage!" My friend laughed and said, "That was a great example of how American's exaggerate, Kevin. Thank you." I could only grumble quietly.

"你是没有眼睛的人吗？"

"Are you a person with no eyes?"

我躺在按摩床上问按摩师："你是没有眼睛的人吗？"他笑着回答："你是想问我是不是盲人？"那次错误之后，我永远也忘不了怎么称呼看不见的人。我一边再三抱歉一边惭愧地把脸埋进床洞里。

幸好，他看不见我的脸是什么颜色！

Lying on a massage bed I asked the masseuse, "Are you a person with no eyes?" He laughed and answered, "Do you mean am I blind?" After that mistake, I would never forget how to address a person who cannot see. I repeatedly said I was sorry as I buried my face in the bed's face hole ashamed.

Fortunately, he couldn't see the color of my face!

"妈在家里。"

"Mom's at home."

在澳门看赛马时我问坐在我旁边的人："你妈在哪里？"他回答："在家里。"我："在家里？""不，你的妈，"我指向赛马说。他说："哦，我的马，"他重读了"马"的第三声，"不是我的妈。"他重读了"妈"的第一声调。

我们的马都输了。到于他的老妈，谁知道呢。

In Macau watching a horse race I asked the person sitting next to me,

"Where's your mom?" He answered, "At home." Me, "At home?" I asked again, "No, your mother," and pointed towards the horse race. He said, "Oh, my horse," he emphasized the third tone on 'horse', "not my mom," he said emphasizing the first tone on 'mom.'

Our horses both lost. And his mother, well who knows.

"什么时候当鸡？"
"When were you a chicken？"

教成人学生（都是女生）一些美国俚语的时候我问她们："你们什么时候当鸡？"（按照美国俚语，叫别人"鸡"的时候，意思是那个人怕什么东西：你什么时候害怕？）没有人回答。我又问了几次，但是真的不明白为什么她们都不敢回答。我们以前都曾被什么东西吓到过，不是吗？最后，我的助教在我耳边小声地说："在中文里鸡有妓女的意思。"

明显我的学生是害怕她们的老师问出很尴尬的问题。

While teaching adult students (they were all female) some American slang, I asked them, "When were you a chicken?" (According to American slang, when someone calls another chicken, the meaning is that they are afraid of something: as in when were you afraid?) But no one answered. I asked a few more times, but I really couldn't understand why no one dared to answer. Haven't we all been frightened by something before? Finally, my assistant whispered in my ear, "In Chinese, chicken means prostitute."

Apparently my students' only fear is their teacher asking embarrassing questions.

"你的坟墓在哪里？"

"Where is your tomb?"

清明节时我问工厂的总经理："你的坟墓在哪里？"他脸都发白了，认真地说："阿文先生，不要那样说。该说：'你的祖先的坟墓在哪里？'"我才意识到自己犯了错。

好像我刚才在自掘坟墓！

During Tomb Sweeping Festival I asked a factory's managing director, "Where is your tomb?" His face blanching, he said earnestly, "Mr. Kevin, don't say it like that. You should say, 'Where is your ancestor's tomb?'" I realized my mistake.

It would seem I had just dug my own grave!

"都是中文，你还是笨。"

"They're both Chinese and you're still stupid."

有一次我带外婆和其他亲戚一起去我老家的唐人街（特别小，只有两个饭店）吃饭。外婆认为我住在中国有点浪费时间，住了三年多，可是还不会说中文，她说我该给他们表演一下，用中文跟服务员交流。我对服务员说："一瓶啤酒。"他茫然地盯着我。我又放慢语速重复了一遍，可他仍然听不懂。最后经理出来了，说："不好意思，服务员不懂普通话，只懂广东话。"我给外婆一个简短的解释："他们只懂广东话，不懂普通话。"

外婆讽刺地回答："都是中文，你还是笨。"

One time I brought my grandmother and relatives to the Chinatown (it's really small, only two restaurants) in my hometown to eat. Because my grandmother thought my living in China was a waste of my time as she felt I had lived there for three years, and still couldn't speak Chinese, my grandmother said I should give them a little performance and use Chinese to communicate with the waiters. I said to the waiter in Chinese, "One bottle of beer." He stared blankly at me. I repeated it again slower, but again he didn't understand. Finally the manager came out and said, "Sorry, the waiters don't understand Mandarin, they can only understand Cantonese." I gave my grandmother a short and simple explanation, "They could only speak Cantonese, not Mandarin."

My grandmother responded sarcastically, "They're both Chinese and you're still stupid."

Chapter 23

"老内"在说什么?
What Did the Chinese Person Say?

当您碰到来自地球的另一头,一个文化完全不一样、语言一点也不熟悉的国家的人时,有时候会说错、做错或想错并不意外。可是,孔子不是曾经说过:不迁怒,不贰过?不管你认为丢不丢脸,根据中国古人的思想和德国的哲学家尼采的理论:大难不死,必有后福,我们怕什么?因此,您还在等什么?马上出门,把你的脸皮锻炼一下,越丢脸,脸皮越厚!

When you run into someone who is from the other side of the world, especially in a country where the culture is completely different and the language is totally unfamiliar, sometimes saying the wrong thing, doing the wrong thing or misunderstanding certainly isn't surprising. But hadn't Confucius once said, "There are no errors, only lessons"? No matter who thought who lost face, following Ancient Chinese and according to the

German philosopher Friedrich Nietzsche's opinion: what doesn't kill you only makes you stronger; what are we afraid of? Therefore, what are you waiting for? Everyone, head out at once, and exercise your face a bit. The more you lose face, the thicker-skinned you'll become!

一个迟钝的更衣室服务员： "这个。"
A slow-witted locker room attendant: "This."

在洗浴中心里，我刚洗完澡正用小毛巾擦干身体时，发现一个服务员小伙子一直盯着我。我感觉很尴尬，因为那时候我只穿着我的"天然毛衣"，意思是除了汗毛以外，我全身都裸露着。过了几分钟后，我还能感受到他的余光在我身上，我有点不耐烦地问："你在看什么？"他走到我面前，离我很近，大约二十厘米左右，伸出手，把我的一根胸毛拔了出来，最后说："这个。"离我那么近站着，他居然迟钝到没发现这是我身体的一部分。

不知道我的那根胸毛怎么样了。

In a spa, after showering, using a small hand towel to dry myself off, I noticed a young man staring at me. I felt embarrassed because at the time I was wearing nothing but my "natural sweater", which meant besides my body hair, I was totally naked. After a few minutes, still feeling his eyes on my body, I really couldn't take it anymore. Slightly impatient I asked, "What are you looking at?" He walked up to me, standing too close, about twenty centimeters, and reaching out his hand, he plucked out one of my chest hairs and then said, "This." Standing so close to me I could finally see that he was slow-witted.

I don't know whatever became of that hair.

一个姑娘： "你吃吧，你是外国人，外国人喜欢吃面包。"
A girl: "Eat, you are a foreigner, foreigners like to eat bread."

有一次一个姑娘开摩托车到我家接我。我开门的时候，看到她站在门外，双手拿着一大条面包。我问她："这是什么？"她回答："面包，送给你。"我："好吧，谢谢。"我准备把面包放在家里，然后陪她去外面，可她说："嘿，你不想吃？"我："现在？"她："是啊，你吃吧，你是外国人，外国人喜欢吃面包。"我笑着问："嘿，如果我拿着一大碗米饭走到你家门口，说：'你吃吧，你是中国人，中国人喜欢吃米饭。'你会怎么想？是不是很奇怪？"她一下子回答："当然，是非常奇……"

她没说完，已经领会了我的意思。

One time a girl rode her motorbike over to pick me up. When I opened the door, I saw her standing outside of the door holding a loaf of bread in her hands. I asked her, "What's this?" She answered, "Bread for you." Me, "Okay, thanks." Planning to place the bread inside and head out with her, she said, "Hey, don't you want to eat it?" Me, "Now?" Her, "Yes, go ahead and eat, you are a foreigner, foreigners like to eat bread." Laughing I asked, "Hey, if I walked up to your front door holding a big bowl of rice and said, 'Go ahead and eat, you are Chinese, Chinese like eating rice.' What would you think?

That's not a little strange?" She immediately responded with, "Of course, that's really stra—."

She didn't need to finish as she got my point.

好几个美女："你像孙悟空。"
More than one pretty girl: "You look like the Monkey King."

有女孩问我道："你知道你像孙悟空吗？"我惊讶地回答："孙悟空？好恐怖！"她说："不，孙悟空很幽默，而且非常聪明。"我最后可怜地说："可是，他是猴子。"

I was asked, "Do you know you look like the Monkey King?" I could only respond in shock, "The Monkey King? That's terrible!" She said, "But no, the Monkey King is very funny and very clever." I finally said pathetically, "But, he's a monkey."

一个过度保护的轮渡保安："有风，你会感冒！"
An over-protective guard on a ferry: "You will catch a cold."

有一次，我和其他五个男人站在渡轮的甲板上吸烟，保安让我们进船舱去，其他人都进去了。我问道："为什么？"他厉声叫道："为什么？！"所以，我又问："是，为什么？"他有点自言自语地反问道："他问为什么？"此时，那些吸烟者们都决定留在外面继续抽烟。然后保安喊道："外面很危险！"那天风和日丽。所以，我问道："为什么危险？"他愤怒地反驳："会掉进水里！"我说："但是我会游泳。"
他回答："水很咸！"我不知道怎么回答，有点沮丧。他终于说："有
风，你会感冒的！"因为他说得很体贴，我服了。我们都走进船舱了。
然后，保安锁上了主舱门。密封在船舱里，即使轮渡沉没都没办法逃跑，
我感觉更"安全"了。

不过至少我不会感冒了。

Once while standing on the deck at the back of a ferry waiting to depart,
a guard told me and five men who were smoking to go inside. The five
men started to head into the main cabin. I asked, "Why?"He snapped back,
"WHY?" So I repeated myself, "Yes, why?" He retorted, more to himself, "He
asked WHY?" At this point, the five men decided to stay outside and continue
smoking. Then the guard shouted, "It's dangerous out here!" It was a clear,
sunny day. So I asked, "Why is it dangerous?" With indignation he snapped,
"You could fall in the water!" I said, "But I can swim." He responded with,
"But it is salty!" I didn't know how to respond to that. A little dejected, he
finally said, "It's windy, you will catch a cold!" That was considerate of him
and I relented. We headed into the main cabin. The guard locked the door.
Sealing us in, with no chance of escape if the ferry sank, I felt much "safer".

At least I wouldn't catch a cold.

亚裔女学生："她阿姨四了。"
A female Asian-American student: "Her aunt 4' ed."

我在美国一所高中的中国俱乐部当领导时，一个三年级的亚裔美国

女学生用英文对我说："阿文，玛利亚今天不能来上课，她阿姨四了。"我不明白。她提醒我："阿文，你没听说在中文里数字四有两个意思，一个就是数字 4，另一个象征'死'的意思？"我："是，中国人不喜欢四号，因为他们认为那个四字的发音听起来像死字。"

她转动了一下眼睛说："所以，她阿姨四了。"

In America acting as the head of a high school's Chinese club, a female Asian-American junior said to me in English, "Kevin, Maria can't come today, her aunt 4'ed." I didn't understand. She reminded me, "Kevin, didn't you say that in Chinese the number 4 has two meanings, one is the number four, and the other can symbolize 'death'?" Me, "Yes, Chinese don't like the number 4 because they believe it sounds similar to the character for death."

Rolling her eyes, she said, "So, her aunt 4'ed."

成人学生："你是……野蛮人。"
Adult student: "You are…savage."

在我第一年来到中国，跟几个成人学生一起吃饭的时候，除了我以外他们吃炸鸡都戴上了一次性手套。当我舔着我油腻的手指时他们都盯着我看，一个学生开始用英文说："你是……"可不知道她想表达的东西用英文怎么说，所以她把想说的单词输入了翻译机器，然后她把翻译机器递给我。那上面显示着一个英文单词：野蛮人。那天我才意识到，在中国，舔手指很不礼貌。

从那时起，吃炸鸡没有以前好玩了，可我至少成了更礼貌的人！好郁闷。

During my first year in China while eating with a few adult students, everyone put on disposable gloves to eat fried chicken except for me. While I was licking my greasy fingers they were all staring at me, and one student began to say in English, "You are…" But not knowing how to say what she wanted to, she used an electronic translator to input the word she wanted to say. She then handed me the electronic translator. It displayed a single English word: savage. That day I realized that in China it was really rude to lick your fingers.

From then on, eating fried chicken just wasn't as fun as before. But at least I was a more polite person! How depressing.

本地官员："我听不懂英文。"
Local officer: "I don't understand English."

有一次，做英语比赛的裁判时，我用英文对另外一个裁判说："哇，这个学生的英文真不错。"那个裁判，一个秃顶的把两侧头发横着梳的中年人用中文懒散地回答："什么？"我又说慢一点。他又回答道："什么？我听不懂英语。"因为这是一场本地学校的重大赛事，我回身问坐在我后面的老板："嘿，这不是一场英文比赛吗？"她说："是啊。"我说："但是我旁边的裁判不懂英文。"她说："没有关系。"我讽刺地说："没有关系？"她平静地说："他是一个本地官员。没有关系。"

第一百遍听学生演唱来自著名电影《音乐之声》版本的《雪绒花》时，我把握到了"关系"的含义：对于有些人来说，没有关系就是因为他们有"关系"。

Acting as a judge for an English competition, I said in English to another judge, "Wow, this student's English is really good." The judge, a middle-aged man with a combover, responded lazily in Chinese, "What?" I repeated myself slowly. He again responded with, "What? I don't understand English." Shocked, as he was a judge for a local school's major English competition, I turned around and asked my boss who was sitting behind, "Hey, isn't this an English competition?" She said, "Yes." And I said, "But the judge next to me doesn't understand English." She said, "It doesn't matter." I said sarcastically, "It doesn't matter?" She said calmly, "He's a local official. It doesn't matter."

Listening to yet another student sing the dreaded song *Edelweiss* from the movie *Sound of Music* for the hundredth time, I grasped the implications of "Guanxi": for some, it really doesn't matter because they "mattered".

一个好奇心很重的小男孩："你是外国人吗？"

A curious little boy: "Are you a foreigner?"

我在上海市的松江郊区骑自行车，中途在一家小商店门口停车买水。商店外有一个小男孩，大约十岁左右。他上下打量着我，问道："你是外国人？"我反问道："你看不出来？"他说："不一定。"我说："我个子挺高。"他说："是的。""我的鼻子很大。"他点了点头同意了。我弯下腰让他看我的眼睛，问："我的眼睛是什么颜色？"他说："蓝色或者绿色。"然后我说:"我的脸很红。"他问:"那正常吗?"我说:"对我来说正常。"他指向我胳膊上的汗毛,并摸了一下,似乎想证实他的怀疑,接着又点了点头。最后,他说:"嘿,如果你真是外国人,你为什么没说外国话?"

Biking in Songjiang, one of Shanghai's suburbs, I stopped to buy water at a small shop. Outside of the shop was a small boy, perhaps ten years old or so. He looked me up and down and asked, "Are you a foreigner?" I then asked him, "Can't you tell?" He said, "I'm not sure." So I said, "I'm quite tall." He said, "Yep." "My nose is fairly large." He nodded his head in agreement. Bending down so he could see my eyes, I asked, "What color are my eyes?" He said, "blue or green." Then I said, "And my face is quite red." He asked, "Is that normal?" I said, "Well, only for me." He pointed towards the hair on my arm and started to touch them. He then nodded his head up and down as if confirming his suspicions. Finally, he said, "Hey, if you really are a foreigner, why aren't you speaking a foreign language?"

九岁的小朋友:有时候,行动胜于言辞。
Seven-year old child: Sometimes, actions speak louder than words.

在昆明市留学的时候,我兼职做英语老师。有一天,在一个初级班上,小学生都在考试。十个小孩在答题,其中一个想做其他事:那个小女孩先偷看右边,再看左边,接下来发现没有同学注意到她时,在桌子下她慢慢把一些纸卷成几个球。然后她一边假装考试,一边把纸球一个一个地装进她的衬衫胸袋里。因为她太注意同学是否看到她在干什么，所以完全忘记了还有老师站在教室里。把纸球装好后，她用小手从衬衫外把里面的纸团塑造成了一个小"馒头"。最后她试着把她的小胸部突起来，抬起了头，露出一个非常骄傲的笑容，有点像是在说："大家看看，我长大了，你们的同学成为女人了！"她想显示她作为女人的一小部分，可是有一个问题：在她的小胸膛上只有一个"馒头"长出来了。

好像第二个还在蒸笼里蒸着。

While in Kunming as an overseas student, I was a part-time English teacher. One day in a beginner's class all of the primary school students were taking a test. Ten were taking the test, but one wanted to do something else. A little girl first sneaked a glance right and then left and once she was satisfied that her classmates weren't paying attention to what she planned to do, she slowly crumpled a piece of paper into a ball beneath her desk. Then while pretending to take the test, one after another, she stuffed the paper balls inside her shirt. Because she was focusing on whether or not her classmates could see what she was doing, she completely forgot about the teacher standing in front of the classroom. At first I didn't know what she wanted to do, but with each additional ball stuffed beneath her shirt, her "plan" quite literally began to take shape. After she finished stuffing paper balls, from the outside of her shirt she used her little hand to shape what appeared to be a small "steamed bun". Finally she tried to stick her small chest outwards, and lifting her head she revealed a very proud smile as if she wanted to say, "Look, everyone, I've grown up, your classmate has become a woman!" She wanted to display her little womanly part, but there was one problem: in the center of her little chest there was only one "steamed bun" growing outwards.

It would seem the second one was still in the steamer steaming.

好奇的服务员："为什么你们老外的姓名中间有一个点？"
A curious waitress: "Why do you foreigners have a dot between the family and given name?"

在一家机场的饭店，一个服务员很真诚地问我："为什么你们老外的姓名中间有一个点？"一开始我不懂她的意思。她解释说："比如，在报纸或杂志里我看到在你们姓名的中间有一个点。那个点代表什么？"直到她举了个例子，我才明白她的意思。我说："这样让读者理解名在哪里结束，姓在哪里开始，没什么代表，举个例子：凯文·史密斯。"

又一次，神秘比现实更有趣。

At an airport restaurant, a waitress asked sincerely, "Why do you foreigners have a dot between the family and given name?" At first I didn't understand her. She explained, "For example, in a newspaper or a magazine I've seen a dot between your family names and given names. What does the dot represent?" I still didn't understand until she actually wrote down an example. Then I understood what she meant. I said, "It allows the reader to know where the given name ends and where the family name begins, it doesn't represent anything, for example Kevin · Smith."

Once again, a mystery is preferable over reality.

隔壁的老人：“不比姚明高。”
An old neighbor："Not taller than Yao Ming."

在电梯里跟一个老人上楼的时候，他看了我一眼。然后他把手伸到头上说："你多高？"我回答："一米八九。"走出电梯，他摇了摇头，仿佛我的答案不尽人意。他骄傲地说："不比姚明高。"

While in an elevator with an old man, he looked at me. Then he stretched his hand over his head and said, "How tall are you?" I answered, "One-hundred and eighty-nine centimeters." Walking out of the elevator, shaking his head as my answer failed to impress, he responded proudly, "Not taller than Yao Ming."

中国商人：“前面的老外做错了！”
Chinese businessman："The foreigner upfront made a mistake."

我在韩国海关排队，几个中国商人站在我前面。一个指向前排说："你看，前面的老外造成延迟了。"在前排的是一个白人。我忍不住有点调皮地说："对不起，先生，在这里你也是老外。"他没回答，但是表情在说：给我闭嘴！

Standing in line at South Korean immigration, a few Chinese businessmen were standing in front of me. One pointed to the front of the line and said, "Look, the foreigner upfront is causing a delay." In front of the line was a white person. A little unable to resist, I said a little mischievously, "Excuse me, sir, you are also a foreigner here." He didn't respond, but his expression shouted: would you shut-up?!

很多人："外国？"
Many people："Foreign country?"

"在中国我们用筷子。在外国呢？" "我听不懂外国话。" "中国人用筷子，外国呢？" "中国人喜欢吃辣椒。外国人呢？" 我还不是很清楚"外国"在什么地方，那里的总统／总理／主席是谁，那里的国歌怎么唱，那里的国旗是什么样子或那里人讲什么语言。我只知道那里不在中国，那里的人不会说中文，不会用筷子，也很可能不会吃辣椒。

"In China we use chopsticks. What about in 'foreign country'?" "I don't understand 'foreign language.'" "China uses chopsticks, what about 'foreign country'?" "China likes chili peppers. Do 'Foreigners' like to eat them?" I'm not exactly clear where "foreign country" is, who their president/prime minister/chairman is, how to sing their national song, what the flag looks like, what language the people speak, but I know it's not in China, they don't speak Chinese, don't use chopsticks and probably don't eat chili peppers.

Chapter 24

神秘的现象：10 度和 20 度没有区别？

A Mysterious Phenomenon: No Difference Between Ten and Twenty Degrees?

　　每年大约三月中旬，气温达到 15 度到 20 度的时候，在我周围常常能听到这样的声音："你看，因为老外从小吃牛肉所以身体很强壮"或"外国人喜欢喝牛奶所以不怕冷"或"因为有汗毛"或简言之"他有毛病！"

　　Every year around the middle of March, when the temperatures surpass fifteen to twenty degrees, I regularly hear, "Look! It is because foreigners ate meat since they were little, their bodies are strong," or "Foreigners like to drink milk so they aren't afraid of the cold," or "because they have body hair," or simply, "They're crazy!"

　　他们指的是什么？不过就是一个外国人的小腿和手臂露出来了。

　　And what exactly are they referring to? I can only imagine it is the exposed calves and arms of a foreigner.

在冬天转向春天的过程中，我骑着自行车，再一次遇到这非常神秘的、有点奇怪的中国现象：10度到20度的气温下，人们穿衣看起来没有区别。

During that period, when winter gives way to spring, peddling my bike, I'm once again able to come across this very mysterious, fairly strange Chinese phenomenon: there is seemingly no difference in temperature between ten degrees and twenty degrees.

首先我想说，各位——我的读者们，应该更理解我的天性。在我看来世界上有两种人：花和蘑菇。我是花，需要去外面感受阳光；蘑菇不需要介绍，大家也知道，他们像"宅男""宅女"一样，都更喜欢留在室内。因为花在冬天很难过，所以当温度达到15到20度时，我就出门把花开起来！穿得少，让我多毛的花瓣晒一会，振作被冬天偷走的精神！

I'd like to take a moment to explain to you, the readers, my nature so that you may better understand. In my opinion there are two kinds of people in the world: flowers and mushrooms. I'm a flower. Flowers need to go outside and feel the sunshine. Mushrooms don't need an introduction as everyone knows mushrooms are akin to homebodies, they prefer staying indoors. Because it is very hard for this flower in the winter, it is no surprise that when coming across temperatures exceeding fifteen to twenty degrees, I will go outside and blossom! Wearing less, I allow my hairy petals to bask in the sun, invigorating the energy that was stolen from the winter to return!

可是我没时间回答，我只能让他们指指点点，仿佛我是一只从动物园里逃出来的长臂猿。

But I was having too good a time riding my bike and had no time to respond. I could only allow them to point at me as if I was an escaped gibbon from the zoo.

但是，我也有我感到奇怪的问题："如果上星期温度是 10 度，而这星期升温到 20 度，为什么你们衣服的穿法却没有改变？"

But, thinking about it, this gibbon had his own question he wanted to ask, "If the temperature was ten degrees last week, but this week it's twenty degrees, why hasn't your dressing style changed?"

我没说清楚？好吧，我再解释一下。我的意思是，不管温度是 10 度还是 20 度，大多数本地人的穿着都一样，包括：内裤、上下身保暖内衣、T 恤、衬衫、毛衣、夹克、外套、手套、针织帽。跟我相比，他们是能走路的胖棉花球，而我是半裸体！因此，对我来说，这种行为不太正常：温度有 10 度的差异，但是穿衣没差别。

Did I not make myself clear? Okay, let me try to explain again: what I mean is, no matter if the temperature is ten degrees or twenty degrees, most of the locals are wearing the same: a few layers of clothing, including underwear, long underwear, both tops and bottoms, a t-shirt, a shirt, a sweater, a jacket, a coat, gloves and a knit cap. Compared to how I dressed, they looked like big, fat walking cotton balls where as I was half-naked! Therefore, to me, this kind of behavior wasn't normal: there was a ten-degree difference, but the clothes were no different.

请让我给你讲一个现实生活中的例子：

Please allow me to give you a real life example:

有一天在办公室里，同事走进来抱怨说："天啊，我热死了，被汗水湿透了！"我转身问道："你还穿着保暖内衣？"她说："当然！"我说："今天气温不是有 20 度？"她说："是啊，20 度，怎么了？"

One day at our office a coworker came in complaining, "My gosh, I'm burning up and soaked in sweat!" I turned around and asked, "Are you still wearing long underwear?" She said, "Of course!" And I said, "Isn't the temperature today twenty degrees?" She said, "Yep, it's twenty, what about it?"

另外一个同事说："没错，阿文，这几天有点暖和，可还是冬天。"

Another coworker said, "That's right, Kevin, these days it's fairly warm, but it's still winter."

我回答："但是天气很好，可以穿得少一点！"

I answered, "But the weather is quite nice, you can wear a bit less!"

她："那不行，还是冬天。"

Her, "Nope, it's still winter."

我："但是温度变了，增加了 10 度！"

Me, "But the temperature has changed and has gone up ten degrees!"

她："但还是冬天。这些天的暖和温度不是真的。这是一种假热。"

Her, "But its still winter. These days the warmer temperatures aren't real. This is a kind of fake heat."

暖和温度不是真的？一种假热？我知道中国的"山寨"市场比较有创意，但是没想到暖和也被"山寨"过！连上帝都没有版权！

The warm temperatures aren't real? A kind of fake heat? I know the Chinese knock-off market is quite creative, but I never would have thought that warmth could also be copied? Even God doesn't possess a copyright!

我也听说过一个原因是根据传统中医理论：人类必须保护内火。如果内火发泄出来就很危险，对健康不利，很容易感冒。有道理，该尊重特定的古老做法，比如我由衷地相信和坚信针灸和中草药。但是，对温度现象，人类身体难道不能自然适应？中国人和西方人的内火条件不一样吗？是因为我们西方人从小喝牛奶和吃牛肉比较多，对外面条件的抵抗力就比东方人更强？这是为什么牦牛特别暖和，能在山顶上生存的原因？是因为它们就是牛肉和牛奶做的，而且毛特别多？我真的不太懂。

I've also heard a reason is due to following traditional Chinese medicine: people must protect their warmth, an internal heat. And if the heat escapes it is very dangerous and bad for their health and it's easy to catch a cold. This makes sense and certain ancient practices deserve respect, for example I sincerely believe and support acupuncture and herbal medicine. But, in regards to the temperature phenomenon, don't people's bodies naturally adjust? Aren't Chinese and western people's internal heat conditions the same? Was it because we've fed our own internal heat with milk and beef since we were children making our resistance to outside conditions stronger than Easterner? Is this why yak fur is so warm and they can survive on the mountaintops? Is it because they are made of beef and milk, and they have a lot of fur? I really don't understand.

　　这将引向另一个重要概念：脚底是整个身体的"火气门"。起初我也不能明白为什么本地人一看我在 20 度穿着拖鞋，就说："他疯了！"我原来认为头是最重要的，必须好好戴上帽子，但是在中国这种想法被颠覆了，火气能从脚底下排泄出来。因此，我们的最下面——脚是最重要的。在冬天，这方面我很能理解。可是，顺便问一下，在夏天我也常常看到美女穿着很漂亮的高跟鞋，同时穿着一双比较适合老奶奶穿的到脚踝的丝袜，这是为了不让火气排泄出去吗？如果我们的火气那么弱的话，一层薄薄的尼龙就能担当身体的守门人？

　　This leads me to another important concept: the bottoms of our feet are the entire body's "gateway for internal heat". At first I couldn't understand why upon seeing me wearing sandals in twenty degrees the locals would say, "You're crazy!" I originally thought that the top was the most important, and you must make sure to wear a hat, but in China this kind of thinking is turned on its head. It wasn't the very top part that needed good protection, but I discovered that in fact internal heat is released through the bottom of our feet. Therefore, the lowest part, our feet are the most important. In the winter I can really comprehend this. But, is this also why in the summer I often see beautiful girls wearing very attractive high heels, while at the same time wearing a pair of ankle stockings that are more suitable for old grannies, because they are worried their internal heat will leak out? If it is, is our internal heat so weak that a flimsy layer of nylon can act as the body's gatekeeper?

我以前也跟朋友开玩笑："你们是要等到国家新闻机构播出正式公告说：各位，今天可以把保暖内衣脱掉！"但是几年过后我意识到那不是一种玩笑，是现实。严格说来，四季是四季，分成四部分，春夏秋冬，每一部分有三个月。但是，新闻媒体和气象学家会公开宣布各个季节什么时候开始，什么时候结束，比如：连续 5 天平均温度 10 度以下就是冬天了，中国的冬天开始！或者连续 5 天平均温度 10 度以上就是春天，中国的春天开始！因此，我的理解是，在新闻报道冬天开始时，大家就都把保暖内衣拿出来穿上。在美国，每年 12 月 21 日——冬至，我们的冬天开始；3 月 20 日——春分，冬天结束。因此，每年在日历上都标记了一样的日期，电视或政府都不需要提醒我们。

Previously I joked with friends, "You must wait until the state-run news agency makes a public announcement: 'Masses, today it is okay to take off your long underwear!'" But a few years later I realized that it wasn't a joke but reality. Technically, four seasons are four seasons, divided into four parts, spring, summer, fall and winter, and each has three months, but officially the government, the news and meteorologists must announce when each begins and ends, for example: five consecutive days of temperatures below ten degrees is winter, and Chinese winter begins! Or five consecutive days of temperatures above ten degrees is spring, Chinese spring begins! Therefore, my understanding is, when the news reports that winter has begun, everyone pulls out their long underwear and puts them on. Perhaps this is why people wait for the news report. In America winter begins every year on December twenty-first, the winter solstice. And on March twentieth, the vernal equinox, winter ends. Therefore, as the dates are the same every year and marked as such on all printed calendars, neither the television nor the government needs to remind us.

可是，如果是按照正式公告，我该接着问："按照哪里的温度计算？"我估计是北京，因为虽然根据国家的面积，中国应该拥有四五个时区，但事实上不管在哪里，人们基本都以北京时间为准。在我的想象中，故宫又宽广又位于城市中心，在故宫的后院里立着一个巨大的温度计，天天通知温度是多少。

But, if it is in accordance with the official announcement, then I should ask, "According to whose thermometer?" I figure this would be in Beijing because, even though China should have four to five time zones based on its size, it only has one and Chinese time is basically in accordance with Beijing time no matter where you are in China. In my imagination, because the Forbidden Palace is so wide and centralized, in its back courtyard stands a giant thermometer and everyday it notifies the heads in charge what the temperature is.

但这就又提出了另外一个很复杂的问题：因为中国挺大，很多地方离北京挺远，所以那个巨大的温度计怎么能准确地预见在那些遥远的地方冬天什么时候开始、什么时候结束？举个例子，在中国的最南方地区之一：广西壮族自治区北海市，我教孩子的时候，老板常对我说："请你不要穿短袖的衬衫，会让学生的父母认为你有毛病。""但是温度超过20度了。"我反驳。她认为我太过分了，不耐烦地说："你看看，小学生们都穿着两三条裤子！"我忍不住说："但是，你看看，在他们小毛衣领后都有一条小毛巾，因为他们都出了很多汗。"

But this only brings up yet another very complicated question: because China is so big, and many places are far from Beijing, how could that giant thermometer accurately predict when winter begins and ends in those distant places? For example, in one of China's most southern parts: Guangxi, Beihai, when I was teaching children, the boss would often said to me, "Please don't wear short sleeve shirts, you'll make the students' parents think you are crazy." "But it's over twenty-some degrees," I'd retort. Believing I was being unreasonable, she'd say impatiently, "Look, the students are wearing two to three pairs of pants!" Unable to resist, I'd say, "But, look, they all have small towels stuffed behind the collars of their little sweaters because they are all sweating."

好的，我不说了，我越思考这种现象就越复杂！但是我真希望某一天能明白它。我的个性已经被我在中国的亲身经历改变了很多，比如：我变成了更谦虚的人，耐心也稍有提升了，我甚至认为温水比冰水好喝。我非常感谢这些改变，中国，我实在是喜欢！所以，如果对这种神秘的10度和20度没差别的现象有误解之处，请你谅解，因为我总是想明白发生在我周围的事情。

Okay, I won't say anymore, the more I think about this phenomenon, the more complex the phenomenon becomes! But I really hope that someday I will be able to understand it. My experiences in China have already influenced my personality in many ways, for example: I've become a more humble person, my patience has increased slightly and I now prefer drinking warm water to cold. I really appreciate these changes, China, I really do! So if there is something I'm misunderstanding about the mysterious ten-degree non-differential phenomenon, please let me know as I'm always trying to better understand what takes place around me.

如果某一天，你又一次发现自己指着一头穿着短裤、T 恤、拖鞋，骑自行车的牦牛说："那个骑自行车的半裸体的老外有毛病吗？穿那么少，今天又不热！"事先想一想，有可能那个老外也看着你说："那个走路的厚厚胖胖的棉花球准备爬珠峰吗？穿了那么多，今天又不冷呀！"

Until that day, the next time you find yourself pointing at a yak dressed in shorts, a t-shirt and sandals riding a bicycle saying, "Is that half-naked foreigner riding a bicycle crazy? Wearing so little, when it isn't even that warm today!" First think for a moment, perhaps that foreigner is looking at you saying, "Is that big, fat walking cotton ball getting ready to climb Mt. Qomolangma ? Wearing so much, when it isn't even that cold today!"

Chapter 25

摩登的上海有条古老的龙？
An Ancient Dragon in Modern Shanghai?

如果每一个国家都要选一个城市走上世界的 T 型台，跟伦敦、纽约、巴黎等超级名模在一起挺胸抬头，张扬自己的才华，中国一定会选上海作为国家最现代、最时尚的城市，充当那位超级名模。不幸的是，追求名与利，是很容易忘记自己的草根出身的。城市被以进步与现代化的名义重新塑造了，而自己的历史和文化却可能丢失了。这意味着中国最现代的城市做出了它的决定，别无选择地牺牲了很多风俗、文物和建筑。好像这是现代化所付出的代价，但中国的一句老话却支持这个论点：旧的不去，新的不来。

If every country could choose a city to walk on the world runway alongside the supermodels of London, New York and Paris, each flaunting their own assets, chest out, head held high, as the country's most modern, as well as most fashionable, China would choose Shanghai to act as that supermodel. Unfortunately, alongside fame and fortune it's easy to forget one's background, and reinvented by others in the name of progress and modernization, it's own history and culture can be lost. The implications are that China's most modern city has made the decision that it has no other choice but to sacrifice some of its customs and cultural architecture. It would seem that this is the price of modernization, and an old Chinese saying seems to support the belief: if the old does not fade away, the new cannot come forward.

但是，即使像许多超级名模一样变得太自我膨胀，她的内心深处仍应有一些很珍贵的秘密躲过了整形医生的手术刀，被保留了下来。不管在哪里发生改变，造了多少大厦，拆了多少老房子，在整个城市中，总有一些小块的地方还藏着那里独有的历史。可惜，由于在大城市的生活压力很大，而且实际上大家都一直忙着跑来跑去赚钱、花钱，所以那些独有的特征始终在无数宽大的广告牌和闪烁的霓虹灯中躲藏着。它们非常难找，因为它们躲藏在高楼大厦和高架道路中；我们看不见它们是因为已经忘记了"过去"的含义。

But, even if it had become as self-absorbed as many a supermodel, shouldn't a few precious secretes remain buried deep within her heart, hidden from the plastic surgeon's scalpel? No matter where the changes took place, how many buildings were built, or how many old buildings were knocked down, throughout the city, buried within small pockets, its own unique history and past superstitions can survive. Sadly, due to the heavy pressure of living in a big city, and given the fact that everyone is too busy running around making money, spending money, these forgotten, but unique characteristics continue to hide themselves amongst countless massive billboards and flickering neon lights. They are really hard to find because they are hidden amongst the skyscrapers and overpasses. We simply can't see them because our brains already have forgotten the meaning of "the past".

希望上海人不介意我替他们介绍一下一个在我们面前躲藏着的、被古老迷信与城市发展所创造的、非常有趣的并且因为能象征中国历史如何跟现代的文明融合而显得尤其迷人的东西：上海龙柱！

I hope the Shanghainese will not mind my introducing on their behalf something that is hiding before our very eyes, created by ancient superstition and urban development, and really quite fascinating as it symbolizes China's history and how it reached an agreement with modern day China: Shanghai's Dragon Pillar!

首先我想说，如果有些细节弄错了，请原谅我，因为其中有些是二手叙述，那时候我不在现场。

First I'd like to say, if I get some of the details wrong, please forgive me, some of which are a second-hand account, as I wasn't around at that time.

在 20 世纪 90 年代中期，上海政府打算造一条高架道路：延安高架路。但不巧在静安区，在成都路与西藏路的十字路口的交叉点上，工程队遇到一个障碍：他们突然无缘无故地打不下去桩。我的意思是，在此之前工程进展得很顺利：先挖个洞，打下去，再把水泥柱子放进去。但是，到成都路和西藏路的十字路口，打桩机打不下去，柱子也放不下去。不管增加多少工人，或者多少工程师、地质学家、建筑经理和其他专家到建筑工地集思广益，都想不出办法解决。后面的路段都没有问题，打得下，也放得下，可为什么在这特定的地点打不下？上海的地下不是像流沙一样，不仅不稳定，而且特别软吗？蓝领们只能白费力气，白领们只能一根又一根地吸烟考虑怎么办。直到有一天，大家都在建筑工地里站着抽烟的时候，一个穿着黄色长袍的和尚出现在了烟云中。

During the 1990s, the Shanghai government planned to build an overpass: the Yan'an Overpass. But, as luck would have it, in Jing'an District, while crossing over the intersection of Chengdu and Xizang Roads, the construction team ran into an obstacle: suddenly for no apparent reason they could no longer dig downwards. What I mean to say is, previously, the construction of the overpass was developing quite smoothly: first excavate the hole, digging downwards, and then place a concrete pillar in the hole. But, upon reaching the Chengdu/Xizang intersection, the excavator couldn't excavate, and the pillars couldn't be set. No matter how many workers were put into the hole or how many engineers, geologists, site managers or other similarly related specialists came to the construction site to pool their ideas together, no one could come up with a solution. The following were dug and set without problem, so why couldn't they dig at this particular spot? Wasn't the ground beneath Shanghai like quicksand, not only unstable, but also extremely soft? The blue collars could only waste their strength digging. The white collars could only smoke one cigarette after another while contemplating the problem, yet again, contemplating how this mysterious dilemma came about. Until one day, while everyone was at the construction site standing around smoking cigarettes, out of the cloud of smoke, a monk wearing a long, yellow robe appeared.

大家都呆呆地望着他，他打破沉默，说自己是静安寺的住持法师。白领们你看我，我看你，都不知是某个同事请来的住持或是他自行前来的。后来，一个地质学家告诉了本地记者法师对白领们说的话："问题不是地面太硬了或另外一些地质条件。其实，地下住着一条龙魂，你们的打桩机打在了龙魂背上，打扰了它的休眠。这龙魂不允许你们继续。"

Everyone stared blankly at him, and he broke the silence by saying that he was the master of Jing'an Temple. The white collars looked at one another, looking to discover whether or not he had come because someone had sought him out or whether he came on his own. Afterwards, a geologist had told a local reporter that the master had said to the white collars, "The problem isn't that the ground is too hard or something else related to the geological conditions. Actually, it is due to the fact that a dragon spirit is living below the earth, and your excavating machines have struck the dragon spirit on the back and have interrupted its sleep. The dragon's spirit will not allow you to continue."

有些人忍不住笑了，认为和尚胡说八道，其他对和尚尊敬一点的人没笑，但是认为他简直太迷信，并不懂地质学。老实说，如果我也在场，不管我是白领、蓝领或其他领，我也不敢相信。

Some of those lacking class couldn't help but laugh at him, believing he was talking nonsense, while others didn't laugh out of respect for the monk, but who also believed he was being too superstitious and really didn't understand geology. Honestly speaking, if I had also been there, it wouldn't matter if I was a white collar, blue collar or any other color collar, I also wouldn't have believed it.

据一位工程师的助手报告，法师耐心地用眼神跟每个人交流后，很郑重地说："哪怕你们是无神论者或者认为我是一个老糊涂，都需要听我讲。" 他的态度和语气引起了他们的注意。他低声严肃地说："你们再靠近一些吧。"无论相信不相信的，大家都饶有兴致地围拢来听。

According to an assistant engineer's report, after the sage patiently made eye contact with each and every one, in a very solemn voice, he said, "It doesn't matter if you don't believe in religion or you think I'm a senile old man, you all need to hear what I have to say." His gentle manner and tone of voice grabbed everyone's attention. Whispering, he said solemnly, "Come closer." Regardless of who believed and who didn't, everyone crowded around with interest to hear him.

他很神秘地说："我知道如何安抚这被你们的大型机器扰乱的龙魂。很遗憾，我也知道你们的现代的行事方式就是：一建新楼，就把旧的拆掉，毫不考虑这种行为是否会把古老的传统和风俗永远丢掉。也许我跟地下的龙魂一样，都被现今的时代忘记了。无论如何，如果你们愿意听从我的意愿行事，为了古老的存在——龙魂，我愿意用我的命来换。"

He said mysteriously, "I know how to appease the dragon spirit that was disturbed by your great machines. Sadly, I also know the modern way of doing things is like this: to build one must destroy, without regard that such actions may or may not cast aside ancient traditions and customs forever. Perhaps I'm the same as the dragon spirit beneath the earth, both have been forgotten by modern times. In any event, if you are wiling to do so according to my wishes, for the sake of another ancient being, the dragon spirit's appeasement, I am willing to exchange my life."

连刚刚取笑他的人都不知道该怎么回答。

Including those who had just laughed at him, no one knew how to respond.

第二天，那些白领们都回到各自的办公室向上级汇报。因为都关着门，所以没人清楚下级是怎么汇报的，或上级做出了什么样的反应。可是可以想见下级永远忘不了他们领导的反应："龙魂？！法师？！孙悟空和猪八戒也在那儿吧？！"

On the second day, the white collars returned to their respective offices to report to their superiors. Because everything took place behind closed doors, it's not clear how the subordinates reported the matter or how the superiors reacted. But, you can guess that the subordinates would never forget their leader's reaction: "Dragon spirit?! A sage?! Were the Monkey King and Piggy there as well!?"

然后，又浪费了一个月，人们还没找到好办法，他们没有别的选择，只好又跟法师联系。他们问法师需要多少钱帮助他们安抚龙魂。法师说自己什么都不需要。可是，寺庙好久没整修，如果愿意给寺庙捐款，他可以试试。

Then, after wasting yet another month, and still having not found a good solution, they had no other choice but to once again get in touch with the master sage. They asked the sage how much money he would need to appease the dragon spirit. The sage said he didn't need anything. But, as the temple had not been renovated in a long time, if they were willing to offer a donation, he would help them.

不知道最后经过什么政府机构批准，通过什么部门的处理——公关部、税务部或者其他有关部门——各方达成了约定。尽管我不在，但我可以肯定地说没有人会真的相信法师会付出生命的代价。

I don't know which government organization approved it, what department handled it—the public relations bureau, the tax bureau or a "relevant bureau", but all parties were in agreement. Even though I wasn't there, I can say with certainty that no one seriously believed the sage actually had to exchange his life.

按照他所说的：一支由工程师组成的小队伍先要制作一个特殊镀层。然后从上到下，利用那张特殊镀层把水泥柱完全包装一下。在镀层表面焊接上一些法师选的金色符号和九龙飞天的形象。根据那位法师精确的说明，无论多么小的细节，工程师们和设计者们都要尽快地把那张特殊镀层一丝不苟地生产出来。工人们拼命苦干，终于把以前打不碎的岩层打碎了。日复一日，在令人窒息的尘雾和重型机械发出的巨大轰隆声中，法师一直不断地在建筑工地中祈祷。

According to his instructions: a small contingent of engineers first needed to create a special plating. Then from top to bottom, they'd wrap the entire concrete pillar in the special plating. On the plate's surface they had to weld golden symbols and the image of nine dragons flying towards the heavens all chosen by the sage. Following the sage's exact instructions, no matter how small the detail, the engineers and designers quickly produced the special plating with not a single hair out of place. The workers toiled away as if their lives counted on it and finally broke through the rocky layer they earlier could not. Day after day, amongst the choking dust and the relentless deafening crash BANG! BANG! of the heavy machinery, the sage prayed continuously at the center of the construction site.

据传闻，洞完全挖掘好了，柱子安装完成以后，仿佛精力全部都用尽了，那位法师像一块被拧干了的抹布：体重大大地减轻，他瘦成了皮包骨头，面孔比月亮还苍白，他老迈了很多。

It is rumored that after the hole was completely excavated and the pillar was installed, as if he had been completely drained of all energy, the sage resembled a rag wrung dry: weight having decreased drastically, he was all skin and bones and his face paler than the moon, he'd aged many years.

那条"龙柱"终于装好以后，像建筑工地上漂浮着的灰尘一样，那位法师渐渐消失了。

Once the "dragon pillar" was finally complete, the sage slowly faded away like so much dust found floating around the construction site.

过了一段时间以后，那位一个月前健康状况还非常好，没有明显的疾病迹象的法师，突然离开了世界。

After some time, the sage whose state of health had been very good a month prior, with no obvious signs of illness, suddenly departed this world.

不知道这个故事是不是真的，但我愿意相信。我相信那位法师足够明智，理解现代化是必然的过程，但是有些古老的遗风也必须保持完好。因此，为了保留中国文化的一小部分，那位法师愿意付出生命的代价。

Is it a true story? I prefer to think so. I would like to believe that the sage was wise enough to know that modernization was an inevitable step, but also that a remnant of the old ways must remain intact. Therefore, in order to preserve a piece of Chinese culture, he was willing to pay the ultimate price: his life.

所以，我请求大家下一次开车，或者坐在出租车、公共汽车中，或在自行车上，经过一条被特殊镀层完全包装，从上到下有金色符号和九龙飞天图的巨大柱子的时候，记住这个现代传说、那位法师的牺牲和这个纪念碑——上海的龙柱。

So, the next time you're driving in car or sitting in a taxi, a public bus or on a bicycle, and you pass the pillar wrapped in extraordinary plating, covered from top to bottom in golden symbols and flying dragons heading towards the heavens, I ask you to remember if even just for a moment this modern legend, the sage's sacrifice and a tribute to the past: Shanghai's Dragon Pillar.

信不信由你!

Believe it or not!

Chapter 26

中式专心：声音的考验
Chinese Concentration: Trial by Sound

大约是大年初五或者初六，我躺在床上，不知道当下是白天还是黑夜。眼球里的血丝像蜘蛛网般密布，眼袋比熊猫的更黑，我能感到睡魔的呼吸，可无法施展他的魔术。我整个身体因为窗外一轮又一轮的巨响抽搐着。楼上的大锤不停地打中水泥墙，听起来像是从各个方向发出一声声巨响：轰！随着每一个令人懊恼的震动，我的牙齿不由自主地嘎吱摩擦。在楼下，一把工业钻机慢慢地钻进水泥墙。同时，那个声音也慢慢地挖洞挖到我的耳朵里，开始进入我的脑子了。它在我的头颅表面凿着这个词：神经错乱！我对着墙壁骂了一声，喊道："难道工人不需要回家过一两个星期春节？"

On around the fifth or the sixth day of the Chinese New Year, lying in bed, I no longer knew whether it was day or night. My eyeballs looking as if they were wrapped in a spider's red web, and the bags below my eyes blacker than a panda's, I was able to feel the breath of the sandman, but unable to feel his magic. My entire body twitched beneath another round of explosive noise outside my window. The sledgehammer on the floor above was crashing repeatedly into a concrete wall, emitting a massive BOOM from seemingly every direction. My teeth couldn't help but grind against one another alongside each irritating vibration. Down below, an industrial drill slowly bore into its own concrete wall. At the same time, that sound slowly dug into my ears and began to enter my brain, as it chiseled onto the surface of my skull the word: INSANITY! Cursing the wall, I shouted, "Didn't the workers have to go home for the holidays for two weeks?"

反应迟钝的脑子跟着摇摇晃晃的身子站起来，我发觉自己向窗户走去了。也许希望暂时逃离这人间地狱，寻找平静，我感觉到我的两条胳臂把窗帘猛然拉开，并推开了窗户。

My brain responded sluggishly, following my shambling body as it stood itself upright. I found myself moving towards the window. Possibly hoping to temporarily escape this hell on earth, searching for peace and quiet, I felt my arms throw open the curtains and slide the window open.

不幸的是，一打开窗户，我的整个感官都被一把来自未来的机枪射出的"声音弹"攻击了！首先脑袋被一辆巴士的喇叭声"叭叭"地击中，接着一辆救护车的警报声环绕在我耳边。对面一个声音开得很大的扩音器把"便宜皮鞋五折"的广告声重重地打在我额头上。在一家水饺馆门口，两个戴着厨师帽的人和一个大胖子男人在互相指着对骂。在绝望之中我发出无声的尖叫，砰的一声关上窗户，猛地拉上了窗帘。

Unfortunately, the second I opened the window, my senses were under assault by what must have been some kind of futuristic machine gun that could fire "sound" bullets! First my head was struck by the horn of a bus, BAA, BAA! Followed by an ambulance's wailing siren, which encircled my ears. Across the street a very loud speaker broadcasting an advertisement for "cheap high heel shoes, 50% off!" pounded heavily against my forehead. In the entrance of a dumpling restaurant two men in chef hats and a fat man were pointing fingers at one another and cursing. In desperation, I released a soundless scream, slamming the window shut and yanked the curtains closed.

尽管是冬天，我还在寻找能令人凉快点的东西。我开了电风扇，想听一会儿它发出的安慰的、柔和的嗡嗡声。我塞了两个棉花球在耳朵里，头上蒙了两条被子和一个枕头，想通过睡眠逃避噪音。我开始数羊，可思绪一片混乱，竟然忘记怎么数。我也试图用中文祈祷，平常只要才一开始，我就睡着了，可是似乎上帝也已经离弃我了——祈祷结束了，而我还躺着睡不着。当第一滴眼泪从紧闭的眼皮中间慢慢挤压出来的时候，我听到电风扇咔嚓关机了。

Even though it was winter, searching for something that would allow me to relax a little, I turned on the fan, hoping to hear its soothing, gentle hum. Stuffing two cotton balls in my ears, covering my head with two blankets and a pillow, I sought an escape through sleep. I began by counting sheep. But my mind muddled, I had forgotten how to count. I even tried praying in Chinese, which always put me to sleep immediately, but it seemed as if even God had forsaken me—my prayers were finished and I still lie awake. As the first tear squeezed out of tightly shut eyelids, I heard the fan click as it turned off.

我用虚弱的胳膊肘，勉强地支撑起身体，我那双疲倦的眼睛开始欺骗它们的主人。为了试一下自己做梦了没有，我眨了几次眼。没有做梦啊，我还是醒着。可是当我还没准备好相信自己的眼睛的时候，在我面前，一位看上去很古老的圣人出现了。

On weak elbows, begrudgingly supporting my body, a pair of exhausted eyes began to play tricks on their master. Checking to see if I was dreaming or not, I blinked my eyes a few times. Nope. Sadly I was still awake. But I still wasn't ready to believe what I was seeing: in front of me, seemingly out of thin air, a very ancient-looking sage had appeared.

他靠在一根手杖上，在他长着很长的白胡子的面孔上有着很多象征着智慧的皱纹，还有像中国龙一样突出的额头。那位老幽灵从一件布满灰尘的长袍里拿出一捆古代文书手卷并把它展开来指向我，嘶哑地说：

"你……"但一说"你"字，他就好像被那个词呛到了，停了下来。他愁眉苦脸地举起食指，表示我要等一下他。他摸了摸嗓子，又张开嘴巴，但是他一开始嘶哑地说"你……"效果还是一样。他的嗓音像他拿着的那捆文书一样干燥。他立马发出一阵咳嗽，咳出来一些黄色灰尘。突然我发现我的卧室闻起来有点臭，有腐烂的洋葱和皮蛋的臭气飘浮在空中。我吐出一些雾状的棕色尘埃在卧室的地板上，忍不住说："嘿，你是什么老鬼？太恶心了！"他很客气地回答："很抱歉，小伙子，倘若你睡了一千多年，你的口气还会像玫瑰那么清新吗？"他的嗓子似乎总算从千百年的粉尘和蜘蛛网中解脱了，其实他说话的声音很好听。

Beneath a long beard as white as snow, face covered in wrinkles, symbolizing wisdom, his forehead protruding like that of the Chinese dragon's, he leaned against a knotty cane. The old ghost pulled a bundled scroll out from his dusty robe and opening it, he pointed towards me and said in a hoarse voice, "You…" But as soon as he said the word "you" he immediately stopped as if choking on the word. Grimacing, lifting up his index finger, implying that I should wait for a moment, he rubbed his throat. Once again opening his mouth, he began by saying in a hoarse voice, "You…" but the results were the same. His voice sounded as dried out as the bundled scroll he held. All at once he began hacking, coughing up yellow dust. The room suddenly smelled foul, leaving the stench of old onions and preserved eggs hanging in the air. Spitting up some hazy brown ash onto my bedroom floor, I couldn't help but say, "Hey, what kind of old ghost are you? That's disgusting!" He responded politely with, "Very sorry, young man, but suppose you had slept for one thousand years, would your breath smell like roses?" His throat finally free of what must have been ages of dust and cobwebs actually left him with a relatively nice sounding voice.

我得承认他说得有道理。他引起了我的注意，我耸了耸肩膀，让他继续说。他用很温和、充满智慧的声音说："在每个人的一生中，我们都不得不学着如何控制自己的耳朵。看上去你还没掌握好。"

I had to admit he had a point. Having caught my interest, I shrugged my shoulders and let him speak. In a soft, sagacious voice he said, "In every man's life, we have no choice but to learn how to control one's own ears. And it would seem that you have yet to have mastered this."

窗外，又一轮鞭炮爆发了。

From outside the window, another round of firecrackers erupted.

"不好意思，我没注意，你刚说什么？" 我问。

"Pardon me, I wasn't paying attention, what did you just say?" I asked.

"确实，你没注意。小伙子，你知道该如何使用自己的耳朵吗？"

"Exactly. You didn't pay attention. Young man, do you know how to use your own ears?"

"当然知道该如何使用。这就是我的烦恼！"

"Of course I know how to use them. That IS the problem!"

"没错。你学会了如何聆听，但是我对你提出的问题是：一扇能开但是不能关的门，还可以视为一扇门吗？同样的逻辑也适用于你的耳朵：你会开，却不会关。遵循阴阳平衡的指导原则，一切都有其正面和反面：日和月，男和女，蜜蜂与花，水饺与醋，一个都不能少。总而言之，你还没学会如何闭上耳朵。"

"Correct. You have mastered how to listen. But, my question to you: is a door that can only open and never close still considered a door? And the same applies to your ears: you may be able to open your ears, but you are incapable of closing them. Following the principles of Yin and Yang, everything has its opposite: the sun and the moon, man and woman, the bees and the flowers, dumplings and vinegar, and without one there isn't the other. Simply put, you have yet to have mastered how to close your ears."

"我不懂。"

"I don't understand."

"我的意思是，耳朵不只具有一个功能——听，有时候也具有其他更重要的功能：听而不闻。为了解决你无法集中注意力和无法入睡的问题，请让我给你介绍你的饺子要的醋。"

"What I mean to say is, the ear doesn't just have a single function: listening. It also possesses another function that is sometimes even more important: the ability to listen, but not hear. For the sake of your inability to concentration, and your failure to sleep, please allow me to introduce to you the vinegar to your dumpling."

我还是不太懂他的话，他把一副老花眼镜从长袍里拿出来，放在鼻尖上。"听我说，"他开始朗读手里的古代文书手卷的标题，"通过声音启迪，通往古老中国的道路。"

Still not really understanding his words, I watched as he pulled out a pair of bifocals from his robe. Resting them on the tip of his nose, he started by saying, "Listen to me," and then began to read aloud the title of the scroll he held in his hand titled, "Enlightenment through sound, leads to China's ancient path."

"有点太戏剧化了，你不觉得吗？"我说。

"Slightly over-dramatic, don't you think?" I said.

他咳了一下，清了清喉咙。我认为那个动作是故意的。我向他点了点头，让他继续。

Coughing a little, he cleared his throat. I believe this time it was intentional. I nodded towards him, giving him the okay to continue.

他摇摇头含糊不清地说："野蛮人。"

He shook his head and mumbled, "Barbarians."

我说了："什么？"可他又开始读。

I said, "What?" But he ignored me and once again began to read.

第一层：和睦
First Level: Harmony

人类都是在这一层产生的：在母亲的子宫里，随着她抚慰的语音，感受她稳定的心脏一直跳动。不幸的是，从子宫出来之后，我们的脑子立刻被外部的杂乱刺激了，而我们天生的对世界上最轻松的声音的鉴赏能力却离我们越来越远：闷热的夜晚电扇发出的呼呼声响，风铃被和风轻送的叮叮当当声，海浪拍打沙滩的声音。一段时间之后，我们只能在身心疲惫的时候捕捉这些声音并欣赏一小会儿。

All of mankind begins life on this level, within a mother's womb, alongside her soothing voice, you feel her steady heart continually beating. Unfortunately, after exiting the womb, our brains are upset by external chaos, and our innate ability to hear and appreciate the world's most soothing sounds grows more distant: a stifling evening's electric fan as it sends forth its whirring sounds; wind chimes tinkling softly beneath the breeze; waves crashing on to a beach. After a short period of time, we are only able to seize and appreciate these sounds when we are mentally and physically exhausted.

第二层：熟悉
Second Level: Familiarity

第二层是像我穿着的这件很熟悉的、仿佛是一个亲爱的朋友披挂在我身上的旧长袍带来的舒适、熟悉的感觉：母亲的哼唱，父亲的温柔建议，隔壁的低沉的收音机里的广播节目，奶奶烧饭锅下的沙沙炊火声，小女孩诚实的吃吃低笑，自行车的铃声，小鸟啁啾声。

Similar to this familiar old robe that hangs from me as if it were a dear friend, the second level also provides a comfortable, familiar feeling: a mother's humming; a father's gentle suggestions; the broadcast of a neighbor's muffled radio; the hissing flame beneath Grandma's wok as she cooks; a little sister's innocent giggling; a bicycle's bell; a small bird's chirp.

第三层：热闹
Third Level: Liveliness

对中国人来说，这层是精华。就像任意一道菜，大笑和喧哗取代了盐和胡椒粉，再加一点调料就让气氛活跃起来：阿姨们一边八卦，一边围坐在一张麻将桌旁把麻将在毡布上滑来滑去的嘘嘘声；在餐桌上哥们开心地互相敬酒碰杯，地上的空酒瓶被他们的脚绊倒发出的哐啷声；顽皮的孩子高高兴兴地放小鞭炮；在背景中，无论是古典的京剧或现代的流行音乐，越闹越好！

To the Chinese, this level is essential. As with any dish, in this case noise and laughter replacing salt and chili pepper, adding a little more seasoning will always create a livelier dish and/or atmosphere: the aunties gossiping as they sit around a table playing mahjong, sliding their tablets back and forth over the felt fabric; at the dinner table dear friends clinking glasses together as they happily toast one another, the empty bottles on the floor knocked over by their feet, clanging as they bounce; mischievous children setting off small firecrackers; and in the background, no matter if classical Beijing Opera or modern day popular music, the louder the better!

第四层：吵闹
Fourth Level: Noise

不出所料，加了太多"调料"，热闹就会成为吵闹，然后导致耳朵消化不良：现代交通的奔放不羁的交响乐团坚持吹奏喇叭；在卡拉OK里品位不高的人大喊大叫；有些人无缘无故地朝手机里大声喊叫！

As expected, adding too much "seasoning" can turn lively into noisy, which leads to ear indigestion: modern traffic's unrestrained and uninhibited orchestra persistently blowing their horns as one; in karaoke bars screaming and shouting, showing one knows nothing of the classics or has any respect towards good taste; and even when there is no apparent reason for doing so, some people insist on hollering into their electrical cell phones!

尽管有点不好意思，我插嘴怀疑地问："在你的年代有汽车和喇叭、卡拉 OK、手机吗？"

A little embarrassed, I interrupted and asked skeptically, "There were cars with horns and karaoke back in your time? And what is an electrical cell phone?"

他不耐烦地说："专注些！小伙子，你真是不可救药。蚊子的注意力都比你的强多了。"

He said impatiently, "Pay attention! This boy really is hopeless. A mosquito has a better attention span than you!"

我抱歉地说："对不起，老鬼，请继续吧。"

I said apologetically, "I'm sorry, old ghost, please continue."

他向天花板嘟哝着一些我听不清楚的话后又接着说。

He looked to the ceiling muttering some words I couldn't hear clearly and then continued to speak.

第五层：折磨
Fifth Level: Torture

为了考验你的耐心，你要加大力度，直到慢慢地切入你心里：楼上的切肉刀不停地在砧板上喀喀喀喀；早上五点钟一连串鞭炮噼里啪啦的爆炸声；窗外的猫发情哭喊；寂寞的狗一直汪汪叫！

In order to truly test one's patience, you need to increase the intensity as it slowly and deliberately cuts into your psyche: the meat cleaver upstairs chopping incessantly against a cutting board, ka-ka-ka; at five o'clock in the morning a string of firecrackers explode, bang-bang-bang; a cat in heat cries outside your window; a lonely dog barks nonstop.

第六层：癫狂
Sixth Level: Madness

根据事物的自然秩序，危机跟随着考验：楼上的切肉刀变成大锤撞碎了墙，发出轰轰巨响；楼下的工业钻机发出尖锐的嘎嘎声。你的身心开始退到一个不和谐的令人怀疑现实的黑暗角落去。

According to the natural order of things, crisis follows the test: under the meat cleaver that has become a sledgehammer as it crashes into the wall upstairs emitting a massive boom, and beneath the industrial drill's penetrating, grating noise downstairs, your body and mind begin to retreat to a dark place of discord where you begin to question reality.

第七：解脱
Seventh Level: Liberation

像熊冬眠、鸵鸟把头埋进沙漠里或者仓鼠装死一样，你认为只有一个方法：完全逃避。换句话说，让自己陷入一种休眠状态。不要误解，我的意思不是正常情况下的睡觉或小憩，而是在一个远远不够理想的环境下，你本人还能进入一个幸福的梦境，而把任何形式的吵闹屏蔽。

Like a bear in hibernation, an ostrich burying it's head in the sand or a hamster playing dead, you believe there is only one solution: total avoidance. In other words, you allow yourself to fall into a state of dormancy. Don't misunderstand, it doesn't mean the act of sleeping or napping under normal conditions, but that in one that is far from ideal, a person may pass into a blissful dreamland and are shielded from any form of noise.

第八层：启示
Eighth Level: Enlightenment

此时，他全身开始发出金色的亮光，老者接下来说："经过这一层，你已经学会了睡眠功夫。如果你愿意，你也可以在菩萨旁边打坐。你终于拥有把全部的外界刺激都阻隔的能力了。在达到这一层的时候，如果你愿意，你可以在一个又拥挤又吵闹的夜店里写出一篇值得鲁迅称赞的论文，或者在建筑工地中思路明确地练习太极拳，你将发现你终于获得启示！"

At this point, his entire body began to emit a golden light, and the old ghost continued, "Through this stage, the ability to sleep has been mastered, and you could even meditate alongside the Buddha himself if you so desired. And you finally possess the ability to block out all sound and outside stimulation. Upon obtaining this final stage, if one fancied writing forth an essay worthy of Lu Xun's praise while sitting in this modern world's crowded, noisy nightclubs or perhaps practicing Tai Chi with a clear mind in the middle of a construction site you could, and only then will you have finally obtained enlightenment."

终于说完了，老鬼把古代文书手卷卷起来，放进长袍里。

Finally finishing his words, the old ghost rolled up the scroll and put it back into his robe.

"那么小的古代文书手卷能包含那么多内容？"我问。

"An ancient scroll that small can contain all that?" I asked.

他揉了揉太阳穴，摇了摇头，有点烦躁地说："我即兴加了点。"

Rubbing his temple, he shook his head, and said somewhat impatiently, "I improvised a bit."

然后他立刻恢复镇静，耐心地说："不幸的是，你离第八层还非常非常远。然而，别心灰意冷，你打开窗帘瞧瞧外面，到处有大师等着。从娘胎里出来之后，中国人一直生活在喧闹中，特别是在我们发明炸药之后。在烟火的吵闹声音下，许多人到七岁左右就已经得道了。这就是中华最基本的生存技能。如果没得道，怎么能在那么吵的环境中专心下来？怎么能听见自己的思想？你们洋人珍爱平静，这种想法没有错。可是，'玉不琢，不成器；人不学，不知义'。这句话的意思是：如果嘴没尝过醋味，任何人都无法真正鉴别甜味。你前面的道路还很遥远。拉开窗帘，寻找启示吧！"

He immediately regained his composure and said patiently, "Unfortunately, you still remain far, far removed from Level Eight. However, don't be discouraged, open the window and take a look outside. Everywhere a master waits. After exiting the womb, the Chinese live within constant commotion, especially after we had invented dynamite. And soon beneath noisy fireworks, by the age of seven or so, most have already found The Path. This is a fundamental survival skill for the Chinese. If you haven't found The Path, how could you concentrate in such a noisy environment? How could one even hear his or her own thoughts? You westerners cherish tranquility, and there's nothing wrong with that kind of thinking. But, as a jade is not complete without chiseling, a man without experience cannot know. What I mean to say is: if your mouth has never tasted vinegar, how can one truly identify what is sweet? The road before you is still quite long. Open your window, seek enlightenment!"

我特别渴望相信他的话，从床上跳了起来。一拉开窗帘，我就得到了他给我的信息，仿佛是我第一次睁开眼睛，我亲眼看到了无数大师：

回收工人在自己改装的电子卡车上睡得正香，有一个人在他的宝马车里打盹，小娃娃在婴儿车里做梦，打扫马路的清洁工靠着墙在看广告纸，银行附近的一群老人在练习太极拳！难怪他们全部对周围疯狂的吵闹无动于衷，他们达到一定境界了！实在是处处都有高手啊！

Desperate to believe in his words, I jumped up from my bed. And as soon as I opened the curtains, I immediately recognized his message and as if my eyes were open for the first time, I saw before me countless masters: a recyclables collector sleeping deeply in the back of his personally customized electric cart; another napping in his BMW; a baby dreaming within its stroller; a street sweeper leaning up against a wall reading an advertisement; a group of old people practicing Tai Chi near the bank! No wonder each and every one of them was oblivious to the insane levels of noise happening around them, they had all reached enlightenment! There really were masters everywhere!

我转身开始对老圣人说："大师，我看到了，终于能看到了！"但是他已经消失了。

I turned around and started to say to the old spirit, "Master, I see them, I'm finally able to see them!" But he had already disappeared.

楼下又有烟火爆炸的声音。

Down below some more fireworks exploded.

谁愿意当我师傅？！

Who's willing to act as my master?

一位公共汽车司机靠在他的喇叭上。

A bus driver leaned on his horn.

谁，任何人！帮帮我！

Someone, anyone, please! Help me!

Chapter 27

中美的差别
Differences Between China and America

事物之间的差别有好处也有坏处。好处是能让人了解之前不熟悉的领域，或是更理解自己已经熟悉的方面。坏处是容易让人产生误会。

Differences can be both positive and negative. A positive is it allows people to better understand aspects they are unfamiliar with, as well as becoming more familiar to one's own aspects. A negative is it creates room for misunderstandings.

可是，各国之间的差别非常重要。如果没有了这些差异，我们怎么能体验新的文化、体验其他的生活方式？还有最重要的是，差异让我们反思自己。

But, each country's differences are very important. If there wasn't any, how could we taste the new and experience other styles? And possibly most important, it allows us to reflect upon on our own.

谁看过调味品架上只摆着一种调料？生活应该丰富多彩。

Who has ever seen a spice rack with only one spice? Life should be rich and colorful.

大多数人已经比较熟悉的中美的差别包括：筷子与刀叉、米饭面条与面包土豆等。我想尝试介绍一些一般人不太熟悉的差别。

And while most of us know the familiar differences between China and the USA: chopsticks versus fork and knife, rice and noodles compared to bread and potatoes, etc., I will attempt to introduce some of the more unfamiliar differences.

第一：
First:

在中国，道路清扫车播放欢快的音乐，警告着行人："小心，我要扫路了。"

In China, street sweepers play happy music: it can warn pedestrians, "Be careful, I need to clean the road."

在美国，冰淇淋车播放欢快的音乐，为了吸引小孩子从家里出来。

In America, ice cream trucks play happy music: it can attract children from their home.

每年有多少来到中国的美国小孩因为误追赶道路清扫车而走失呢？

Every year, how many American children who have come to China go missing because they mistakenly chased a street sweeper?

第二:
Second:

在美国，锻炼身体的时候，大多数人更喜欢喝冷水或冰水，特别是户外锻炼时，不管什么季节。

In America, when exercising, most people prefer drinking cold water, especially when exercising outside, no matter the season.

在中国，锻炼身体的时候，大多数人更喜欢喝热水或温水，不管在户外还是室内，不管什么季节。

In China, when exercising, most people prefer drinking hot or warm water, no matter if inside or out, or what season it is.

我现在更喜欢喝温水——难道这是中美融合的副产品？

I now like drinking warm water—a byproduct of Sino-America?

第三:
Third:

在中国，下飞机时，人们都推推搡搡的，匆匆离去。

In China, when exiting a plane, people all push and shove, getting off quickly.

在美国，下飞机时，人们都礼貌地等别人先下，于是会等半天才下来。

In America, when exiting a plane, people politely allow others off first, spending half the day getting off.

如果能把两者混在一起就好了：下飞机时，人们都礼貌地说"对不起，不好意思，抱歉"，然后推推搡搡地下飞机。

A combination would be best: when exiting a plane, everyone can politely say, "Excuse me, pardon me, sorry." as they push and shove their way off.

第四：
Fourth:

在美国，大家先吃早饭，再刷牙。

In America, people eat breakfast first, brushing their teeth second.

在中国，大家先刷牙，再吃早饭。

In China, people brush their teeth first, eating breakfast second.

第五：
Fifth:

在中国，老百姓在阳台上晾衣服或晒被子。

In China, the average person dries clothes or bedspreads on the balcony.

在美国，我们的老百姓喜欢在阳台上聊天、喝酒、吃早午晚饭和烧烤。

In America, the "average joe" likes to talk, drink, eat breakfast, lunch and dinner or barbecue on the balcony.

第六：
Sixth:

在中国，很多男士把他们的钥匙挂在皮带上，令他们看起来肩负很多责任，有面子。

In China, many men hang their keys from their belts, letting others know how many responsibilities they have, gaining face.

在美国，除了学校大楼的看门人和监狱的保安，没有人会把钥匙挂在皮带上。

In America, besides a school's janitor or a prison guard, no one hangs keys from their belt.

第七：
Seventh:

在美国，除了一个被称为"老师的宠儿"的非正式角色，小学教室里都没有班干部。

In America, besides the informal role known as the "teacher's pet", elementary school classrooms have no small departments.

在中国，小学教室里有各种各样的班干部：学习委员、体育委员、劳动委员、一二三道杠。

In China, elementary school classrooms have all kinds of mini-departments: homework committee, sports committee, labor committee, class monitor 1, 2 and 3, etc.

第八
Eighth:

在美国，肥胖大多是贫穷群体中的现象。

In America, obesity is a problem for the impoverished areas.

在中国，肥胖大多是有钱人群体中的现象。

In China, obesity is a problem in wealthy areas.

第九：
Ninth:

在中国，和陌生人打招呼，会令人觉得有点奇怪。

In China, if you greet a stranger you are considered mentally ill.

在美国，和陌生人打招呼，别人会认为很正常。

In America, if you greet a stranger you are considered normal.

第十：
Tenth:

在中国，中国人吃面条的时候，用嘴唇"吸吮"，发出呲溜的声音。

In China, when Chinese eat noodles, they use their lips to suck, releasing a slurping sound.

在美国，美国人吃面条的时候，用牙齿"咬断"，不敢发出声音。

In America, when Americans eat noodles, they use their teeth to cut, not daring to release a sound.

第十一：
Eleventh:

在美国，人们更喜欢早上洗澡，让中国人认为我们睡觉时很脏。

In America, people prefer to shower in the morning, leaving Chinese to believe they go to bed dirty.

在中国，人们更喜欢晚上洗澡，让美国人认为他们是一个头发很乱的国家。

In China, people prefer to shower in the evening, leaving Americans to believe China is a nation of bed heads.

第十二：
Twelfth:

在中国，一部分人受孔子影响很深。

In China, a portion of society is influenced by Confucius.

在美国，一部分人受本·富兰克林影响很深。

In America, a portion of society is influenced by Ben Franklin.

第十三：
Thirteenth:

在美国，有一个流行的说法是："努力工作，努力玩儿。"

In America, a popular saying is: "Work hard, play hard."

在中国，好像有一个流行的说法是："努力工作，努力休息。"

In China, it seems the popular saying is: "Work hard, rest hard."

第十四：
Fourteenth:

在中国，也许间接地要强调集体主义，连地址都是从大到小：国家、省、市、路、号、楼、室、姓名。

In China, perhaps indirectly emphasizing collectivism, an address is listed from biggest to smallest: country, province, city, road, number, building, room, name.

在美国，也许间接地要强调个人主义，地址是从小到大：姓名、室、楼、号、路、市、州、国家。

In America, perhaps indirectly emphasizing individualism, an address is listed from smallest to biggest: name, room, building, number, street, state, country.

第十五:
Fifteenth:

在美国，满月的时候，大多数人能在月球上看见一个男人的脸。

In America, when it's a full moon, most people can see a man's face on the moon's surface.

在中国，满月的时候，大多数人能在月球上看见一个兔子的身影。

In China, when it's a full moon, most people can see a rabbit's body on the moon's surface.

第十六:
Sixteenth:

在美国，大多数人，特别是爱尔兰裔美国人，认为绿色是一种幸运色。

In America, most people, especially Irish-Americans, believe green is a lucky color.

在中国，大多数人都不敢戴绿帽子！

In China, most people would not dare to wear a green hat!

第十七:

Seventeenth:

在中国，大多数人送礼物的时候，收礼的人不在对方面前拆礼物。

In China, when most people give gifts, the receiver does not open the gift in front of the other.

在美国，大多数人送礼物的时候，收礼的人一定会在对方面前拆礼物。

In America, when most people give gifts, the receiver will open the gift in front of the other.

第十八：
Eighteenth:

在美国，为了尊敬老师，学生在课堂上都主动提问题。

In America, to show respect to their teacher, students will always ask questions in class.

在中国，为了尊敬老师，学生在课堂上都不主动提问。

In China, to show respect to their teacher, students will never ask questions in class.

第十九：
Nineteenth:

在美国，司机用嘴巴骂人。

In America, drivers use their mouths to shout at others.

在中国，司机用喇叭骂人。

In China, drivers use the horn to shout at others.

第二十：
Twentieth:

在美国，复制别人的作品是一种犯罪。

In America, copying someone else's work is a kind of crime: plagiarism.

在中国，复制别人的作品有时是一种表扬。

In China, copying someone else's work is sometimes a kind of flattery.

第二十一：
Twenty-first:

在美国，向与你很亲密的人说"谢谢"是应该的，因为这表示你的感谢，无论行为大小。

In America, saying thank you to someone you are close to is expected as it shows appreciation to your loved one no matter the act.

在中国，向与你很亲密的人说"谢谢"不是必需的，因为只需要对陌生人表示你的感谢，亲密的人不用这么做。

In China, saying thank you to someone close is not expected as it does not need to be said to someone you care about as they already know and it is saved for strangers.

第二十二:
Twenty-second:

在美国，人们喜欢顺着鸡的翅膀和腿部的关节部位切块。

In America, people like to cut chicken along the arm and leg joints.

在中国，人们喜欢把除了鸡头以外的部位都切成小块。

In China, besides the head, everything is chopped into bite-sized pieces.

第二十三:
Twenty-third:

在美国，除了口香糖和牙膏以外，能吃的东西都不吐出来。

In America, outside of gum and toothpaste, nothing you eat is acceptable to spit out.

在中国，能吃的东西都可以吐出来。

In China, anything you can eat is acceptable to spit out.

第二十四:
Twenty-fourth:

在美国，女朋友／老婆不让男朋友／老公拿着她们的包包，因为要给他们面子。

In America, girlfriends/wives don't allow their boyfriends/husbands to carry their purses because they want to give them face.

在中国，女朋友／老婆可以让男朋友／老公拿着她们的包包，因为可以给他们面子。

In China, girlfriends/wives allow their boyfriends/husbands to carry their purses, because they want to give them face.

第二十五：
Twenty-fifth:

在美国，最受欢迎的口号是：自由。

In America, the favorite catchphrase seems to be: freedom.

在中国，最受欢迎的口号是：和谐。

In China, the favorite catchphrase seems to be: harmonious.

作 者 附 言
Note from the Author

读者们，首先我要感谢你们对我的书感兴趣。但是，我也要提醒你们，这本书就是一个人的经历，是我个人的观点。我不敢代表"外国"。只想告诉大家一个外国人所看到的。

Readers, let me begin by saying I appreciate your interest in my book. But, I'd also like to remind you that this book is the experience of one, my individual perspective. I don't dare represent the world outside of China. I only offer a glimpse into the mind of a foreigner.

所以，尽管享受，别想太多……

So, please just enjoy and don't think too much...

谢谢您，中国！

Thank you, China!

图书在版编目（CIP）数据

你好，米饭，我是汉堡！ / （美）阿文
（Kevin Smith）著. — 杭州 ：浙江大学出版社，2016.12
ISBN 978-7-308-16262-3

Ⅰ. ①你… Ⅱ. ①阿… Ⅲ. ①散文集—美国—现代—
英、汉 Ⅳ. ①I712.65

中国版本图书馆CIP数据核字(2016)第233671号

你好，米饭，我是汉堡！

【美】阿文（Kevin Smith）　著

责任编辑	蔡圆圆
责任校对	韦　伟
封面设计	项梦怡
出版发行	浙江大学出版社
	（杭州市天目山路148号　　邮政编码　310007）
	（网址：http://www.zjupress.com）
排　　版	杭州林智广告有限公司
印　　刷	杭州杭新印务有限公司
开　　本	710mm×1000mm　1/24
印　　张	16.75
字　　数	260千
版 印 次	2016年12月第1版　2016年12月第1次印刷
书　　号	ISBN 978-7-308-16262-3
定　　价	42.00元